Formal Methods for Managing and Processing Ontology Alignments

Ontologies are formal knowledge representation methods that can provide means for a shared understanding of a given domain. To enable meaningful communication and interoperability between two or more information systems that utilize independently created ontologies, a bridge between them is necessary, often referred to as an ontology alignment. *Formal Methods for Managing and Processing Ontology Alignments* provides a complete ontology alignment lifecycle, including modelling, methods, and maintenance processes.

Summarizing the author's research from the past ten years, this book consolidates findings previously published in prestigious international journals and presented at leading conferences. Each chapter is designed to be self-contained, allowing readers to approach the material modularly. The text introduces basic mathematical concepts, and later chapters build upon these foundations, but each focuses on specific aspects of ontology alignment, making the content accessible and easy to follow.

Key Features:

• Includes formal definitions of ontologies and ontology alignment along with a set of methods for providing semantics of attributes and relations.
• Provides application of fuzzy logic in the task of ontology alignment.
• Contains methods of managing the evolution of ontologies and their alignments.
• Proposes novel methods of assessing the quality ontology alignment.

Situated in the fields of knowledge representation and semantic technologies, this book is an invaluable resource for both academic researchers and practitioners, as well as students looking to deepen their understanding.

Marcin Pietranik is an assistant professor at Wrocław University of Science and Technology. He holds a deep interest in the areas of knowledge management and intelligent data processing technologies. He has published more than 50 articles and participated in organizing several scientific conferences devoted to his research interests. His academic expertise is enriched by practical knowledge of modern web technologies, particularly within medical and telecommunication projects.

Formal Methods for Managing and Processing Ontology Alignments

Marcin Pietranik

CRC Press
Taylor & Francis Group
Boca Raton London New York

CRC Press is an imprint of the
Taylor & Francis Group, an **informa** business

First edition published 2025
by CRC Press
2385 NW Executive Center Drive, Suite 320, Boca Raton FL 33431

and by CRC Press
4 Park Square, Milton Park, Abingdon, Oxon, OX14 4RN

CRC Press is an imprint of Taylor & Francis Group, LLC

Library of Congress Cataloging-in-Publication Data
Names: Pietranik, Marcin, author.
Title: Formal methods for managing and processing ontology alignments /
  Marcin Pietranik.
Description: First edition. | Boca Raton, FL : CRC Press, 2024. | Includes
  bibliographical references and index. | Summary: "Ontologies are formal
  knowledge representation methods that can provide means for a shared
  understanding of a given domain. To enable meaningful communication and
  interoperability between two or more information systems that utilize
  independently created ontologies, a bridge between them is necessary,
  often referred to as an ontology alignment. This book provides complete
  ontology alignment lifecycle, including modelling, methods, and
  maintenance processes. Summarizing the author's research from the past
  ten years, this book consolidates findings previously published in
  prestigious international journals and presented at leading conferences.
  Each book chapter is designed to be self-contained, allowing readers to
  approach the material modularly. The book introduces basic mathematical
  concepts, and later chapters build upon these foundations, but each
  focusses on specific aspects of ontology alignment, making the content
  accessible and easy to follow. Key Features: Includes formal definitions
  of ontologies and ontology alignment along with a set of methods for
  providing semantics of attributes and relations. Provides application of
  fuzzy logic in the task of ontology alignment. Contains methods of
  managing the evolution of ontologies and their alignments. Proposes
  novel methods of assessing the quality ontology alignment. Situated in
  the fields of knowledge representation and semantic technologies, this
  book is an invaluable resource for both academic researchers and
  practitioners, as well as students looking to deepen their
  understanding"-- Provided by publisher.
Identifiers: LCCN 2024019523 | ISBN 9781032571171 (hardback) | ISBN
  9781032571201 (paperback) | ISBN 9781003437888 (ebook)
Subjects: LCSH: Ontologies (Information retrieval) | Semantic Web.
Classification: LCC Q387.4 .P54 2024 | DDC 006.3/32--dc23/eng/20240531
LC record available at https://lccn.loc.gov/2024019523

ISBN: 978-1-032-57117-1 (hbk)
ISBN: 978-1-032-57120-1 (pbk)
ISBN: 978-1-003-43788-8 (ebk)

DOI: 10.1201/9781003437888

Typeset in CMR10 font
by KnowledgeWorks Global Ltd.

Publisher's note: This book has been prepared from camera-ready copy provided by the authors.

To the wisest people I know,
my wife and my parents

Contents

Foreword   ix

Preface   xi

Author   xiii

List of Algorithms   xv

I   Introduction and Background   1

1   Introduction   **3**
1.1   Understanding ontology alignment 3
1.2   The subject of this book 5
1.3   The contributions of this work 6
1.4   The structure of this book 8

2   A formal model of ontology and ontology alignment   **10**
2.1   Basic notions 10
2.2   Methods of providing semantics of attributes and relations 18
2.3   Ontology alignment 27
2.4   Conclusions 32

II   Techniques and Frameworks   33

3   Classification of ontology alignment techniques   **35**
3.1   Designating ontology alignments 36
3.2   Managing ontology evolution and maintaining ontology alignments over time   56
3.3   Evaluating the quality of ontology alignments 60
3.4   Conclusions 64

4   Fuzzy logic framework for ontology alignment   **66**
4.1   Introduction 66
4.2   Aligning ontologies on the concept level 68
4.3   Aligning ontologies on the relation level 76
4.4   Aligning ontologies on the instance level 86
4.5   Conclusions 103

III   Maintenance and Evaluation   105

5   Ontology evolution and version management in ontology alignment   **107**

  5.1   Introduction 107
  5.2   Tracking changes in evolving ontologies 108
  5.3   Assessing the significance of ontology modifications 111
  5.4   Methods for updating ontology alignment 116
  5.5   Measuring the level of knowledge about ontology interoperability 131
  5.6   Conclusions 140

6   Advanced methods of assessing ontology alignment   142
  6.1   Content-based methods of assessing ontology alignment quality 142
  6.2   Applicability analysis 154
  6.3   Conclusions 167

IV   Final Remarks   169

7   Conclusions   171

Bibliography   173

Index   193

Foreword

This book addresses the field of ontologies and ontology alignment, covering a range of topics from basic concepts to the more complex issues related to ontology evolution. The book aims to provide a systematic overview of the literature but primarily presents novel findings proposed by the author, who has devoted over ten years of research in this area.

Initially, it introduces a formal model of ontology divided into the levels of concepts, relations, and instances. The crated formal foundations are used throughout the book, forming a backbone for every method presented further. Subsequently, it gives a set of methods for defining the semantics of attributes and relations. Then, the focus is put on defining ontology alignments and a comprehensive set of formal criteria for detecting inconsistencies in ontology mappings. This is what clearly distinguishes this book from other books on the ontology subject.

A significant part of the book addresses a fuzzy logic framework for designating ontology alignment. It is based on a set of similarity measures that allow calculating the degree to which two ontologies are related, which are then fed into custom fuzzy inference rules. The presented approach has been experimentally verified using state-of-the-art benchmark data from the Ontology Alignment Evaluation Initiative.

The book also introduces a formal model for tracking changes in evolving ontologies, offering tools for understanding and documenting modifications over time. It covers a systematic approach for revalidating and updating ontology alignments, ensuring they remain valid as the underlying ontologies change.

Finally, the book explores a content-based framework for assessing ontology alignment quality, incorporating concept depth and continuity factors. The proposed approach, validated through experimental evaluations against state-of-the-art benchmark datasets taken from the literature, offers new insights into the efficacy and applicability of ontology alignments.

In my opinion, the methods for ontology alignment included in this book are very valuable and many readers such as postgraduate and PhD students in computer science, as well as scientists who are working on knowledge management, information fusion and ontology integration, will find it interesting.

Ngoc Thanh Nguyen

Preface

The domain of ontologies and ontology engineering represents one of the branches within the broader field of knowledge representation. It focuses on creating structured methods that allow machines to understand, interpret, and manipulate symbolic information. In this context, ontologies refer to explicit, formal specifications of conceptualizations and provide a shared understanding of a given domain.

To ensure effective communication between two or more information systems that utilize independently created ontologies, some kind of bridge between them is necessary. In the literature, establishing such a bridge is often called ontology alignment. The main aim of this task is to find semantic equivalences or similarities between entities from different ontologies that may not be identical but may share a similar meaning or role. Eventually, semantic interoperability can be achieved by aligning ontologies, enabling diverse information systems to communicate effectively.

The book aims to cover the complete ontology alignment lifecycle, including modelling, methods, and maintenance processes. Such construction offers readers a thorough understanding of every aspect of the considered subject. It aspires to be a valuable resource for both academic researchers and practitioners in the field of knowledge representation and semantic technologies.

This book summarizes the author's research achievements over the past seven years. Some of these findings have been published in esteemed international journals and presented at prominent conferences. However, within this book, the results have also been expanded and thoroughly explained in a cohesive and detailed manner. The material of each chapter is self-contained, assuming familiarity with the basic mathematical notions introduced in the initial sections of the book.

I wish to extend my deepest appreciation to my wife and daughter, whose encouragement, patience, and understanding have been my greatest support during the writing of this book. Special thanks go to Professor Ngoc Thanh Nguyen, whose invaluable insights and engaging discussions have significantly enriched my work. I am also grateful to Professor Zbigniew Huzar for his inspiring commentaries, and to Professor Marcin Hernes for his detailed feedback. Finally, my sincere thanks go to Randi Slack, the editor of this series, for her help and guidance.

Author

Dr. Marcin Pietranik has been an assistant professor at Wrocław University of Science and Technology since 2016. He obtained his MSc and PhD degrees in computer science in 2008 and 2014, respectively. Dr. Pietranik is passionate about knowledge integration and is interested in ontology management, particularly ontology evolution and alignment. He has published more than 45 articles and co-organized several conferences, demonstrating his significant contribution to the field. In addition to his academic pursuits, Dr. Pietranik has a practical background in modern web technologies, especially in the context of medical and telecommunication projects, which provide him with a unique perspective in his research.

List of Algorithms

1	Designating attribute's semantics	21
2	Select attribute entry	23
3	Prepare candidate entries	23
4	Naive approach to relations semantics	25
5	Determining semantics of relations	26
6	Get single word semantics	27
7	Fuzzy-based approach for concept alignment	69
8	Fuzzy-based approach to ontology alignment on relation level	77
9	Fuzzy-based approach to ontology alignment on instance level	89
10	Calculating $prsim$	92
11	Updating the existing alignment with new mappings	117
12	Updating alignments of modified concepts	118
13	Removing stale mappings of deleted concepts from the existing alignment	120
14	Adding new mappings on the level of relations	121
15	Revalidating the existing mappings of relations	123
16	Removing stale mappings of deleted relations from the existing alignment	124
17	Applying effects of instance and concept removals in ontology alignment on the instance level alignment	125
18	Applying effects of concept additions in ontology alignment on the instance level alignment	127
19	Updating ontology alignment on the instance level	128
20	Refining ontology alignment on the instance level	130
21	Procedure for calculating values of Γ_C	150
22	Procedure for calculating values of Γ_I	153

Part I

Introduction and Background

1

Introduction

1.1 Understanding ontology alignment

In the context of computer science, an often-cited definition of ontologies created by Thomas Gruber describes them as "a formal, explicit specification of a shared conceptualization" ([69]). This definition, while brief, captures the essence of what ontologies aim to achieve. A shared conceptualization refers to an abstract model of a common understanding of elements from some domain of discourse. A formal, explicit specification entails that the conceptualization can be unambiguously described using some kind of formal language that provides both a vocabulary (terms and their meanings) and a grammar (rules for combining terms) to express knowledge about the conceptualization.

In other words, in the base Thomas Gruber's definition, an ontology is a structured representation of knowledge. It is a formal representation that describes concepts that express the knowledge about types of objects within a specific domain, their relationships, and their potential instantiation. These three distinguished types of elements within ontologies together form a stack of abstraction levels (namely, the level of concepts, the level of relations, and the level of instances) that need to be considered when using ontologies spanning a wide range of fields and applications. For example, in the healthcare sector, a medical ontology might include concepts representing symptoms, diseases, and treatments. At the same time, relationships could define how a symptom is related to a disease or which treatment is suitable for a particular disease. Finally, instances might become specific patients, their diagnoses, and performed treatment processes.

In recent years, a new research area of knowledge graphs has emerged ([93]), which focuses on representing knowledge in a graph-like structure. Although the topic originates from the subject of ontologies, Knowledge Graphs differ from them in several key aspects, and the primary distinction lies in their structural focus and expressivity.

As described earlier, ontologies are formal representations of knowledge, which may include a rich set of constraints and annotations that preserve internal consistency. They offer a more comprehensive and detailed framework for understanding and inferring relationships within a domain. On the other hand, Knowledge Graphs focus on factual information, linking specific entities and relationships rather than defining abstract concepts, often rejecting issues concerning redundancy or inconsistency. In simpler terms, Knowledge Graphs can be treated as an instance-focused version of ontologies, making them relatively more straightforward to implement and manage. This makes Knowledge Graphs particularly effective for applications that require rapid traversal and querying, such as search engines and recommendation systems.

The emergence of Knowledge Graphs signifies a shift towards a more practical and accessible means of knowledge representation, rejecting the rigorous formalism of ontologies with the operational needs of modern data-driven applications. This rejection is directly caused by the complexity of developing and maintaining ontologies, which involves several key stages.

DOI: 10.1201/9781003437888-1

It starts with defining its scope, which involves identifying the domain of knowledge the ontology will cover and understanding the level of detail required. Once the scope is established, the next step is to enumerate the essential concepts and relationships within that domain. This process is typically collaborative, involving domain experts and ontology engineers, ensuring that the ontology accurately reflects the consensus understanding of the domain.

The described procedure and its overall complexity (especially if created ontologies cover a large scope of knowledge like the Gene Ontology [25] or FMO [170]) implies that multiple specifications can exist for the same conceptualization. Therefore, if two integrated computer systems exist that use different ontologies, there is a need to establish a shared means of communication and to provide such communication, it is necessary to establish a mapping between the contents of their respective ontologies, which in the literature is often referred to as ontology alignment. In other words, ontology alignment is a seemingly uncomplicated task of finding how different independently developed and maintained ontologies articulate identical or closely related elements of the underlying conceptualization.

One of the practical application examples of ontology alignment is facilitating communication between two medical systems that use different ontologies in their knowledge bases. This scenario is especially visible in healthcare applications where diverse therapeutic devices, like MRI or CT scanners, operate using different healthcare ontologies, such as SNOMED-CT or ICD10 ([169]). These often contain overlapping or related concepts, but they are expressed in different ways, and without the alignment, the systems may interpret the same clinical information differently, leading to potential misunderstandings or errors in patient care. Effective ontology alignment ensures the systems can understand and interpret each other correctly, leading to more cohesive and reliable integration of medical information across various platforms.

Despite being simple to understand, finding good alignments between ontologies entails multiple challenges. First, a solid mathematical definition of ontology is crucial for providing effective alignments as it provides an unambiguous description of ontology content on all of the levels of abstraction aforementioned at the beginning of this chapter. Precise definitions of concepts, relations, and instances and their internal structures ensure they are clearly understood and consistently interpreted. Consequently, it clarifies and streamlines identifying alignments between two distinct ontologies.

Unfortunately, in literature, a majority of publications treat ontology definitions superficially ([195], [94]) or even do not provide one at all ([137], [143]). The most common approach involves accepting OWL[1] (Web Ontology Language) format as the only method of expressing ontologies. These remarks are further supported by [31] and [213].

Even though the OWL itself is a mature and sound tool, it has certain expressivity limits ([63],[152], [198]). One such limitation is negligible attention to attributes that form a structure of concepts. The OWL standard is limited to representing attributes only as simple values assigned with no additional semantics. Obviously, when some attribute is included in different concepts, it acquires different interpretations. For example, an attribute "address" has different semantics if included within a concept "Company" and different when being a part of a concept "Website". As far as we are aware, no existing ontology alignment method has concentrated on how the semantics of attributes affect the process of establishing ontology mappings at various levels of granularity.

An approach to ontology alignment based only on processing OWL format and omitting the formal backbone reduces designating semantically rich alignments to finding mappings between two text files containing OWL documents. This issue is especially visible when some methods for ontology alignment build their approach to analysing elements that appear in

---

[1]https://www.w3.org/OWL/

such files but are outside the scope of ontologies (for example, informal comments added as purely syntatic constructs within files containing ontologies, like solutions proposed in [185], [19]).

A complete formal definition of ontology (like the one that will be presented in Chapter 2), that consistently covers all of its internal elements, entails that finding an alignment involves processing multiple elements on different granularity levels. The ontology alignment framework can be considered complete only if it allows for mapping ontologies on a level of concepts, relations, and instances. However, processing components of ontologies and their internal structure requires a multistrategy approach, with each strategy yielding separate results. These individual outcomes must be combined into a single, unified result.

When some alignments are eventually established, the task of deciding which of them is "the best one" exists. One of the approaches to the topic would involve using a reference alignment, pre-prepared by experts, which would allow the use of classic metrics like Precision and Recall. However, in real-world applications, one cannot expect that there is some gold standard alignment with which competing alignments could be confronted and evaluated. Moreover, what would be the point of finding other alignments if a reference alignment exists? Thus, if multiple different alignments are provided, how do we evaluate their quality? Therefore, it would be beneficial to develop methods of assessing ontology alignments based only on information available within aligned ontologies and their additional properties.

Finally, it is essential to recognize that even a high-quality alignment between two ontologies is not guaranteed to remain valid over time, and the alignments, like every other element of modern information systems, require ongoing maintenance. Ontologies are not static; they may evolve to incorporate new knowledge or changes in their covered domain. Consequently, when an ontology changes, the existing alignment may become unusable. Therefore, one of the most crucial issues that needs to be addressed while maintaining ontology alignment is related to ontology evolution. A straightforward, albeit resource-intensive, solution to this problem would be re-establishing the alignment from the beginning, ensuring good results. However, in scenarios where only parts of an ontology have changed, and most of the existing mappings remain valid, one must consider whether this computationally expensive approach is the sole option. Ideally, the process should consist of two steps: first, evaluating if the modifications substantially affect the alignment's validity, and second, deciding if the alignment can be updated merely by referencing the changes described in the ontologies.

In summary, finding and maintaining alignments between ontologies are complex tasks with a number of challenges. The discussions presented above shed some light on a few of them, providing a foundational understanding of the subject. This book aims to provide comprehensive and detailed solutions to these challenges, rooted in rigorous formal foundations.

1.2 The subject of this book

The main subject of this book is related to formal methods for managing and processing ontology alignments, which include developing a formal, mathematical definition of ontologies, finding alignment between ontologies and maintaining them over a period of time and finally, evaluating their quality. The book aims to provide a systematic overview of the found literature but primarily presents novel findings proposed by the author, who has devoted over ten years of research to these problems.

Overall, the book attempts to answer the following questions:

- How can ontologies be precisely defined at the concept, relation, and instance levels?

- How to precisely define the ontology alignment on a level of concepts, relations, and instances?

- How to detect inconsistencies in ontology mappings?

- Can fuzzy logic be integrated into ontology alignment to incorporate an additional layer of expert knowledge?

- What structure allows for the analysis of changes within ontologies?

- How can the impact of sequential modifications to ontologies be quantitatively assessed?

- What strategies effectively maintain ontology alignments in light of ontology evolution?

- How can the quality of ontology alignments be evaluated independently of reference alignments?

Although some content in this book has previously appeared in various publications, it has been significantly reworked, refined, and organized to form a more structured and comprehensive narrative. Additionally, the book introduces new insights and methodologies not previously published, offering a deeper understanding of the domain. Each chapter's conclusion provides detailed discussions and analyzes of these new materials, highlighting their unique features and importance.

Overall, this book is a valuable resource for scholars and practitioners in the domains of knowledge representation and semantic technologies. It offers a comprehensive and novel perspective on ontology alignment, enriching the academic discourse and advancing practical applications in the field.

1.3   The contributions of this work

The field of ontologies and ontology alignment continues to be a relevant and significant area of research. However, a comprehensive resource that encapsulates this topic from foundational concepts to advanced research issues, such as the evolution of ontology alignment, is absent in current literature. Notably, issues concerning ontology evolution and its impact on ontology alignment are usually neglected.

For example, [8] primarily concentrates on the development aspects of ontologies, predominantly perceiving them as static entities. This perspective disregards the evolving nature of ontologies over time, which is a crucial factor in modern applications. On the other hand, [192] addresses aspects of the Semantic Web, predominantly dealing with OWL language (one of many ontology representation methods), RDF, and description logic. This approach, while insightful, narrows the scope to practical applications of ontologies, omitting broader issues like ontology alignment and the implications of ontology evolution.

A notable contribution can be found in [47], which focuses on classifying primary ontology alignment techniques. It discusses fundamental similarity methods, provides insights into various ontology matching systems, and overviews several evaluation methodologies. However, it does not cover the temporal aspect of ontologies nor does it venture into more generalized techniques for evaluating ontology alignments.

For a broad overview of literature covering topics related to ontologies, ontology alignment, and ontology evolution please refer to Chapter 3, where a critical analysis of a wide array of publications is provided along with their comparison with the solutions presented in this book. The performed research allows us to claim that while the existing literature in the field contains numerous publications in prestigious journals, there is a noticeable gap in continuous and comprehensive research in this domain. Thus, this book aims to fill this gap by providing an extensive overview of ontologies and ontology alignment issues. It brings forth the original contributions of the author, which include the following elements:

- A formal model of ontology, its internal elements (concepts, relations, and instances), and their structures, including a novel notion of attributes' and relations' semantics based on propositional calculus.

- Method of providing attributes' semantics.

- Method of providing relations semantics.

- A formal model of ontology alignment.

- A set of formal criteria for detecting inconsistencies in ontology mappings.

- Fuzzy logic framework for ontology alignment, which includes:

  - Fuzzy logic-based method for aligning ontologies on the concept level (three concept similarity functions with accompanying fuzzyfication functions and a set of fuzzy inference rules).

  - Fuzzy logic-based methods for aligning ontologies on the relation level (two relation similarity functions with accompanying fuzzyfication functions and a set of fuzzy inference rules).

  - Fuzzy logic-based methods for aligning ontologies on the instance level (seven instance similarity functions with accompanying fuzzyfication functions and a set of fuzzy inference rules)

- Results of experimental verification of fuzzy logic framework for ontology alignment and its comparison with competitive solutions in the light of the state-of-the-art benchmark datasets provided by the Ontology Alignment Evaluation Initiative.

- A formal model of time, ontology repository and ontology log used to track changes in evolving ontologies.

- A set of difference functions providing methods to describe changes applied to ontologies throughout their maintenance and evolution.

- A set of functions for assessing the significance of ontology modifications for the concept, relation, and instance levels.

- A framework for revalidating and updating ontology alignments based on information about ontology evolution, which includes

  - A set of methods for updating ontology alignment on the concept level.

  - A set of methods for updating ontology alignment on the relation level.

  - A set of methods for updating ontology alignment on the instance level.

- A method for measuring the level of ontologies interoperability and the results of its experimental evaluation.

- A content-based framework for assessing ontology alignment quality, which includes:
  - The concept depth-based methods for assessing ontology mappings.
  - The continuity-based methods for assessing ontology mappings.

- Experimental evaluation of a content-based framework for assessing ontology alignment quality, which includes:
  - Comparison with traditional metrics in the context of datasets provided by the Ontology Alignment Evaluation Initiative
  - Applicability analysis in ontology evolution utilizing the developed framework for updating ontology alignment.

1.4   The structure of this book

This book is organized into three main sections. The first part (Chapters 1 and 2) introduces the book's main subject and provides mathematical foundations that form the basis for all the subsequent chapters. The second section (Chapters 3 and 4) is devoted to techniques for finding ontology alignments. This includes a comprehensive literature review and a broad description of a novel fuzzy logic-based framework for ontology alignment. The third part (Chapters 5 and 6) discusses topics related to maintaining ontology alignment over time. It provides a set of tools for evaluating their quality. The latter can assess the efforts undertaken while maintaining ontology alignments. The additional, fourth, and final parts conclude the book. A more detailed description of the chapters can be found below.

Chapter 2 serves as a formal foundation for the book and is divided into three subparts. The first contains a general definition of ontology and its components. It introduces the notion of attributes' semantics, which is one of the distinguishing factors of the author's research compared to the literature. As mentioned in the earlier part of this chapter, attributes may have many different explicit and implicit meanings and gain interpretability by being included within concepts. To achieve such flexibility, the author formulated a function that assigns a logic sentence built from a set of symbols and basic logic operators to every inclusion of an attribute within a concept. Such an approach allows not only to express detailed knowledge about attributes but also to track relationships between them. However, the most significant difficulty while using the proposed approach is asserting the consistency of vocabulary used in the aforementioned logic sentences. Thus, the second part of the chapter covers these issues. The third and final part contains definitions of ontology alignment on the level of concepts, relations, and instances.

Chapter 3 provides a systematic overview of ontology alignment techniques in the literature. It includes a description of both classic and temporary approaches to the problem. It starts with a general classification of different methods and eventually provides a detailed summary of ontology alignment systems from theoretical, practical, and application perspectives.

Chapter 4 describes the author's novel fuzzy logic-based approach to ontology alignment. A number of ontology alignment solutions are based on calculating similarities between two elements taken from two ontologies, for example comparing concept names, how their hierarchies are constructed, which instances they include, etc. When used separately, such methods cannot be expected to yield satisfying outcomes. Therefore, there must be a method of combining several different values into one interpretable output. The author proposes a different approach by incorporating fuzzy logic and inference rules, introducing another layer of experts' knowledge to the process. Additionally, a set of similarity functions is also provided along with the experimental evaluation of the developed framework.

Chapter 5 is devoted to the topic of ontology evolution and how it impacts ontology alignment. The author noticed that it is not plausible to expect that the aligned ontologies do not change in time, and it is also not plausible to expect that the established alignment will not become invalid due to those changes. The chapter discusses and describes an ontology alignment maintenance framework developed by the author. It is divided into three parts. The first introduces basic mathematical notions necessary to model ontology evolution. The second part focuses on identifying situations when ontologies evolved significantly enough to potentially invalidate their alignment. The third part of the chapter gives a set of algorithms for updating the established alignment based only on information about how involved ontologies changed. The chapter also contains the results of the experimental verification of the created framework.

Chapter 6 presents the author's novel methods for evaluating ontology alignments based on mapped ontologies' content and independent from preprepared reference alignments. It is divided into three parts. The first provides methods for assessing ontology mappings using the information about concepts' depths. The second part contains a description of continuity-based methods. The third part describes an experimental comparison with traditional metrics (Precision and Recall) using state-of-the-art benchmark datasets taken from the literature, along with the applicability analysis in the context of ontology evolution and the framework described in the earlier chapter.

The book ends with Chapter 7, which provides conclusions and potential future research directions.

2

A formal model of ontology and ontology alignment

The primary goal of this chapter is to establish a mathematical foundation for the remainder of the book. It offers a comprehensive ontology definition, detailing its core elements, including concepts, relations, and instances. It also introduces the notion of semantics of attributes and relations, which is one of the distinguishing factors of the author's research compared to the literature. Methods that can be used to provide these semantics are also discussed. Finally, formal definitions for ontology alignment and its properties are given.

2.1 Basic notions

Definition 2.1 A real world is defined as a pair *(A, V)*, where A is a set of attributes describing objects. Each attribute $a \in A$ has its respective domain denoted as V_a. V is a collection of valuations of all attributes from A, therefore $V = \bigcup_{a \in A} V_a$. This pair *(A, V)* forms the "closed world", on top of which the (A, V)-based domain ontology can be defined as a quintuple:

$$O = (C, R^C, I, R^I, H) \tag{2.1}$$

where:

- C is a finite set of concepts,

- R^C is a set of concepts relations $R^C = \{r_1^C, r_2^C, ..., r_n^C\}$, $(n \in \mathbb{N})$, such that every $r_i^C \in R^C$ is a subset of a cartesian product $C \times C$, which can be formally described as:

$$\forall r_i^C \in R^C : r_i^C \subset C \times C \tag{2.2}$$

Elements of R^C establish the possible types of relations between different concepts within the ontology, which may be treated as a schema that defines how instances of different concepts may relate to each other. For example, in a medical ontology, a relation $diagnoses^C$ in R^C could define that a concept *Physician* can provide diagnoses for concepts *Patient*. Therefore, $R^C = \{diagnoses^C\}$ and $diagnoses^C = \{(Physician, Patient)\}$, setting a framework for how instances of these concepts can interact. However, within R^C there are no specific occurrences of these interactions between instances of concepts *Physician* and *Patient*. These are defined further within the set R^I.

- I represents a collection of unique identifiers assigned to instances. It is essential to understand that these identifiers are not the instances themselves. Instead, they serve

DOI: 10.1201/9781003437888-2

as labels that allow distinguishing one instance from another. These identifiers are utilized within various ontology concepts, each dictating a particular set of attributes for the instances it encompasses (which will be clarified in Definition 2.3). Such an approach allows the same identifier to be applied across different concepts, illustrating the multifaceted nature of an object from the domain of discourse, which not only enhances the flexibility of the ontology by enabling the multifunctional use of a single identifier but also reflects the interconnected and versatile roles that instances can embody in different contexts.

- $R^I = \{r_1^I, r_2^I, ..., r_n^I\}$ is defined as the set of relations detailing specific interactions between instances of concepts, contrasting with R^C, which outlines potential relationships at a conceptual level. In a medical ontology, for example, R^C could include relations such as $diagnoses^C$, indicating possible interactions like $(Physician, Patient)$ among others, thus $R^C = \{diagnoses^C, consults^C, prescribes^C, ...\}$ with $diagnoses^C = \{(Physician, Patient), (Specialist, Patient), ...\}$. Correspondingly, R^I specifies concrete relations between instances such as $diagnoses^I$, encompassing actual pairs like $(John\ Smith, Peter\ Jones)$, $(Alice\ Brown, Mary\ Clark)$, showcasing real-life instances of physicians or specialists diagnosing patients. This structure allows R^I to accurately reflect real-world interactions, following the concept-level schema provided by R^C.

- H represents the hierarchy among concepts within the ontology, formally defined as $H \subseteq C \times C$. This denotes that H is a particular type of relation between concepts from the set C, which delineates the inheritance relationship. For example, in a biological ontology, the concept *Bird* might inherit attributes from the more general concept *Animal*, indicating that *Bird* is a type of *Animal*. Formally, members of the set H must adhere to specific conditions, detailed in Definition 2.10, which ensure the proper organization of H. However, it is essential to note that within the proposed definitions, hierarchy is treated as a partially ordered set, thus allowing for multi-inheritance.

To denote a set of all (A, V)-based ontologies the symbol $\widetilde{O}$ will be used. Additionally, $\widetilde{C}$ will denote a set of all possible concepts.

Definition 2.2 A structure of a concept taken from the set C is defined as a quadruple:

$$c = (id^c, A^c, V^c, I^c) \tag{2.3}$$

where:

- id^c is concept's identifier,

- A^c is a set of concept's attributes, such that:

$$\forall a \in A^c : a \in A \wedge V_a \subset V \tag{2.4}$$

- V^c is a set of domains of concept's attributes, such that:

$$V^c = \bigcup_{a \in A^c} V_a \tag{2.5}$$

- I^c is a set of concepts' c instances.

In isolation, attributes in set A possess no inherent semantic content; they function as placeholders for values. However, in everyday speech, people associate explicit meanings with attributes, and moreover, attribute interpretation changes with the context of their usage. For example, the attribute "size" assumes different meanings based on its contextual application: in the domain of clothing, it typically denotes the dimensions of an article of clothing, whereas in the field of data storage, "size" pertains to the required memory capacity for storing a file.

In other words, if an attribute is a part of different concepts, its semantics are different. In order to achieve such an increased level of expressivity of attributes, let's introduce a attribute language.

Definition 2.3 *Attribute language* is a formal language denoted as EXP_A. It is defined as a set of expressions built from the alphabet $D_A = \{\alpha_1, \alpha_2, ..., \alpha_p\}$ and three propositional connectives: conjunction $\wedge$, disjunction $\vee$, and negation $\neg$. Each member of EXP_A must meet the following conditions:

- every $\alpha \in D_A$ is an expression of EXP_A;

- if α is an expression of EXP_A, then $\neg\alpha$ is also an expression;

- if α_i and α_j are expressions, then $\alpha_i \wedge \alpha_j$ and $\alpha_i \vee \alpha_j$ are also expressions.

The above conditions form the syntax of EXP_A. At this point, it is important to emphasize that multiple ontology developers may work on a single ontology. Therefore, many people may contribute to the content of D_A, which cannot be known beforehand. Consequently, multiple different understandings of elements of D_A may exist.

Let $U = \{u_1, u_2, ..., u_t\}$ denote a finite set of experts. Each expert has his own domain knowledge and may or may not agree with the statement that some expression from EXP_A is valid. An overall perspective on the opinions of all experts is given by the function with the following signature:

$$I_A : EXP_A \times U \rightarrow \{true, false, \emptyset\} \tag{2.6}$$

The above function provides an expert's evaluation of an expression to one of the truth values, namely *true* or *false*. The situation in which $I_A(exp, u) = true$ (such that $exp \in EXP_A$ and $u \in U$) represents the fact that the expert u claims that the expression exp is valid. The opposite occurs if $I_A(exp, u) = false$. The distinguished value $\emptyset$ is used when some experts has no opinion about a given expression (if such is the case, then $I_A(exp, u) = \emptyset$).

Utilizing the definition of attribute language it is possible to define attributes semantics within ontology $O = (C, R^C, I, R^I, H)$ as a function with the following signature:

$$S_A : A \times C \rightarrow EXP_A \tag{2.7}$$

S_A simply assigns a chosen expression of the EXP_A to every inclusion of attributes from the set A to concepts from the given ontology. Such an approach enables a clearer understanding of the role of attributes, and in consequence, it enables the attribute to be employed more precisely and effectively in various scenarios.

For better understanding, imagine an attribute *birthday* included in a concept *Person*. The following value of the function S_A can be accepted: $S_A(birthday, Person) = day\_of\_birth \wedge month\_of\_birth \wedge year\_of\_birth \wedge age \wedge zodiac\_sign$, which allows for more detailed and structured information to be stored and analyzed about a person's birthday. For example, instead of just knowing the date of a person's birthday, we can also store information about their age, what zodiac sign they belong to, and even the specific day and month of their birth.

Moreover, the function S_A entails that it is possible to define relationships between attributes formally:

- Two attributes $a \in A^{c_1}, b \in A^{c_2}$ are *semantically equivalent* from any two concepts c_1, c_2, if the following expression is a tautology $(\neg S_A(a, c_1) \vee S_A(b, c_2)) \wedge (\neg S_A(a, c_2) \vee S_A(b, c_1))$. It will be denoted as $a \equiv b$.

- The attribute $a \in A^{c_1}$ in concept c_1 is *more general* than the attribute $b \in A^{c_2}$ in concept c_2 (denoted as $a \leftarrow b$) if the following expression is a tautology $\neg S_A(b, c_2) \vee S_A(a, c_1)$.

- Two attributes $a \in A^{c_1}, b \in A^{c_2}$ from any two concepts c_1, c_2 are in *semantic contradiction*, denoted as $a \sim b$, if the following expression is a tautology $\neg(S_A(a, c_1) \wedge S_A(b, c_2))$.

The relationships between attributes of a concept refer to how different properties or characteristics of a concept are linked or associated. However, a significant limitation of this approach is the requirement for manual input by ontology authors. The values of S_A and the elements of D_A both require their manual specification. This process can be time-intensive and susceptible to errors, particularly when several people collaborate on developing the same ontology. This issue is significant as it can lead to inconsistencies and inaccuracies in the ontology, ultimately affecting its reliability and effectiveness. In order to remedy this issue, a semi-automatic method of providing values of S_A (and in consequence narrowing the scope of D_A) is presented in Section 2.2 of the book.

Definition 2.4 A context entailed by a concept is its overall semantics, and it can be expressed as a conjunction of the semantics of all attributes included in c. It can be defined as a function with the following signature:

$$ctx : C \rightarrow EXP_A \tag{2.8}$$

Assuming that some concept $c \in C$ contains k attributes ($|A^c| = k$) the considered function ctx can be defined as follows:

$$ctx(c) = S_A(a_1, c) \wedge S_A(a_2, c) \wedge ... \wedge S_A(a_k, c) \tag{2.9}$$

An instance within an ontology denotes a concrete example or specific occurrence that falls under a defined concept within that ontology. To illustrate, consider an ontology that describes various animal species. In this context, an instance could be some individual animal, like a specific dog or cat, representing a real-world embodiment of the concept of "Animal". Similarly, in an ontology focused on fruit types, an instance could be a particular fruit, such as an apple or a banana. In other words, an instance of a concept is a concrete example that helps illustrate and apply the concepts defined within an ontology.

Definition 2.5 The instance i which belongs to the set I^c from some concept $c \in C$ is defined as a pair:

$$i = (id^i, v_c^i) \tag{2.10}$$

where:

- id^i is the instance's identifier,

- v_c^i is a function with a signature:

$$v_c^i : A^c \rightarrow V^c \tag{2.11}$$

The valuation of the function v_c^i is tightly bound to the instance occurrence within a concept. It can be treated as a vector of specific values of attributes from the set A^c. For short, we can write $i \in c$, which expresses that the instance i belongs to the concept c.

Due to the fact that instances can belong to several concepts at the same time, the set I from Equation 2.1, which is a collection of instances' identifiers, can be defined as follows:

$$I = \bigcup_{c \in C} \{id^i | (id^i, v_c^i) \in I^c\} \tag{2.12}$$

Utilizing such approach, it is possible to define two additional functions:

- A function denotes as Ins returns a set of identifiers of instances of the given concept c within ontology O:

$$Ins(O, c) = \{id^i \mid (id^i, v_c^i) \in I^c\} \tag{2.13}$$

- A function Ins^{-1} is a reversed version of Ins, which for a given instance identifier i, returns a set of concepts in which it has been used within ontology O:

$$Ins^{-1}(O, i) = \{c \mid c \in C \wedge i \in c\} \tag{2.14}$$

Definition 2.6 Two concepts c_1 and c_2 are considered semantically equivalent (which will be denoted by the operator $\equiv$) only if:

- the expression $ctx(c_1) \Leftrightarrow ctx(c_2)$ is a tautology

- $Ins(c_1) = Ins(c_2)$

For example, consider an ontology that defines two concepts, *Dog* and *Canine*. These concepts can be considered equivalent as every instance of a *Dog* is also an instance of *Canine* and vice versa.

Definition 2.7 Two concepts c_1 and c_2 are considered disjoint (which will be denoted by the operator $\not\equiv$) only if:

- the expression $\neg(ctx(c_1) \wedge ctx(c_2))$ is a tautology

- $Ins(c_1) \cup Ins(c_2) = \emptyset$

Consider an example of an ontology where two distinct concepts, namely *Vegetarian* and *Carnivore*, are defined as mutually exclusive. In this scenario, an instance classified under the *Vegetarian* concept cannot simultaneously be categorized as a *Carnivore*, and the reverse also holds. This exclusivity extends to any subclasses that emerge from these primary classes. For example, a subclass like *Vegan* originating from *Vegetarian* must also be distinctly separate from *Carnivore* and its related subclasses. This separation is crucial to preserve the logic consistency within the ontology.

Relations from the set R^C in an ontology pertain to the meanings or interpretations of the connections or relationships established between various concepts. These relationships are non-hierarchical, meaning they don't conform to a parent-child or subclass-superclass structure. Non-taxonomic relations instead describe how concepts are interlinked. For example, in an ontology about cars, non-taxonomic relations might include 'part-of' (as in, a steering wheel is part of a car), 'located-in' (a car is located in a garage), 'precedes' (the timing belt precedes the crankshaft), and 'follows' (the battery follows the alternator). Therefore, by analogy to propositional attribute language let's introduce a propositional relation language.

Definition 2.8 *Relation language* is a formal language denoted as EXP_R. It is defined as a set of expressions built from the alphabet $D_R = \{\beta_1, \beta, ..., \beta_q\}$ and three propositional connectives: conjunction $\wedge$, disjunction $\vee$, and negation $\neg$. Each member of EXP_R must meet the following conditions:

- every $\beta \in D_R$ is an expression of EXP_R;

- if β is an expression of EXP_R, then $\neg\beta$ is also an expression;

- if β_i and β_j are expressions, then $\beta_i \wedge \beta_j$ and $\beta_i \vee \beta_j$ are also expressions.

The above conditions form the syntax of EXP_R.

Analogously to EXP_A, multiple understandings of elements of D_R may exist and, consequently, multiple understandings of expressions of EXP_R. Each expert from the set $U = \{u_1, u_2, ..., u_t\}$ has his own domain knowledge and may or may not agree with the statement that some expression from EXP_R is valid. An overall perspective on the opinions of all experts is given by the function with the following signature:

$$I_R : EXP_R \times U \rightarrow \{true, false, \emptyset\} \tag{2.15}$$

The function above assigns an expert's assessment of a given expression to one of the binary truth values, specifically *true* or *false*. When $I_R(exp, u) = true$ (where $exp \in EXP_R$ and $u \in U$), it denotes that the expert u_n asserts the expression exp to be correct. Conversely, if $I_R(exp, u) = false$, the expert disagrees with the expression's validity. The special value $\emptyset$ is employed to represent the absence of an opinion from an expert on the particular expression (in which case, $I_R(exp, u) = \emptyset$).

Utilizing relation language it is possible to define relations semantics as a function that maps each relation in the set R^C to a corresponding expressions of EXP_R. It has a signature:

$$S_R : R^C \rightarrow EXP_R \tag{2.16}$$

This approach enables a more detailed understanding of the relations from R^C. Moreover, having the function S_R it is possible to define relationships between relations, similarly to relationships between attributes:

- Two relations r_1^C, $r_2^C \in R^C$ are equivalent (denoted by $r_1^C \equiv r_2^C$) if the following expression is a tautology $(\neg S_R(r_1^C) \vee S_R(r_2^C)) \wedge (\neg S_R(r_2^C) \vee S_R(r_1^C))$.

- The relation $r_2^C \in R^C$ is more general than the relation $r_1^C \in R^C$ (denoted by $r_2^C \leftarrow r_1^C$) if the following expression is a tautology $\neg S_R(r_1^C) \vee S_R(r_2^C)$

- Two relations r_1^C, $r_2^C \in R^C$ are contradicting $r_1^C \sim r_2^C$ if the following expression is a tautology $\neg(S_R(r_1^C) \wedge S_R(r_2^C))$

Definition 2.9 Each relation r_j^C in R^C has a complementary relation r_j^I in R^I, which contains pairs of instances of concepts linked by the r_j^C relation. Both relations use the same index j for identification purposes. Obviously, $|R^C| = |R^I|$. Formal criteria describing such an approach are defined below:

1. $\forall_{r_j^I \in R^I} : r_j^I \subseteq \bigcup\limits_{(c_1, c_2) \in r_j^C} (Ins(c_1) \times Ins(c_2))$

2. $(i_1, i_2) \in r_j^I \implies \exists(c_1, c_2) \in r_j^C : (c_1 \in Ins^{-1}(i_1)) \wedge (c_2 \in Ins^{-1}(i_2))$; two instances can be connected by some relation only if there is a relation connecting concepts they belong to

3. $(i_1, i_2) \in r_j^I \implies \neg \exists r_i^I \in R^I : ((i_1, i_2) \in r_i^I) \wedge (r_j^C \sim r_i^C)$; two instances cannot be connected by two contradicting relations (e.g. Peter cannot be simultaneously a father and a brother of Jack)

4. $(i_1, i_2) \in r_j^I \wedge \exists r_i^I \in R^I : r_i^C \leftarrow r_j^C \implies (i_1, i_2) \in r_i^I$; if two instances are in a relation and there exists a more general relation, then they are also connected by it (e.g. if Joe is a father of Robert, then he is also his parent).

Consider the relation *reacts_with* from the set R^C, which links concepts representing chemical molecules that can combine to form more complex compounds. This relation is integral in an ontology focusing on chemistry, as it defines the potential for interaction between different molecular entities. The instance relations in the set R^I then describe the specific interactions between instances of these molecules. For example, the pair (hydrogen, oxygen) within R^I signifies that hydrogen molecules react with oxygen molecules, resulting in water compounds. This example illustrates how relations at the concept level (R^C) are instantiated at the instance level (R^I), providing a concrete and specific manifestation of the more abstract relationships.

Definition 2.10 The concept hierarchy H is a unique relation between concepts representing a tree with a root node. Although it is defined similarly to R^C as $H \subset C \times C$, it is not included in the set R^C for clarity. Certain conditions must be met for elements to be added to H. Specifically, a pair of concepts $c_1 = (id^{c_1}, A^{c_1}, V^{c_1}, I^{c_1})$ and $c_2 = (id^{c_2}, A^{c_2}, V^{c_2}, I^{c_2})$ can only be part of H if:

1. $|A^{c_2}| \geq |A^{c_1}|$

2. $\forall a \in A^{c_2} \exists a' \in A^{c_1} : a \leftarrow a'$

3. $Ins(c_2) \subseteq Ins(c_1)$

If a pair of concepts (c_1, c_2) is present in the set H, we can infer that they are connected through a subsumption relation, which implies that c_2 is a subclass of c_1. We can use the following notation $c_1 \leftarrow c_2$ to represent such a relation for clarity purposes.

This relation is also transitive, meaning that if there is a sequence of concepts $c_1, \ldots, c_n$ such that $(c_i, c_{i+1}) \in H$ for all $i \in [1, n-1]$, then we can conclude that the pair (c_1, c_n) also satisfies the conditions for subsumption, and we can represent it as $c_1 \leftarrow c_n$.

Definition 2.11 The set C contains an abstract concept called *Thing*. Utilizing Equation 2.3 its structure is defined as $\{Thing, \emptyset, \emptyset, \bigcup_{i \in I} (i, \emptyset)\}$. This concept acts as the root of the hierarchy H. All other concepts in the set are its subclasses.

The developed formal foundations allow for introducing a set of auxiliary functions that will be used throughout the remainder of the book:

1. $Root(O)$ returns a set of classes in the ontology O which are direct children of the distinguished class *Thing*. In other words- it yields a collection of classes situated at the topmost level within the hierarchy H. It has a signature $Root : \widetilde{O} \to \widetilde{C}$ and is calculated as:

$$Root(O) = \{c \in C | (Thing, c) \in H \wedge \neg \exists c' \in C \setminus \{Thing\} : (c', c) \in H\} \qquad (2.17)$$

2. $Sub_C(c)$ returns a set of all concepts that are descendants of concept c in the concept hierarchy H. For given ontology O it has a signature $Sup_C : C \to C$ and the returned set satisfies the following conditions:

- $\forall_{c' \in Sub_C(c)} c \leftarrow c'$, which ensures that every element in the set produced by the Sub_C function must be a descendant of the concept c.

- $\neg \exists c' \in C \setminus Sub_C(c) : c \leftarrow c'$ which states that no concept that descends from c is present in the ontology outside of the set produced by the $Sub_C(c)$ function.

3. $Sup_C(c)$ returns a set of concepts which are predecessors of the given concept c in the concept hierarchy H. For given ontology O it has a signature $Sup_C : C \rightarrow C$ and the returned set satisfies the following conditions:

   - $\forall_{c' \in Sup_C(c)} c' \leftarrow c$, which ensures that the concept c of every element in the set produced by the Sup_C function

   - $\neg \exists c' \in C \setminus Sup_C(c) : c' \leftarrow c$ which states that no concept of which c is a descendant is present outside of the set produced by the $Sup_C(c)$ function.

4. $Depth(S, c)$ returns the number of subsumption relationships between c and a root concept c_r of a subtree $S = Sub_C(c_r)$. For given ontology O it has a signature $Depth : 2^C \times C \rightarrow N$. It allows to use the notation $Depth(H, c)$ to represent the length of the shortest path in the tree from the root concept *Thing* to a particular concept c belonging to the set C.

5. $Depth(O)$ returns the overall depth of ontology O. It has a signature $Depth : \tilde{O} \rightarrow N$ and is calculated as:

$$Depth(O) = \max_{c \in C} Depth(H, c) \tag{2.18}$$

6. *dom* and *rng* are two contextual helper functions, that can be used to designate a domain and a range of a relation. Those terms refer to two fundamental aspects of defining connections between concepts or instances. The domain of a relation specifies the set of concepts from which the subject of that relation must belong. In other words, it defines the types of instances that can be the starting point of the relation. On the other hand, the range of a relation specifies the set concepts to which the object of that relation belongs. It defines the types of instances that can be the ending point of the relation.

For example, in an ontology about movies, where a relation called "directed_by" exists, the domain of this relationship might be defined as "Person" concept, while its range might be defined as the concept "Movie". In this example, the "directed_by" relation connects directors (persons) to the movies they have directed. The domain specifies that only instances of the class "Person" can be the subject of this relation. The range specifies that only instances of the class "Movie" can be the object of this relation. Such an approach ensures that it is only possible to associate directors with movies they have directed.

If functions *dom* and *rng* are used with a concept relation (thus, having signatures $dom : R^C \rightarrow C$ and $rng : R^C \rightarrow C$) they return set of concepts which are a domain or a range of a given relation:

$$dom(r^C) = \{c \in C | \exists c' \in C : (c, c') \in r^C\} \tag{2.19}$$

$$rng(r^C) = \{c \in C | \exists c' \in C (c', c) \in r^C\} \tag{2.20}$$

When provided with some instance and a specific instance relation, they return sets of instances with which a given instance is connected through a given relation. The former (with a signature $dom : I \times R^I \to I$) returns instances that are a starting point of the given relation. The latter (with a signature $rng : I \times R^I \to I$) provides instances which are an ending point. Formally:

$$dom(i, r^I) = \{i' \in I | (i', i) \in r^I\} \qquad (2.21)$$

$$rng(i, r^I) = \{i' \in I | (i, i') \in r^I\} \qquad (2.22)$$

7. *rel* is a helper function which for given instance extracts all relations in which this instance participates. Is has a signature: $rel : I \to 2^{R^I}$ and is defined below:

$$rel(i) = \{r \in R \mid rng(i, r) \neq \emptyset\} \qquad (2.23)$$

2.2   Methods of providing semantics of attributes and relations

This book section focuses on techniques for assigning meaning to attributes and relations based on their definitions as outlined in Section 2.1. Formally, the developed methods can be used to provide values of functions S_A and S_R from Equation 2.7 and 2.16, which are expected to provide semantics for attributes and relations, as zero-order logic expressions built from elements of respective sets of available atomic symbols.

Initially, the valuations of those functions (actual logic sentences assigned to relations or attributes within concepts) were supposed to be provided directly by experts or ontology developers. This method of manual assignment, however, is prone to becoming burdensome and error-prone as the number of attributes, concepts, and relations expands. To illustrate, in a relatively small-scale scenario involving five concepts, each encompassing five attributes, this process necessitates the manual formulation of twenty-five logical expressions, all needing to be consistent with one another. The considered difficulty would rapidly increase in real-world applications, such as in the sizeable biomedical ontology SNOMED-CT [39], where the number of concepts surpasses 360000, highlighting the impracticality of manual methods in such large-scale applications.

This section of the book presents methods that address the described issues. An external lexical database is necessary to provide the discussed logic sentences in a semi-automatic manner. Moreover, the selected database must contain comprehensive information about word senses, including disambiguation, part of speech, and semantic relations such as synonyms, antonyms, and hypernyms. Therefore, the section will start with a formal definition of thesauri and its internal components that will be used in further parts of the book.

Definition 2.12 By Σ we will denote an alphabet, which can be used to form a set of all finite strings regardless of their length (denoted as Σ^*). The thesauri can be defined as a pair:

$$TH = \langle S, Hyp \rangle \qquad (2.24)$$

where:

- S is a set of entries. Each entry from this set is a structure that represents the potential meaning of a word and is defined as a tuple:

$$\langle name, definition, synonyms, antonyms \rangle \qquad (2.25)$$

where:

- *name* $\in \Sigma^*$ is a unique name of an entry. To indicate that the entry belongs to a specific thesaurus, we use the notation *name* $\in TH$, which means that the entry with the name "name" is a member of the set S. However, since entries represent words from natural language, there may be cases where multiple entries require the same name. To avoid confusion, names are usually supplemented with a symbol representing the type of word (e.g. n denotes a noun, while v denotes verbs), and a number is added to differentiate between multiple entries.
- *definition* is a gloss of the entry – a brief explanation, which can be used to disambiguate the meaning of a word that may be a part of different entries and, therefore, have multiple senses.
- *synonyms* $\subset \Sigma^*$ is a set synonym of the given word
- *antonyms* $\subset \Sigma^*$ is a set of words that carry the opposite meaning of the given entry. For example, for the word "hot", its antonyms can be "cold" or "cool".

In subsequent parts of the chapter, a dot notation will be employed to reference specific components of any given entry within this set. As an example, consider an entry denoted as e. To access the 'name' component of this entry, the notation $e.name$ will be utilized.

- $Hyp \in S \times S$ is a hypernymy relation between entries, which expresses that one entry represents a more general meaning. In contrast, the other represents a more specific one. For example, "animal" is a hypernym of "cat," as "cat" is a type of "animal".

In the specified set S, there is a designated root entry characterized by the tuple $\langle$*entity*, *"that which is perceived or known or inferred to have its distinct existence (living or nonliving)"*, $\emptyset$, $\emptyset$ $\rangle$. This root entry serves as the most general and abstract element within the set S.

Three additional functions can be defined:

1. *tokenize_and_tag* with a signature:

$$tokenize\_and\_tag : 2^{\Sigma^*} \to 2^{\Sigma^*} \qquad (2.26)$$

which preprocesses the given set of words from Σ^*, discarding any appearing stop words, preserving only nouns, verbs, pronouns, adjectives, and adverbs in their base forms. The actual body of this function lies in the field of Natural Language Processing, which is beyond the scope of this book; therefore, in further parts, the external tool Spacy[1] has been used.

2. *get_entries* with a signature:

$$get\_entries : \Sigma^* \to 2^S \qquad (2.27)$$

which for given word from the set Σ^* returns a set of entries which include this word. Formally, the function is defined as:

$$get\_entries(word) = \{e \in S \mid word \in e.synonyms\} \qquad (2.28)$$

3. sim_{ML} with a signature:

$$sim_{ML} : \Sigma^* \times \Sigma^* \to [0, 1] \qquad (2.29)$$

---

[1] https://spacy.io/

which is a similarity function that, given two words from the set Σ^*, returns a value representing the degree to which these two words are similar. This function utilizes a language model to provide a vector representation of given words, where each dimension in the vector corresponds to a particular feature of the word. For example, a dimension may represent the frequency of the word in the corpus, while another may represent the context in which the word is typically used. To calculate the similarity between the words, the cosine similarity between their vector representations is typically used. The choice of language model used to generate the vector can vary, with options such as Word2Vec [21] or FastText [10] being commonly used for this purpose.

Numerous thesauri are available that meet the above definition, with WordNet [138] being a notable example. It was developed at Princeton University in 1985 and covered only english language. However, the accepted methodology and eventual results have led to the creation of analogous thesauris in more than 200 languages, each linked to the foundational Princeton WordNet.

In addition, modern technological advancements have facilitated the development of digital tools for lexical research. A solid example of such an online resource is WordsAPI[2], which provides a comprehensive platform for accessing a wide range of word-related information like synonyms, antonyms, and other lexical data.

The following two sections will discuss techniques for semi-automatically integrating external thesauri into generating attributes' (Section 2.2.1) and rations' semantics (Section 2.2.2). The first approach utilizes WordNet [138], while the second employs the WordsAPI aforementioned above [3].

2.2.1 Method of providing attributes semantics

Attributes do not have any explicit meanings independently. Only through their association with a concept can their meanings be discerned. In order to describe such attribute-concept connection, the previous section introduced in Equation 2.7 a formal mechanism which assigns logic sentences to each inclusion of an attribute within a concept.

However, a critical issue is the complexity of manually generating these logic sentences during the ontology development process. Therefore, the current section proposes a semi-automatic method to ease this process. This method is backed by the observation that the identifiers of attributes and concepts typically follow some naming conventions. By employing external thesauri to analyze the names of concepts and attributes, it becomes feasible to infer how these terms are interrelated and, consequently, provide the valuation of the function in Equation 2.7.

In the previous section, we introduced the hypernymy relation between any two entries in a thesaurus defined in Equation 2.24. By leveraging this concept, if the names of attributes and concepts can be aligned with entries in a thesaurus, it is possible to ascertain the shortest path connecting these entries, which facilitates the identification of their semantic relationship. In other words, this approach uses the structure and relationships inherent in a thesaurus to derive and assign meaning to the attributes and concepts within an ontology, thereby simplifying and enhancing the process of ontology development.

The proposed approach is presented in Algorithm 1. The algorithm takes as input a concept c from a set of concepts C and an attribute a belonging to the set of attributes A

---

[2]https://www.wordsapi.com/
[3]https://www.wordsapi.com/

Algorithm 1 Designating attribute's semantics

Input: $c \in C$, $a \in A^c$
Output: $S_A(a, c)$ (semantics of attribute a in the concept c according to Equation 2.7)
1: $entry(c) :=$ a selected entry for c based on the value of id^c;
2: $entry(a) := select\_attribute\_entry(a, c)$
3: $S_A(a, c) := ''$
4: **for** $node \in shortest\_path(entry(a), entry(c))$ **do**
5:     $S_A(a, c) := S_A(a, c) +' \wedge' + node.name$
6: **end for**
7: **return** $S_A(a, c)$

---

of the concept c ($a \in A^c$). In order to generate the semantics $S_A(a, c)$ of the attribute a in the concept c it takes the following steps:

1. It selects an entry for the concept c based on the value of id^c, where id^c is an identifier of the concept c.

2. It selects an entry for the attribute a by calling the function $select\_attribute\_entry(a, c)$.

3. It initializes the semantics $S_A(a, c)$ to an empty string.

4. It finds the shortest path between the entry of a and the entry of c by traversing the graph build upon the hypernymy relation Hyp from Equation 2.24. The sought shortest path usually leads through the root of the hypernymy relation.

5. For each node on the shortest path, the name of the node is appended to $S_A(a, c)$, separated by the logic operator $\wedge$.

6. Finally, the resulting semantics $S_A(a, c)$ is returned.

The initial step involves pinpointing the thesaurus entries that most accurately represent the names of the given attribute and concept, which is accomplished by comparing the attribute and concept names against the entries in the thesaurus. The comparison is based on the similarity scores generated by the sim_{ML} function, as defined in Equation 2.29. The entries that yield the highest similarity scores are chosen as the best representations. Then, after identifying the most representative entries for the attribute and concept, the algorithm determines the shortest path between these two entries, guided by the hypernymy relation. Following this relation, the algorithm traces a path from the specific entry (representing the attribute) to the second entry (representing the concept). Along the way, the algorithm concatenates the entries' names situated along the identified shortest path. The underlying assumption is that the shortest path between the entries corresponding to the attribute and concept encapsulates the transition from the context of the attribute to the context of the concept and provides the most direct and informative representation of their semantic relationship.

Consider an example given in Figure 2.1. Let us assume that the given concept is represented by the thesauri entry "dog" and the attribute for which we want to provide the value of S_A is represented by the entry "diet". Therefore, an example path the algorithm traverses is [*canine, domestic_animal, animal, entity, physical_entity, matter, substance, food, fare*]. In return it yields the following semantics $S_A(diet, dog) = canine \wedge domestic\_animal \wedge animal \wedge entity \wedge physical\_entity \wedge matter \wedge substance \wedge food \wedge fare$.

It can be easily seen that the algorithm leverages that in any thesauri, the common ancestor of every two words is an entry named "entity", which represents an abstract object

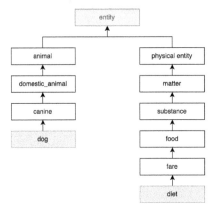

FIGURE 2.1
An example of hypernymy in WordNet thesauri

- the root of the hypernymy relation. If some expert u from the set U (introduced in Definition 2.3) considers the *diet* attribute of the concept *dog* related to the elements of the yielded expression (e.g. *canine*), then $I_A(S_A(diet, dog), u) = true$. Otherwise, I_A returns the value *false* or $\emptyset$ if the expert u doesn't provide any assessment of the considered expressions.

The Algorithm 1 utilizes a function *select_attribute_entry* presented in Algorithm 2. It takes two inputs: $c \in C$ and $a \in A^c$. Its output is an entry, denoted by *syn*, that is the best representation of the attribute a in the concept c. It takes the following steps:

1. It tokenizes and tags the concept name id^c using the *tokenize_and_tag* function, and stores the result in the variable *tagged_concept_name*.

2. It tokenizes and tags the attribute name a using the *tokenize_and_tag* function, and stores the result in the variable *tagged_attribute_name*.

3. It initializes a variable *max* to 0 to keep track of the maximum similarity score.

4. For each candidate entry *candidate* in the set of candidate entries obtained from the thesauri TH using the function *get_candidate_entries* (presented in Algorithm 3):

   (a) It creates a set *pairs* by taking the Cartesian product of the tagged concept name and the tagged candidate definition obtained from TH using the function *tokenize_and_tag*.

   (b) It calculates the partial similarity score *partial_sim* by computing the average of the maximum likelihood similarity score $sim_{ML}(pair)$ for each pair in the set *pairs*.

   (c) If the partial similarity score *partial_sim* is greater than the current maximum similarity score *max*, it updates the maximum similarity score to *partial_sim*. It sets the entry variable *syn* to the current candidate entry *candidate*.

5. Finally, the algorithm returns the entry variable *syn*, which represents the best entry that describes the attribute a in concept c.

The Algorithm 2 incorporates the function *get_candidate_entries* which realization is presented in Algorithm 3. It is essential to identify potential thesaurus entries corresponding to a set of words. It takes as input a tagged attribute name, denoted as *tagged_attribute_name*, and returns a set of entries, denoted as *candidates*. It takes the following steps:

Algorithm 2 Select attribute entry

Input: $c \in C$, $a \in A^c$

Output: $e \in S$ (entry best representing attribute a in the concept c)

1: **function** *select_attribute_entry*(a, c)
2:     $tagged\_concept\_name := tokenize\_and\_tag(id^c)$
3:     $tagged\_attribute\_name := tokenize\_and\_tag(a)$
4:     $max := 0$
5:     **for** $candidate \in get\_candidate\_entries(tagged\_attribute\_name)$ **do**
6:         $pairs := tagged\_concept\_name \times tokenize\_and\_tag(candidate.definition)$
7:         $partial\_sim := \frac{\sum_{pair \in pairs} sim_{ML}(pair)}{|pairs|}$
8:         **if** $partial\_sim > max$ **then**
9:             $max := partial\_sim$
10:            $e := candidate$
11:         **end if**
12:     **end for**
13:     **return** e
14: **end function**

---

1. The algorithm initializes *previous_iteration* as an empty string and *mutations* as an empty set.

2. It enters a loop that iterates over each attribute part in the *tagged_attribute_name* input string. If this is the first iteration of the loop, the *current_iteration* variable is

---

Algorithm 3 Prepare candidate entries

Input: $tagged\_attribute\_name \in \Sigma^*$

Output: $candidates \subseteq S$ (set of candidate entries for given set of words)

1: **function** *get_candidate_entries*$(tagged\_attribute\_name)$
2:     $previous\_iteration := ''$
3:     $mutations := \emptyset$
4:     **for** $attr\_part \in tagged\_attr\_name$ **do**
5:         **if** $previous\_iteration = ''$ **then**
6:             $current\_iteration := attr\_part$
7:         **else**
8:             $current\_iteration := previous\_iteration + '\_' + attr\_part$
9:             $previous\_iteration := current\_iteration$
10:             $mutations := mutations \cup \{current\_iteration\}$
11:         **end if**
12:     **end for**
13:     $candidates := \{\}$
14:     **for** $mut \in mutations$ **do**
15:         $candidates := candidates \cup get\_entries(mut)$
16:     **end for**
17:     **if** $candidates = \emptyset$ **then**
18:         **for** $attr\_part \in tagged\_attribute\_name$ **do**
19:             $candidates := candidates \cup get\_entries(attr\_part)$
20:         **end for**
21:     **end if**
22:     **return** $candidates$
23: **end function**

---

set to the current attribute part. Otherwise, the *current_iteration* variable is set to the concatenation of the previous iteration and the current attribute part, separated by an underscore. The *previous_iteration* variable is then updated to be the current iteration, and the *current_iteration* is added to the *mutations* set. The loop repeats for each attribute part in the *tagged_attribute_name* input string.

3. It initializes an empty set called *candidates*.

4. The algorithm enters a loop that iterates over each element in the *mutations* set. For each element in the *mutations* set, the algorithm retrieves the entries associated with that element using the *get_entries* function, and adds them to the *candidates* set.

5. If the *candidates* set remains empty after the previous step, the algorithm enters another loop that iterates over each attribute part in the *tagged_attribute_name* input string. For each attribute part, the algorithm retrieves the entries associated with that part using the *get_entries* function, adding them to the *candidates* set.

6. Finally, the algorithm returns the *candidates* set as its output.

Overall, the algorithm works by generating all possible mutations of the attribute name and using them to get entries from a function called *get_entries*. If no entries are found using the mutations, it falls back to getting entries using the individual parts of the attribute name. The resulting set of entries is returned as the final output of the algorithm.

This book section presents a semi-automatic technique for generating attribute semantics that significantly improves manual processes. By utilizing external thesauri and exploiting the hypernymy relations contained within, the approach aids in the semantic analysis of attribute and concept names. This advancement not only simplifies the process of ontology development and maintenance but also ensures a more accurate and contextually appropriate interpretation of attributes. Additionally, the method's structured approach to leveraging external thesauri and hypernymy relationships provides a solid foundation for semantic interpretation, which is crucial for successful ontology integration.

For experimental evaluation of the proposed algorithms, interested readers are encouraged to refer to [83] and [87]. These works demonstrate the utility of the proposed technique in providing semantic attributes within the context of ontology integration. The experimental results highlighted in these references suggest that the proposed method is superior to manual approaches in generating attribute semantics. By leveraging thesauri, the technique partially automates the semantic generation process, thereby reducing the likelihood of human error and increasing the consistency of the results. Moreover, a common limitation of a standard thesaurus, such as WordNet, which is the fact that sometimes it does not encompass all necessary terms, has been addressed. A hybrid strategy that merges the initial thesauri-based approach with a caching mechanism has been proposed. This combination enriches the standard thesaurus with new, user-contributed terms, thus bridging lexical gaps and creating a more comprehensive lexical repository.

2.2.2 Method of providing relations semantics

When it comes to developing a method of providing the semantics of relations according to Equation 2.16, it is generally considered a simpler task compared to defining the semantics of attributes and concepts. This is because relations exist independently, meaning that they do not rely on their connection with other elements of ontologies. In other words, they have a more straightforward meaning that is easier to describe.

Simarly to the semantics of attributes, the semantics of relations are provided through logic sentences. These sentences are assigned to each relation by applying the function

---

Algorithm 4 Naive approach to relations semantics

Input: $r \in R^C$
Output: $S_R(r)$ (semantics of relation r according to Equation 2.34)
  1: $S_R(r) :=''$
  2: **for** $(c_1, c_2) \in r$ **do**
  3:     $S_R(r) := S_R(r) +' \vee' + (ctx(c_1) +' \wedge' + ctx(c_2))$
  4: **end for**
  5: **return** $S_R(r)$

---

detailed in Equation 2.16. However, a critical aspect of this process is the maintenance of consistency in the elements that form these logic sentences.

In order to address this issue, it is essential to establish a systematic approach that guarantees the logic sentences assigned to relations are both internally coherent and consistent. A naive approach, presented in Algorithm 4 to designating relations' semantics would be to simply provide an alternative of conjunctions of contexts of concepts from every included pair. The proposed procedure takes as its input a single relation $r \in R^C$ and returns the value of the function $S_R(r)$ which represents the semantics of the relation r according to Equation 2.34. It takes the following steps:

1. It initializes $S_R(r)$ to an empty string.

2. For each concept pair (c_1, c_2) in r it constructs a zero-order logic sentence by concatenating the context of c_1 and the context of c_2 with the conjunction symbol $\wedge$, and then it concatenates the resulting sentence with the disjunction symbol $\vee$ to $S_R(r)$.

3. Finally, it returns $S_R(r)$ as the semantics of the relation r.

The algorithm presented in Algorithm 4 aims to generate the semantics of a given relation r by outputting a set of zero-order logic sentences. However, it utilizes a simplistic approach that may not accurately capture the complete meaning of the relation, potentially resulting in ambiguous or incomplete descriptions. The algorithm primarily focuses on the contexts of the concepts linked by the relation for deriving its semantics. While this strategy offers some initial understanding of the relation's nature, it fails to consider the intricacies of how the involved concepts interact. This omission can lead to a representation of the relation that lacks depth and accuracy.

Addressing this limitation requires an enhancement of the semantic description of relationships. One viable strategy involves incorporating synonyms and antonyms from a thesaurus. Synonyms can contribute to a more comprehensive depiction of the relationship, while antonyms aid in clarifying and removing ambiguities. Utilizing a thesaurus enables the generation of more detailed and expressive relationship descriptions.

However, this approach has its flaws. Since a single thesaurus entry can have multiple meanings, automatically matching the relation's name with the specific context of an ontology can be challenging. This limitation might require human intervention. Nonetheless, integrating the basic approach with human-guided thesaurus input can result in a more robust and nuanced semantic description of relations within the ontology. Algorithm 5 presents such a semi-automatic process addressing the abovementioned concerns. It takes a relationship r from the set R as input and produces its semantics $S_R(r)$ based on Equation 2.16 by taking the following steps:

1. It splits the relation's name r into its constituent single words and stores them in the set *words*.

Algorithm 5 Determining semantics of relations

Input: $r \in R^C$
Output: $S_R(r)$ (semantics of relation r according to Equation 2.34)
  1: split relation's r name into single words and store them in the set $words$
  2: $rel\_labels := \bigcup_{word \in words} tokenize\_and\_tag(word)$
  3: $rel\_symbols := \bigcup_{label \in rel\_labels} get\_single\_word\_semantics(label)$
  4: $S_R(r) := ''$
  5: **for** $elem \in rel\_symbols$ **do**
  6:     $S_R(r) := S_R(r) +' \wedge' + elem$
  7: **end for**
  8: **return** $S_R(r)$

---

2. It uses the function $tokenize\_and\_tag$ which performs the preprocessing of the given set of words from Σ^* discarding any appearing stop words preserving only nouns, verbs, pronouns, adjectives, and adverbs in their base forms. It stores the resulting labels in the set rel_labels.

3. It uses the $get\_single\_word\_semantics$ to obtain the semantics for each label in rel_labels and store the resulting symbols in the set $rel\_symbols$.

4. It initializes the string $S_R(r)$ as an empty string. For each element $elem$ in the set $rel\_symbols$, the procedure concatenates the string "$\wedge$ elem" to the end of $S_R(r)$.

5. Finally, the algorithm returns the value of $S_R(r)$ as the output.

The algorithm employs a function called $get\_single\_word\_semantics$, detailed in Algorithm 6, which is designed to process a single word, represented as $word \in \Sigma^*$ (following Definition 2.12) and outputs a set of potential semantic meanings for that word. The process consists of the following steps:

1. It utilizes the function $get\_entries$ which finds all entries s from the set S in the thesauri TH such that the given word $word$ appears in the list of entries synonyms.

2. It presents the list of candidate entries to the user to select the best one $\tilde{s}$.

3. It constructs the set $semantics$ as a union of two sets:

    (a) The set of names of synonyms' of $\tilde{s}$

    (b) The set of names of antonyms' of $\tilde{s}$, but with a preceding negation symbol ($'\neg'$)

4. Finally, the algorithm returns the $semantics$ set as its output.

The proposed semi-automatic solution, while requiring involvement from the ontology developer, offers several benefits compared to a fully manual approach in which an expert is responsible for defining the semantics of relations. One of the primary advantages is efficiency, mainly when dealing with a large set of relations. In a manual scenario, assigning semantics to numerous relations can become time-consuming, subjective, and prone to errors as the number of relations increases. For example, assigning semantics to ten different relations would entail preparing ten distinct logic sentences. The risk of inconsistency in the manual approach is heightened due to potential discrepancies in the interpretations of different experts, which entail different choices of literals from the set D_R. Although experts might address this issue and manually verify every step to ensure the consistency of the semantics, this process can quickly become complex and unwieldy.

Algorithm 6 Get single word semantics

Input: $word \in \Sigma^*$
Output: $semantics \subset \Sigma^*$
1: **function** $get\_single\_word\_semantics(word)$
2:     $candidates := get\_entries(word)$
3:     present $candidates$ to choose a desired entry $\tilde{s}$
4:     $semantics := \{s.name \mid s \in \tilde{s}.synonyms\} \cup \{'\neg' + s.name \mid s \in \tilde{s}.antonyms\}$
5:     **return** $semantics$
6: **end function**

In contrast, by integrating automated processes with human input, the semi-automatic approach streamlines the considered task. It reduces the time and effort required while minimizing subjective biases and errors. Therefore, the proposed solution is a more pragmatic and efficient method of handling the semantics of relations in an ontology, even though it still relies on some input and verification from the ontology developer.

2.3 Ontology alignment

2.3.1 Basic definitions

In scenarios involving multiple ontologies, a key challenge lies in enabling these distinct ontological structures to communicate and interact with one another effectively. This challenge is addressed through the idea of semantic interoperability, which ensures that different ontologies can seamlessly exchange information and meaningfully relate to each other. In essence, semantic interoperability is about creating a "bridge" between these ontologies, allowing for a mutual understanding of how they correspond and connect. This "bridge" is commonly known as "ontology alignment".

Ontology alignment can be thought of as a collection of paired elements, each drawn from the maintained ontologies. These pairs are known as "mappings". A mapping signifies that the elements it comprises are understood to represent similar or even identical entities or concepts in the real world. Establishing a consistent and sound set of these mappings facilitates a shared understanding and interpretation of the concepts and relationships defined within each ontology.

In practice, achieving semantic interoperability through ontology alignment involves identifying the mappings (also referred to as correspondences), as mentioned above, between concepts, relations, and instances across the different ontologies, which eventually enable various systems and applications that utilize the mapped ontologies to communicate and function harmoniously, even though they may be based on different knowledge structures.

Definition 2.13 Let us denote a set of all potential alignments of all (A, V)-based ontologies as $\widetilde{AL}$. Given two (A, V)-based ontologies $O_1 = (C_1, H_1, R^{C_1}, I_1, R^{I_1})$ and $O_2 = (C_2, H_2, R^{C_2}, I_2, R^{I_2})$ the alignment $Align(O_1, O_2) \in \widetilde{AL}$ between them is a triple:

$$Align(O_1, O_2) = \{Align_C(O_1, O_2), Align_I(O_1, O_2), Align_R(O_1, O_2)\} \qquad (2.30)$$

The above equation enables us to identify distinct sets of correspondences for various levels of conceptualization, specifically for concepts (represented by $Align_C(O_1, O_2)$), instances (represented by $Align_I(O_1, O_2)$), and relations (represented by $Align_R(O_1, O_2)$).

Consequently, sets of all potential alignments on the concept, instance, and relation, levels will be denoted as $\widetilde{AL}_C$, $\widetilde{AL}_I$, $\widetilde{AL}_R$ respectively.

Definition 2.14 *The ontology alignment on the concept level* can be formally defined as a set that consists of tuples with the following structure:

$$Align_C(O_1, O_2) = \{(c_1, c_2) \mid c_1 \in C_1 \land c_2 \in C_2\} \tag{2.31}$$

where c_1, c_2 are concepts from O_1 and O_2 respectively.

Definition 2.15 *The ontology alignment on the instance level* is a set of alignments of instances of two aligned concepts:

$$Align_I(O_1, O_2) = \{AL_{O_1, O_2}(c_1, c_2) \mid (c_1, c_2) \in Align_C(O_1, O_2)\} \tag{2.32}$$

where c_1, c_2 are concepts from O_1 and O_2 respectively, and each $AL_{O_1, O_2}(c_1, c_2)$ is a set defined as follows:

$$AL_{O_1, O_2}(c_1, c_2) = \{(i_1, i_2) \mid i_1 \in c_1 \land i_2 \in c_2\} \tag{2.33}$$

The Equations 2.32 and 2.33 represent the instance-level alignment, denoted as $Align_I(O_1, O_2)$. It is a set that contains alignments of instances belonging to aligned concepts, which implies that if there is an alignment between concepts c_1 in ontology O_1 and c_2 in ontology O_2 (as defined in $Align_C(O_1, O_2)$), then there can exist an alignment of their instances (denoted as $AL_{O_1, O_2}(c_1, c_2)$).

Definition 2.16 *The ontology alignment on the relation level* is a set defined as:

$$Align_R(O_1, O_2) = \{(r_1, r_2) \mid r_1 \in R^{C_1} \land r_2 \in R^{C_2}\} \tag{2.34}$$

where r_1, r_2 are relations from O_1 and O_2 respectively.

In order to determine if two elements from different ontologies (such as a pair of concepts or instances) can be added to the respective alignment, it is necessary to apply some filters. These filters can be understood as first-order predicates, which produce a boolean value given two elements from the ontologies. Only those pairs of elements that yield a "true" value under this predicate are deemed suitable for alignment. Typically, the predicate involves comparing a similarity measure between the elements against a predefined threshold. For example, in the context of concept alignment, a filtering predicate $P_C(c_1, c_2) : \lambda_C(c_1, c_2) \geq T_C$ can be used, where λ_C represents a function that measures the similarity between two concepts, and T_C is the accepted threshold value. Obviously, analogous predicates can be formulated for relations and concepts.

It is important to note that various methods can be used for comparing elements from ontologies, as highlighted in literature [151]. Additionally, the author has previously developed a more sophisticated technique for ontology alignment that leverages the semantics of attributes. While the specifics of the developed framework are beyond the scope of this book, readers can refer to [157] for a detailed explanation.

Furthermore, it is crucial to emphasize that our approach excludes the alignment of relations between instances. As defined in Definition 2.9, these relations establish connections between specific instances using their unique identifiers. When an ontology alignment at the instance level exists (which connects instance identifiers from the source ontology with identifiers from the target ontology), it becomes relatively straightforward to identify corresponding pairs of instance relationships within the target ontology.

In conclusion, the definition of ontology alignment presented here, which will be consistently applied throughout the rest of the book, distinguishes itself from other definitions in the existing literature by emphasizing a clear distinction in alignments at different levels: concepts, relations, and instances. Aligning ontologies at the concept level involves matching the general ideas or classes of different ontologies. At the relational level, it focuses on how these concepts are interrelated, ensuring that these connections are consistently understood across the aligned ontologies. Finally, instance-level alignment deals with the specific occurrences or examples of these concepts, further solidifying the comprehensive understanding of how these entities are represented and used in various contexts. Therefore, categorizing alignments into separate layers allows for a more precise and comprehensive alignment of ontologies.

2.3.2 Inconsistencies in ontology mappings

Ontology alignment is fundamental for integrating heterogeneous knowledge systems, ensuring that disparate ontologies can effectively communicate and share information. The success of this integration heavily relies on the consistency of the ontology alignment mappings with the constraints of the mapped ontologies. This section of the book discusses two types of inconsistencies that can occur in ontology alignments.

The first kind of inconsistency that may be found in ontology alignment is based on circular inheritance. This issue arises when there is a loop in the inheritance hierarchy among two or more concepts across the ontologies being aligned. Figure 2.2 shows an example of this inconsistency. Consider Ontology O_1, which includes a concept c_1 that is a descendant of another concept c_2. In Ontology O_2, there is a concept c_2', a subclass of concept c_1'. If the ontology alignment includes the pairs of concepts (c_1, c_1') and (c_2, c_2'), a circular inheritance loop is inadvertently created between concepts c_1 and c_2. This loop violates the basic understanding of inheritance hierarchies where a concept cannot be both a descendant and an ancestor of another concept.

The discussed inconsistency may lead to significant issues, particularly for reasoning engines. For example, when an inference engine tries to deduce the properties of concept c_1, it may find itself in a continuous loop, moving back and forth between c_1 and c_2 without

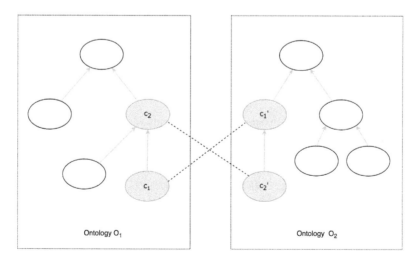

FIGURE 2.2
An example of circular inheritance

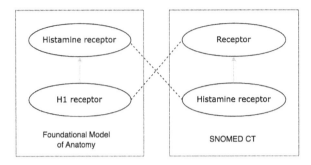

FIGURE 2.3
Circular inheritance in alignment of biomedical ontologies

reaching a conclusion. This not only prevents the engine from producing valid results but also impacts the overall functionality and reliability of the system.

Definition 2.17 Assuming the existence of ontologies O_1 and O_2, concepts $c_1, c_2 \in C_1$, $c_1', c_2' \in C_2$ and alignment $Align_C(O_1, O_2)$, correspondences $corr_{c_1 c_1'} = \langle c_1, c_1' \rangle$ and $corr_{c_2 c_2'} = \langle c_2, c_2' \rangle$ (such that $corr_{c_1 c_1'}, corr_{c_2 c_2'} \in Align_C(O_1, O_2)$) are *inconsistent because of circular inheritance* if:

$$c_1 \in Sup_C(c_2) \wedge c_2' \in Sup_C(c_1') \tag{2.35}$$

To denote this inconsistency $\not\equiv_C$ symbol will be used. Therefore, for the given example, a statement $corr_{c_1 c_1'} \not\equiv_C corr_{c_2 c_2'}$ is true

Figure 2.3 shows the actual example of such inconsistency which can be found in the alignment of two medical ontologies: *Foundational Model of Anatomy* ([170]) and *SNOMED-CT* ([39]) created by the KEPLER ontology alignment system ([103]). In *Foundational Model of Anatomy*, a concept *H1 receptor* is a subclass of concept *Histamine receptor*, while in the ontology *SNOMED-CT*, a concept *Histamine receptor* is a descendant of a concept *Receptor*. The considered alignment includes pairs (*Histamine receptor, Histamine receptor*) and (*H1 receptor, Receptor*), which entails the inconsistency based on circular inheritance.

The second type of inconsistency in ontology alignment arises from violating disjoint class restrictions following Definition 2.7. An example of this inconsistency is illustrated in Figure 2.4. In this scenario, Ontology O_1 contains a concept c_2, a descendant of concept c_1. Meanwhile, Ontology O_2 includes a concept c_2', a descendant of another concept c_3'. If in Ontology O_2, concepts c_1' and c_3' are considered as disjoint, then the alignment, which includes pairs of concepts (c_1, c_1') and (c_2, c_2'), is inconsistent.

Definition 2.18 Assuming the existence of ontologies O_1 and O_2, concepts $c_1, c_2 \in C_1$, $c_1', c_2' \in C_2$ and alignment $Align_C(O_1, O_2)$, correspondences $\langle c_1, c_1' \rangle$ and $\langle c_2, c_2' \rangle$ (such that $\langle c_1, c_1' \rangle, \langle c_2, c_2' \rangle \in Align_C(O_1, O_2)$) are *inconsistent because of inheritance from disjoint class* if:

$$(c_1, c_2) \in H \wedge \exists c_3' \in Sup_C(b') : c_3' \not\equiv c_1' \tag{2.36}$$

To denote this inconsistency $\not\equiv_R$ symbol is used and therefore, a statement $\langle c_1, c_1' \rangle \not\equiv_R \langle c_2, c_2' \rangle$ is true for the given example.

Figure 2.5 provides an example of such inconsistency found in the alignment of ontologies: *Adult Mouse Anatomy* ([73]) and *NCI Thesaurus* ([182]) created by the FCAMapX ontology alignment system ([18]). In *Adult Mouse Anatomy*, a concept *respiratory_system* is a subclass of concept *organ system*. In the ontology *NCI Thesaurus*

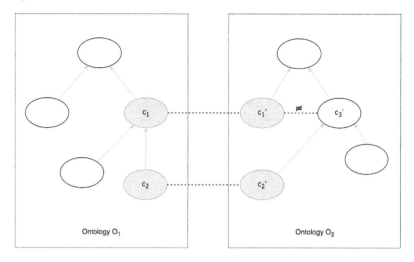

FIGURE 2.4
An example of inheritance from disjoint concepts in aligned ontologies

a concept *Head_and_neck* is a subclass of a concept *Body_Region*, which is disjoint with the concept *Organ_System*. The analyzed alignment includes mappings of concepts (*organ system*, *Organ_System*) and (*respiratory_system*, *Head_and_neck*) which entails the considered inconsistency.

Definitions 2.17 and 2.18 can be used to identify inconsistent correspondences. However, when a newly designated pair of concepts is about to be included in the alignment, one needs a tool to check if it will not be a source of any inconsistency with existing correspondences.

Definition 2.19 Assuming the existence of ontologies O_1 and O_2, concepts $c_1 \in C_1$, $c'_1 \in C_2$ and an alignment $Align_C(O_1, O_2)$, a correspondence $\langle c_1, c'_1 \rangle$ is inconsistent with the alignment $Align_C(O_1, O_2)$ if:

$$\exists \langle c_2, c'_2 \rangle \in Align_C(O_1, O_2) : (c_2 \in Sup_C(c_1) \lor c'_2 \in Sup_C(c'_1)) \land \\ (\langle c_1, c'_1 \rangle \not\equiv_C \langle c_2, c'_2 \rangle \lor \langle c_1, c'_1 \rangle \not\equiv_R \langle c_2, c'_2 \rangle) \tag{2.37}$$

To denote this, the operator $\not\sim$ will be used. Therefore, to express the fact that the corresponce $\langle c_1, c'_2 \rangle$ is inconsistent with the alignment $Align_C(O_1, O_2)$ a following statement can be used: $\langle c_1, c'_1 \rangle \not\sim Align_C(O_1, O_2)$. To denote the opposite fact (the corresponce $\langle c_1, c'_1 \rangle$ is consistent with the alignment $Align_C(O_1, O_2)$), the operator $\sim$ will be used ($\langle c_1, c'_1 \rangle \sim Align_C(O_1, O_2)$).

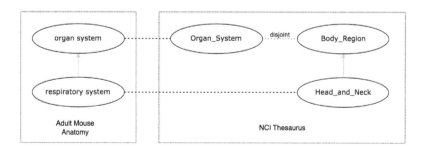

FIGURE 2.5
Inheritance from disjoint classes in alignment of biomedical ontologies

It is obvious that ontology alignments should not contain any inconsistencies. Ideally, an inconsistent mapping is never a part of the alignment $Align_C(O_1, O_2)$ ($\langle a, a' \rangle \notin Align_C(O_1, O_2)$), however, in many cases, methods of designating ontology alignment do not verify the above conditions and allow for their presence within $Align_C(O_1, O_2)$ (as shown on real-world example in Figures 2.3 and 2.5).

We claim it is essential to consider the alignment with fewer inconsistencies better than the one with multiple such flaws. This remark is an inspiration for developing sophisticated techniques for evaluating the quality of ontology alignments, which go beyond standard measures like Precision or Recall. These methods and various other factors are discussed in detail in Chapter 6, which focuses on advanced methods for assessing ontology alignments.

2.4   Conclusions

This chapter offers a comprehensive overview of a general model of ontologies and ontology alignment. Its main objective is to familiarize readers with ontologies and ontology alignment's key terminology and definitions. It defines ontology as a whole and its internal parts, including concepts, relations, and instances. Moreover, the chapter introduces the concept of attributes' semantics, which distinguishes the author's research from existing literature. It also discusses various approaches for providing semantics to attributes and presents formal definitions of ontology alignment.

While some of the elements discussed in this chapter may have already been presented in the author's previous works, there are also new and original elements that have been introduced here:

- The fundamental concepts presented in Section 2.1 have been previously provided in various publications ([114], [116], [117], [119], [157]), each focusing on different aspects of ontologies and ontology alignments. None of the previous publications contained a complete and comprehensive set of definitions for these concepts. Therefore, this chapter aims to provide a complete and overall set of definitions for these basic notions.

- Section 2.2 describes the methods for providing attributes and relations semantics, which were previously discussed in the author's other publications ([84], [83], [87]). However, this chapter takes a step further. It presents a more comprehensive and generalized view of these methods by introducing the concept of a thesaurus, which can be applied to different domains. Unlike in previous publications, the presented methods are consistent and can work independently without external tools. Furthermore, the chapter introduces a new approach to assigning semantics to relations.

- The final part of the chapter, given in Section 2.3, focuses on the topic of ontology alignment, which is presented in a precise mathematical framework. The section introduces formal criteria for detecting inconsistencies while providing a deeper understanding of the key concepts through real-world examples. Although specific components of this section have been published previously ([156]), this chapter incorporates a more extensive perspective grounded in the definitions offered in Section 2.1.

In conclusion, this chapter establishes a formal groundwork by introducing fundamental mathematical concepts. The definitions provided here will serve as a basis for all the following chapters, making it an essential prerequisite for comprehending the remainder of the book.

Part II

Techniques and Frameworks

3

Classification of ontology alignment techniques

Ontology alignment, in essence, can be understood as finding a bridge connecting heterogeneous, independent ontologies. It consequently allows for interoperability of computer systems, which utilize them as a backbone of their knowledge bases. This chapter provides a comprehensive overview of both classic and recent research concerning the topic. Its purpose is to clearly show that the field of ontology alignment plays a pivotal role in knowledge engineering and semantic technologies. It is organized around three main questions:

1. **How can ontology alignments be designated?** Section 3.1 offers a comprehensive and organized insight into the methodologies employed for designating ontology alignments across conceptual, relational, and instance levels. The discussion concerns various strategies, from linguistics-based techniques utilizing lexical and linguistic similarity through structure-based methods to approaches incorporating external knowledge sources such as WordNet. Additionally, the chapter explores modern machine learning-based methodologies and delivers an in-depth description of a range of noteworthy and actively developed ontology alignment systems.

2. **What are the methods for managing ontology evolution and maintaining ontology alignments over time?** As ontologies are subjected to continuous updates, ensuring that ontology alignments remain consistent and verified over time is critical. Section 3.2 gives insights into effective practices for managing the dynamic nature of ontologies. It explores various techniques and strategies for issues like tracking ontology changes, detecting emerging inconsistencies, or updating existing alignments.

3. **What are the approaches to evaluating the quality of ontology alignments?** Typically, the reliability of ontology alignments is measured using some prepared benchmark datasets and broadly known metrics like Precision or Recall. Section 3.3 contains an overview of these basic methods. Simultaneously, it explores alternative approaches beyond usually incorporated solutions, allowing for a more nuanced evaluation of ontology alignments.

In summary, this chapter surveys the state of literature about ontology alignment techniques and related topics. It serves as a background, laying the groundwork and justification for the author's methods presented in the remainder of this book.

DOI: 10.1201/9781003437888-3

3.1   Designating ontology alignments

3.1.1   Problem overview

One of the earliest works on the topic of ontology alignment can be found in [148], where authors were one of the first who coined the terms "ontology alignment" and "ontology merging", taking inspiration in the field of automatic database schema matching ([167]). The developed tool, PROMPT, is built on top of an algorithm performing a semi-automatic process of ontology merging and alignment. It automates specific tasks while offering user guidance for actions requiring manual intervention. Additionally, the tool identifies potential inconsistencies in the ontology state that may arise from user actions and proposes solutions to rectify these inconsistencies.

The novelty of the topic at the time and the absence of a standardized benchmark for verification led the authors of [148] to conduct experiments involving human experts. These experts were tasked with merging two ontologies using PROMPT and Chimaera ([132]), an entirely manual ontology integration tool. The merged ontologies were compared and evaluated manually, revealing that PROMPT successfully met experts' expectations.

What sets PROMPT apart from methods proposed in the author's research is its close integration with OWL and the Protege platform[1], as PROMPT was implemented as a plugin on this platform. These features constrain PROMPT's applicability to the OWL representation format and the Protege platform, limiting its adaptability to other ontology representation formats due to a lack of formal foundations.

The OWL standard by itself, as extensively discussed in literature [63], [67], has some limitations. One significant drawback lies in its inability to support dedicated datatypes for attributes, necessitating the creation of additional concepts and relations to express more intricate property relationships. Moreover, OWL lacks the capability to represent negations of values, limiting its capacity to capture certain logic constructs effectively.

While OWL allows the definition of restrictions on relations between concepts, it falls short in enabling similar restrictions on attributes and their values. Attributes, specifically those defined with the owl:DatatypeProperty tag, cannot be expressed with more granularity than a simple key-value pair or an explicitly given taxonomy. Consequently, OWL lacks a refined mechanism to define the semantics of attributes in a more nuanced manner.

Moreover, OWL provides informal annotation mechanisms, such as rdfs:comment and rdfs:seeAlso, for elements in ontologies. However, these annotations are not considered formal parts of ontology definitions. Relying on such mechanisms when constructing ontology alignment tools is a workaround rather than a genuine solution, as these annotations neither contribute to nor follow the formal and precise representation of ontological elements.

Since PROMPT, many different approaches to finding ontology alignments (also known as "ontology matching") have been proposed and extensively discussed in the literature. In essence, the process involves comparing various aspects expressed in two or more ontologies and, based on that, establishing correspondences between them. For a simplified representation focused on a pair of ontologies, please refer to Figure 3.1 for a high-level overview.

---

[1]https://protege.stanford.edu/

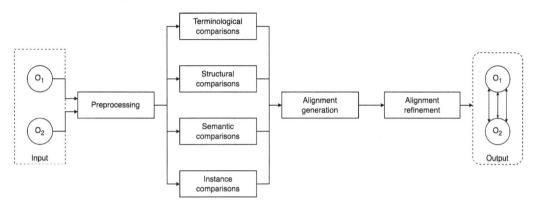

FIGURE 3.1
An overview of ontology alignment procedure elements

The process begins with identifying the types of elements to be considered in the ontologies. Then, for the extracted elements, the procedure ensures their uniform representation. Variations in labels or naming conventions are normalized to establish consistency, while redundant information, such as duplicate elements or unnecessary details, is discarded. The step may also include standardizing date formats, numerical representations, or other data types. Some ontologies may require specific additional preprocessing steps based on their characteristics or the nature of the matching task.

Consequently, preprocessed contents of ontologies are compared on the **terminological**, **structural**, **semantic**, and **instance** levels. This categorization of core techniques is based on a taxonomy ontology alignment method found in [48] and [151], adjusted and updated to the current state of available literature.

The terminological comparisons are based on the syntactic analysis of ontology content, treating all encountered elements as strings. Therefore, the techniques from this group may be based on assessing string similarity, comparing the names and descriptions of entities using different string distance metrics such as Jaccard, Jaro-Winkler, Euclidean, and TFIDF ([24]).

In the work of [2], the authors introduce a modified Levenshtein distance termed AFB. This adaptation addresses scenarios where compared strings contain non-letter characters, incorporating specific adjustments such as conversion to bags of words, removal of unwanted elements, and selective application of base Levenshtein distance to ensure robust similarity calculation.

A comparative evaluation of the applicability of various methods (Edit, Monge-Elkan, Jaro-Winkler, ISUB, n-gram, and Jaccard distances) can be found in [189]. Authors show a wide disparity among the performance of string similarity metrics when used as a single method for ontology alignment. The results show that these types of metrics should not be used as the only technique in more elaborate ontology alignment solutions. However, despite acknowledged limitations in the context of semantically rich ontology comparisons, these methods find widespread application in sophisticated alignment systems, exemplified by AgreementMaker as described in [27] and its subsequent evolution AML/AMLC ([51], [53]).

In order to overcome the issue posed by treating every ontology element as a mere string, specific approaches integrate Natural Language Processing (NLP) methodologies. These methods consider entity names not as isolated strings but as words embedded within the context of natural language. Techniques like tokenization, lemmatization, and removing stopwords are commonly employed to refine the analysis ([15]). Additionally, incorporating external resources such as lexicons or dictionaries further augments matching capabilities, contributing to a more nuanced and contextually informed understanding of the analysis ([74]).

Moreover, using NLP techniques is critical if modern techniques based on word embedding are applied. For example, in [195], authors developed a method that initially extracts lexical and structural information from processed ontologies using the baseline NLP methods, fed to pre-trained language models to compute the vector representations of concepts – the experimental evaluation showed promising results. An overview of several additional linguistic similarity functions can be found in [108].

Several endeavours propose to incorporate BERT in the process of ontology alignment. BERT, which stands for Bidirectional Encoder Representations from Transformers, is a natural language processing model developed by Google and introduced in [107]. Authors of [143] developed a method based solely on terminological comparisons, discarding every other aspect of ontologies. The BERT model then processes the extracted lexical information. It has been observed that the proposed method did not produce meaningful alignment independently. However, it generally outperformed other approaches based on word embeddings.

On the other hand, in [77], authors introduced BERTMap, a BERT-based ontology alignment system that outperforms existing methods, particularly in the biomedical domain. The technique first predicts mappings using a classifier based on fine-tuning BERT on text semantics corpora from ontologies and then refines the mappings using information about ontology structure. The experimental verification showed that such a hybrid approach led to a solution that can often yield better results than other prominent ontology alignment systems such as LogMap or AML.

It is worth noting that several publications on modern machine learning solutions ([76], [203]) claim that they are not suited for the ontology alignment task as a sole technique. These solutions often overlook the contextual element of the problem, resulting in an inability to distinguish between different word senses or capture nuanced distinctions within a particular sense. This limitation directly results in their inability to distinguish between different word senses or capture nuanced distinctions within a particular sense, as they neglect additional knowledge expressed in aligned ontologies.

Methods of ontology alignment based on **structural comparisons** focus on processing hierarchical and relational information within ontologies. These methods treat the ontologies to be aligned as labelled graphs, treating the ontology matching task as a graph homomorphism problem. A range of approaches have been proposed. The most basic one can be found in [129], where authors formulate a similarity measure called "semantic cotopy". The developed function uses information about specialization relation (hierarchy of concepts) and provides means for calculating how similarly embedded within respective taxonomies two compared concepts are.

In [101], an approach based on a metric order theory is proposed. It involves measuring the amount of structural distortion carried by an alignment between two taxonomic cores of ontologies represented as semantic hierarchies—the preliminary experimental evaluation showed promising results for ontologies with extensive hierarchical content.

In [60] and [59], authors introduce a novel matching operation termed "structure-preserving semantic matching," designed to assess correspondences between entire graph structures while maintaining specific structural properties. Unlike typical ontology matching applications focusing on node correspondences, this operation is crucial for applications like web service integration, where the global similarity of entire graph structures is essential. The approach relies on a formal theory of abstraction and employs a tree edit distance measure to ensure efficiency and effectiveness in various scenarios, as validated through experimental evaluations. The solution's practical applicability in service integration in SOA-based distributed systems was demonstrated in [134].

Moreover, there exist several attempts at ontology alignments which are based on more refined information about ontology structures, like techniques which consider criteria regarding the internal structure of the concepts, such as the domain and range of the relations or the types of the attributes ([62]). Nevertheless, a notable concern arises from utilizing the OWL format as the formal foundation for such methods, as it treats both relations and attributes uniformly as properties. This assumption may need to be more balanced with the nuanced distinctions between attributes and relations, potentially compromising the needed granularity of expressiveness.

The **semantic comparisons** are usually built on top of incorporating external resources. For example, ontologies may be linked to informal resources through annotating online wiki pages or images. In this context, the employed methods infer correspondences between ontology entities based on their relationships with analyzed external resources. For example, two concepts annotating the same set of pictures may be treated as equivalent. These techniques commonly leverage data analysis and statistical methods to identify patterns and variations among them ([48]).

Some techniques use formal resources to support the matching process, such as upper-level ontologies ([131]), domain-specific ontologies ([37], [197]), or the alignments of already matched ontologies. The last approach is usually called alignment reuse ([177]). However, both types of methods heavily depend on structured external resources, which, in consequence, makes them impractical; therefore, no recent research has been devoted to these kinds of solutions.

Other techniques falling under the category of semantic comparison leverage the semantic interpretations associated with input ontologies. An illustration of this category uses description logic reasoning techniques, as exemplified in [173]. The authors introduce a metric for evaluating similarity in Description Logic (DL) through refinement operators and a refinement graph. The process involves determining the most specific concepts of two individuals, identifying their least common subsumer, and gauging their distances in the refinement graph. In an extension of this work presented in [172], there is an exploration of measuring similarity in the space of Conjunctive Queries, independent of the underlying description logic and computationally more efficient.

Authors of [94] took a different route by developing an approach based on Normalized Google Distance ([22]) to quantify the degree to which semantic characteristics of two concepts are related. Another approach can be found in [191], where a similarity measure for the EL class of description logic is computed, providing a numerical degree of similarity between two concept descriptions. EL by itself is a lightweight description logic that asserts sound and complete reasoning in polytime and is a syntactic fragment of OWL. Therefore, the considered approach is tightly bound to this format and lacks versatility.

Another group of comparison methods is **instance based techniques**, also referred to as **extensional methods**, which follow the intuition that if the instances of concepts are similar, then the concepts to which they belong are also similar ([128]). In other words, the characteristics and relationships observed at the instance level can provide insights into the similarity between concepts.

All of the solutions preliminarily require finding correspondences between instances. In [111], the authors present an approach that leverages ontology reasoning to generate a corpus of shared instances, built on the assumption that ontologies typically have only a few or no common instances. The experimental results demonstrate the effectiveness of the authors' method, revealing notable performance enhancements compared to other ontology alignment systems, particularly in the context of instance-based and reasoning-based methods.

Authors of [210] developed an approach to instance-based ontology aligning based on NSGA-II – the Non-dominated Sorting Genetic Algorithm ([36]). The method identifies the most efficient connections between instances. It incorporates a propagation process that uses different semantic relations to extend similarity values to other entities within the ontologies, including concepts and additional instances. The effectiveness of the proposed approach is supported by the experiments that have been carried out, which highlight its usefulness and its ability to identify alignments that are characterized by high values of Precision.

Both [187] and [5] emphasize the importance of considering knowledge about instances in ontology alignment, with the former presenting a holistic approach that aligns instances, relations and concepts and the latter extending a hybrid evolutionary approach to incorporate instances. An extension of the work can be found in [188], where authors describe a holistic ontology alignment system based on the assumption that alignments at the instance level cross-fertilize with alignments at the schema level.

In recent years, the topic of instance alignment has shifted towards research focused on knowledge graph alignment ([207], [190], [212]). This field shows some resemblance with ontology alignment; however, while ontologies provide a formal and structured representation of knowledge with a focus on concepts, properties, and instances using formal logic, knowledge graphs, on the other hand, are graph-based structures that emphasize the relationships between entities and are often built from diverse data sources. Thus, ontologies and knowledge graphs share common goals, such as organizing information and enhancing interoperability, but they differ in their formalisms and emphasis on logic versus graph structure. Therefore, designating mappings between knowledge graphs falls outside the scope of this book.

The next step in the process involves initial **generating ontology alignments** based on multiple comparison techniques, which may include several different techniques from core categories overviewed above (**terminological, structural, semantic**, and **instance-based**). Numerous strategies exist for selecting suitable similarity measures and their effective integration ([13]). For instance, some hybrid methodologies combine multiple comparison techniques by assigning weights or employing machine learning algorithms to discover their optimal combination ([146]). Alternatively, specific approaches dynamically choose similarity measures based on the ontologies' characteristics or integrate fuzzy logic and fuzzy inference rules into the alignment process.

Regardless of the chosen strategy, the considered step concludes with the initial version of alignment between the given ontologies. This initial alignment is then evaluated and undergoes **a refinement and repair step**, which aims to address any potential inconsistencies that might arise in the first version of the alignment ([135]). It may involve adjusting similarity thresholds, incorporating user feedback ([122]), providing interactive visual representations of alignments ([92]) or applying alignment repair techniques.

There exist multiple approaches to alignment repair. For example, in [175], authors observe that alignments generated for extensive ontologies frequently exhibit logic inconsistencies. The paper presents a set of rules for identifying such inconsistencies and a modularisation technique for repairing ontology alignments. It involves extracting segments from the input ontologies containing only the essential concepts and their relationships necessary to resolve all identified inconsistencies.

The paper introduces an alignment repair algorithm based on a global repair strategy, which aims to minimize incoherence and the number of mappings eliminated from the alignment. Therefore, the authors emphasize a potential trade-off between correctness and coherence in the repair processes, noting that many correct mappings may be accidentally removed during the alignment repair process. This observation has also been supported in [154]. Recent progress in the field can be found in [40], where a repair and review tool for ontology alignment is introduced. The tool aims to provide an assistance process designed to aid experts in tasks related to repairing alignments.

The article [46] explores agents' use of ontology alignments to communicate knowledge represented in different ontologies. The research demonstrates that agents, through simple interaction games, can effectively repair random ontology networks. The study reproduces experiments already known in the literature ([9]) but introduces new measures and reveals that earlier results were underestimated. The authors introduce enhanced adaptation operators, examine agents' abilities to generate new correspondences when discarding incorrect ones, and provide less precise answers.

The research has been developed in [199] and its direct continuation [200]. The Alignment Repair Game (ARG) was proposed to enable agents to communicate and repair alignments concurrently through adaptation operators during communication failures. Experimental evaluations demonstrated that agents converge towards successful communication and improving their alignments. Moreover, a logic model called Dynamic Epistemic Ontology Logic (DEOL) is introduced. This framework allows for expressing ontologies and alignments by translating ARG to DEOL and modelling ARG adaptation operators as dynamic modalities. Finally, the authors proposed a formal definition of the adaptation operators' correctness, partial redundancy, and incompleteness in ARG.

One of the most prominent and respected ontology alignment systems that holistically approach the task at hand is LogMap ([99]). Besides a complex method of designating ontology alignment itself (which will be further described in detail in the following parts of this chapter), LogMap LogMap leverages the well-known Dowling-Gallier algorithm ([41]) for propositional Horn satisfiability verification. After producing the initial alignment version, it uses a Horn propositional logic representation of the extended hierarchy of each ontology created from found mappings. Each mapping is split into two propositional rules, and then LogMap uses the well-known Dowling-Gallier algorithm ([41]) for propositional Horn satisfiability verification. Such an approach allows us to identify nodes from both ontologies that are a source of incoherence. Consequently, these identified nodes are excluded from the final alignment, ensuring the coherence and quality of the final ontology alignment.

Regardless of the specific refinement strategies chosen from the extensive techniques available in the literature, completing all selected actions concludes the ontology alignment designation process. Subsequently, this process produces the final set of mappings.

In summary, a comprehensive ontology alignment solution rarely relies only on a single technique. It is more common for a prominent approach to the task to incorporate various techniques (e.g. terminological and structural, like the method proposed in [144]), each accompanied by its modifications ([1]). Moreover, the choice of comparison techniques, the overall matching strategy, and refinement techniques may vary depending on the characteristics of the ontologies and some specific requirements. Thus, overviewing various independent techniques does not answer how ontology alignments can be designated.

Therefore, below, we will examine various ontology alignment systems incorporating techniques and strategies to produce high-quality outcomes. Their selection is based on their active participation in the Ontology Alignment Evaluation Initiative (*OAEI*), a non-profit organisation that since 2004 has been hosting annual campaigns devoted to comparing different, complex ontology alignment solutions. These campaigns provide researchers and developers with a platform to evaluate their ontology alignment solutions and compare them with others in the field.

The assessment process revolves around a prepared benchmark dataset encompassing various ontology pairs. These pairs are categorized into thematic tracks, each addressing different aspects of ontology alignment that must be addressed to achieve satisfactory results. For instance, the Anatomy track focuses on aligning ontologies describing Adult Mouse Anatomy and a part of the NCI Thesaurus describing human anatomy. Another example is the Multifarm track, which assesses systems' proficiency in handling ontologies in different natural languages.

Regardless of the track, each ontology pair is accompanied by a reference alignment, facilitating a straightforward validation of the alignment generated by a particular system. It is achieved using well-known metrics, Precision, Recall, and F-measure, taken from the information retrieval field ([130]). Both will be further described and characterized in Section 3.3.

To the best of the author's knowledge, it is the most widely recognized and respected methodology for verifying the quality of ontology alignment solutions. Thus, the systems described in this section have been chosen based on their participation in the OAEI campaigns held in 2021 ([162]), 2022 ([164]), and 2023 ([165]). The additional requirement is at least one publication (including the OAEI result overview) explicitly devoted to the solution. Such an approach yielded 25 ontology alignment systems that will be overviewed below.

A-LIOn

A-LIOn ([4]) is an ontology alignment system employing a combination of terminological, semantic, and machine-learning approaches. The methodology of A-LIOn is structured around three components: element-wise, structure-wise, and formal semantics learning techniques. Element-wise evaluation involves independently assessing entities based on explicitly given information like textual annotations and labels. Structure-wise analysis considers concepts within their structural context, focusing on the adjacency in the concept taxonomy.

A-LIOn's distinguishing feature lies in its use of external automated reasoner ELK ([105]), facilitated by expressing ontologies in OWL-DL. This approach addresses inconsistencies in initially found alignments by merging ontologies, adding predicted alignments as equivalence class axioms, and using reasoners to detect unsatisfiable classes. In case of unsatisfiability, explanations are generated, and problematic equivalence class axioms are iteratively removed.

However, A-LIOn has limitations. It is shown in the formal definition of ontology accepted in the methodology that the system can only generate mappings for concepts, neglecting relations and instances. The exclusive focus on concepts is identified as a factor impacting the quality of mappings, emphasizing the importance of analyzing concepts in conjunction with their broader context. The results from OAEI campaigns ([164]) suggest that A-LIOn falls short compared to baseline methods – the average Precision from three tracks A-LIOn has participated (Anatomy, Conference, and mse) was equal to 0.66 and the obtained average Recall was equal to 0.19.

The most significant difference between A-LIOn and the methods described in this book is the rejection of formal definitions. That reduces processing ontologies to processing OWL files. Focusing on concepts alone also impacts the quality of mappings since concepts should not be analyzed in isolation. Moreover, A-LIOn's exclusive focus on processing OWL files and concepts is identified as a factor impacting the quality of mappings, emphasizing the need for a more comprehensive analysis that includes relations and instances.

ALIN

ALIN ([28]) is an interactive ontology alignment system. Unlike fully automated ontology alignment systems, interactive ontology matching includes active participation from users or domain experts. Users may guide the matching process, review and validate suggested alignments, or provide additional information to improve accuracy.

During the alignment procedure, ALIN manages three sets of mappings: (i) Accepted, which includes mappings definitively retained in the alignment; (ii) Selected, which includes mappings pending a decision on inclusion in the alignment; and (iii) Suspended, which includes mappings previously chosen but temporarily or permanently filtered out of the selected set. ALIN's main procedure consists of 5 Steps. Initially, ALIN executes scanners and parsers for each ontology's concept name, modifying and standardizing them. Employing a blocking strategy, ALIN focuses solely on concept mappings, utilizing linguistic similarities among standardized concept names. Automatic acceptance occurs for concept mappings with synonymous standardized names, leveraging resources like Wordnet and domain-specific ontologies. ALIN also incorporates Natural Language Processing (NLP) resources, including regular and context-free grammar and their corresponding lexical and syntax analyzers, enhancing its capability to handle diverse linguistic and structural aspects during the alignment process.

Next, ALIN suspends selected mappings with entities exhibiting low lexical and semantic similarity, employing metrics such as Jaccard, Jaro-Winkler, and n-grams. Suspended mappings may be revisited later, potentially returning to the selected status.

In the subsequent step, domain expert involvement begins. ALIN sorts selected mappings based on the cumulative similarity metric values. The sorted mappings are presented to the expert, with up to three mappings shown together if they share full entity names. The set of selected mappings evolves with expert interactions. Accepted mappings trigger the removal of mappings constituting instantiations of anti-patterns, the selection of data property and object property mappings related to accepted concepts, and the unsuspension of concept mappings with entities subsuming the concept of accepted mappings. The interaction phase persists until there are no more selected mappings, ensuring thorough expert validation of the alignment.

The analysis of the results of subsequent OAEI campaigns ([30], [29]) shows a steady quality increase of mappings produced by ALIN. Obtained metrics of Precision demonstrate the correctness of designated mappings. However, as shown by mediocre value of average Recall equal to 0.44, there is still room for improvement in the amount of found mappings. The obtained value of average Precision was equal to 0.82. Additionally, the authors of ALIN point out the sensitivity to experts' feedback, which frequently becomes ALIN's biggest weakness.

In summary, ALIN distinguishes itself from the ontology alignment methods discussed in this book primarily through two key characteristics. Firstly, it focuses exclusively on mapping concepts, neglecting the inclusion of mappings for relations and instances. Secondly, its interactive nature in the primary mapping process sets it apart, as it involves human intervention and expertise to a greater extent than the other methods discussed here.

ALOD2Vec

ALOD2Vec Matcher([161]) is a label-based matcher. It uses terminological methods and WebIsALOD – a large-scale Web-crawled RDF data set of hypernymy relations as background knowledge ([78]).

In the alignment process, the matcher retrieves textual descriptions for all elements within the processed ontologies. It then establishes links between the ontology labels and concepts in the WebIsALOD dataset. This linkage is achieved through string operations on the labels, verifying their presence in WebIsALOD. In cases where a label is not found, labels comprising multiple words are progressively truncated from the right, and the process is reiterated to identify concepts positioned as descendants of the currently processed ones.

With the established links between the ontologies and WebIsALOD, ALOD2Vec utilizes pre-calculated embedding vectors extracted from WebIsALOD. The cosine similarity between these vectors is computed, resulting in the final alignment. Similar to the author's methods described in this book, ALOD2Vec produces homogenous alignment – concepts, attributes, relationships, and instances are handled and mapped separately.

In the OAEI campaigns ([30], [29]), ALOD2Vec participated in several tracks obtaining average results. For example, in the Anatomy track, the system scored a Precision of 0.828 and a Recall of 0.766. On the conference track, it achieved a Recall of 0.49 and a Precision equal to 0.64. Thus, ALOD2Vec outperformed only baseline solutions, and the mappings are simplistic and designated based only on shared labels. It is also worth noting that since 2021, it has not participated in OAEI campaigns, and its further development appears to be abandoned.

AgreementMaker

The literature illustrates that the alignment system family, called AgreementMaker, comprises multiple subsolutions. The initial version ([27]) relies on a set of matchers, each offering a fundamental method for calculating a similarity between elements extracted from mapped ontologies. These matchers are organized into a cascade and are responsible for similarity calculation, execution of a multi-strategy aligning procedure, and final result composition. AgreementMaker incorporates three propagation methods for base similarities: the basic Similarity Flooding algorithm, descendant's similarity inheritance, and sibling similarity contribution. The resulting values are compared to a predefined threshold, and the eventual mappings are returned. It is one of the oldest alignment systems (created in 2007) that is not under active development and has not participated in OAEI campaigns since 2011.

AgreementMakerLight ([52]), also referred to as AML or AMLC, is a general-purpose ontology alignment system heavily inspired by its predecessor, the original AgreementMaker. It primarily relies on terminological matching methods, incorporating structural and logic-based repair algorithms. AML begins by utilizing the Lexical Matcher, which seeks direct matches of labels (extracted from concepts) in an external lexicon. Subsequently, AML uses the Mediating Matcher, which incorporates an external ontology as a mediator in addition to direct label matching. Thirdly, the Word Matcher is applied, based on a word-based string similarity algorithm that gauges the similarity between two concepts' names through a weighted Jaccard index of the present words. Finally, the Parametric String Matcher is activated, comprising a selection of metrics directly derived from the original AgreementMaker. Throughout subsequent OAEI campaigns, AML proved itself to be one of the systems that successfully solved most challenges hidden within the OAEI dataset and one of the best-performing systems.

AgreementMakerDeep ([208]), also called AMD, extends previous solutions with deep learning techniques – terminological comparison methods are enhanced with BERT-like pre-train language model for textual matching, and structural matchers utilized knowledge graph embedding techniques based on a modified TransR model ([125]). AMD is capable of providing mappings of concepts and relations, which is its distinguishing feature among other ontology alignment systems. AMD has shown its potential as a relative newcomer to the OAEI competitions, especially in the Anatomy, Largebio, and Knowledge Graph tracks regarding obtained Precision and the time required to generate mappings. However, the results produced by AMD in the generic Conference track are below expectations, which is caused by the choice language models, which were focused entirely on medical terminology.

AROA

AROA (Association Rule-based Ontology Alignment) is an instance-based ontology alignment system ([219]). It is based on association rule mining and requires ontologies that will be aligned to share common instance data. Initially, AROA extracts triples in the format of (Subject, Predicate, Object) from both the source and target ontologies. Subsequently, these triples are cleaned based on information concerning concept assignments. Following the filtering step, AROA constructs a transaction database, serving as input for the association rule mining algorithm. AROA then enhances the content of these databases by incorporating information about the concepts to which specific instances are assigned. The modified data is utilized in the Frequent Pattern Growth Algorithm ([12]) to generate association rules between the ontologies. Finally, AROA incorporates a pattern-based approach for correspondence detection ([168]) to produce the final result.

According to the results of OAEI campaigns, AROA is one of the three systems capable of producing complex alignments (a set of mappings containing logic constructors rather than literal, direct mappings). AROA achieved relatively good results (average Precision equal to 0.84 and average Recall equal to 0.42) in the corresponding track dedicated to this issue. However, it did not participate in other tracks. Moreover, since AROA is an instance-based system which relies on the shared instances between ontologies, it can be assumed that the quality of alignments of ontologies without instances would not be satisfactory, which is the most significant limitation of AROA, which distances it from solutions provided in the book.

ATMatcher

ATMatcher, also referred to as ATBox, is an ontology alignment system capable of mapping concepts and instances ([79]). Dedicated procedures that solve these two aspects of ontology alignment are run in parallel. Eventually, the produced correspondences are combined to get the final results.

The process begins by preprocessing information related to concepts. Initially, all stop words are eliminated, and the textual content of each concept is enriched with synonyms sourced from the English Wiktionary ([178]). Subsequently, a cascade of six different string-matching strategies is applied for every pair of concepts from input ontologies. Even if a match is identified, the process continues to discover additional candidate mappings. Finally, bound path matching is executed, linking concepts between two already mapped classes in the taxonomy.

The instance-mapping procedure starts with the string-matching cascade, following the same strategy as in concept matching, with the omission of stopword removal and synonym enrichment. The initial alignment often includes excessive mappings; therefore, ATMatcher uses a set of heuristic filters to select the most suitable mappings.

During the OAEI campaign in 2022 ([164]), ATMatcher scored a Precision of 0.978 but only a Recall of 0.669 in the Anatomy track. Similarly, in the Conference track, ATMatcher achieved a Precision of 0.69, with a Recall of only 0.51. Therefore, ATMatcher demonstrates proficiency in ontology alignment, however, while achieving notable Precision scores, its Recall performance shows an area for potential improvement. This observation is supported by results of OAEI from different years ([163], [162]).

CIDER-LM

CIDER-LM (Language Model-based Context and Inference basED ontology alignER) is a cross-lingual ontology alignment system which leverages BERT([107]) – a transformer-based pretrained multilingual language model ([201]). It proceeds through the following steps.

Initially, CIDER-LM processes source and target ontologies using the HermiT semantic reasoner ([61]) and extends them by inferring initially undeclared semantic relations. CIDER-LM then focuses on concepts and their attributes, extracting associated labels to construct corresponding sentence embeddings. Labels from the concepts within the direct taxonomic neighbourhood are included to enhance the semantic representation.

Subsequently, CIDER-LM incorporates the BERT language model and cosine similarity to determine distances between vector embeddings associated with concepts from the two ontologies. This step generates a set of potential correspondences, each assigned a confidence level. Eventually, a straightforward threshold filtering is applied to eliminate correspondences with low confidence levels.

The applicability of CIDER-LM is limited, as it was specifically developed for the Multifarm track in the OAEI. This track assesses systems' capabilities in handling ontologies in different natural languages. The results obtained by CIDER-LM in the 2022 OAEI campaign are only moderately satisfactory, with a Precision of 0.16 and a Recall of 0.58. Given these results, there is much room for further development. Unfortunately, CIDER-LM's participation has been restricted to the 2022 OAEI campaign, with no subsequent publications.

DLinker

DLinker ([70]) is an ontology alignment system dedicated only to finding correspondences of instances. The primary approach adopted by DLinker relies on utilizing the Longest Common Subsequence (LCS) method for effective matching. The alignment process in DLinker is conducted in two steps.

In the initial step, known as the training phase, DLinker undergoes a learning process utilizing the given hyperparameters. Subsequently, in the prediction step, DLinker leverages the insights gained during the training phase to make predictions about similar instances. Unfortunately, only one very brief article is available in the literature. Therefore, providing a more precise description of the procedure utilized in DLinker is impossible.

During the 2022 OAEI campaign, DLinker participated in two tracks devoted to aligning instances – SPATIAL and SPIMBENCH. DLinker was ranked first on the SPACIAL track and second on the SPIMBENCH track. However, it is worth noting that the collected values of Precision and Recall, respectively equal to 0.791 and 0.632, are only average. Thus, similar to CIDER-LM, there is much room for further development. Regrettably, similar to CIDER-LM, no subsequent developments or advancements have been documented in the existing literature at the moment of writing, leaving the potential for future enhancements unexplored.

GMap

GMap ([123], [124]) is an ontology alignment system that combines lexical, semantic, and stochastic approaches in a multi-step procedure. It starts by computing lexical similarities between concepts from two input ontologies, using edit-distance calculations, external lexicons like WordNet, and the TFID method with a maximalization strategy. After computing these similarities, GMap employs Sum-Product Networks (SPN) to encode them, determining their significance through Maximum A Posteriori (MAP) inference. Using the noisy-or model, it further encodes the values from SPN and probabilistic matching rules.

The process GMap follows is iterative. It starts by collecting initial concept mappings, which are then refined in subsequent iterations to identify additional matches. If no new correspondences are found, the alignment process concludes.

GMap's performance varied in the OAEI campaigns of 2021 ([162]). The anatomy track demonstrated high Precision (0.916) and substantial Recall (0.812), benefiting from the ontologies' similar shared terminology, which facilitated the identification of sound correspondences. However, in the conference track, where ontologies used similar terminology but in different contexts, GMap's performance was notably lower, with Precision and Recall at 0.61. This lower performance in the conference track is attributed to the system's reliance on terminological methods, which are less effective in contexts where the same terminology is used differently. Since 2021, no further developments have been reported on GMap, suggesting that its methodologies and capabilities have remained the same since then.

GraphMatcher

GraphMatcher ([42]) is an ontology alignment system that leverages graph representation learning, specifically through graph attention networks ([202]), in combination with a neighbourhood aggregation approach. The system starts by preprocessing ontology content, which includes tokenization and stop word removal. It then employs the Universal Sentence Encoder to create word embedding vectors for concepts, attributes, and relations within the ontology. GraphMatcher utilizes graph attention within a supervised machine-learning framework for representation learning. This approach generates advanced representations of concepts and related elements, enabling the system to determine similarity scores between concept pairs.

The primary advancements of GraphMatcher lie in addressing two key challenges in machine learning-based ontology matching: the need for enhanced contextual information about properties and concepts and the difficulties in effectively representing ontology data. GraphMatcher aggregates neighbouring terms around a central concept or property to overcome the first challenge, providing richer context. For the second, it represents ontology data as an arbitrary graph. The overarching objective is to develop a graph representation learning model, incorporating Siamese networks and a graph attention mechanism, to identify semantically corresponding concepts within different ontologies.

GraphMatcher's performance in the Ontology Alignment Evaluation Initiative (OAEI) campaigns of 2022 ([29]) and 2023 ([43]) has shown promising results. Particularly in the Conference track, the system achieved high F1-measure scores (equal to 0.71), indicating a balanced performance in Precision (equal to 0.82) and Recall (equal to 0.62). These results suggest that GraphMatcher was competitive among other campaign participants, though not necessarily the top performer. However, as of the time of writing, the limited number of publications (only two) focusing on GraphMatcher makes providing a more detailed and comprehensive description of the system challenging.

KGMatcher

KGMatcher is a system designed to align domain-independent Knowledge Graphs, which could be treated as ontologies containing only instances ([49]). It employs a hybrid approach to find correspondences between concepts, involving two primary techniques: an instance-based matcher and a name matcher, both preceded by initial preprocessing. The process begins with KGMatcher parsing and indexing the lexical content of two input ontologies. Each concept within these ontologies is indexed as a 'document,' with its content derived from concatenated instance labels. Word segmentation methods are then applied to refine these labels.

The Instance-based Matcher, the first key component of KGMatcher, uses a self-supervised machine-learning approach to map concepts based on the overlap of their instances. This matcher excludes concepts with identical labels across both ontologies and then calculates the maximum similarity between concept pairs. The second component, the element-level matcher, evaluates the similarity of concept labels using edit distance, Levenshtein distance, and a pre-trained word2vec model to measure cosine similarities through word embeddings.

KGMatcher constructs an alignment matrix with confidence values representing different concept pairs, ultimately selecting pairs with the highest similarity scores for its final output. The process includes standard text preprocessing methods, like removing stopwords, and generates potential instance pairs by analyzing label presence in the ontologies.

During the 2022 OAEI campaign, KGMatcher's performance varied across different tracks ([50]). In the Conference track, it achieved a Precision of 0.83 but a lower Recall of 0.38. The system performed better in the Knowledge Graph and Common Knowledge Graphs tracks, with notably higher Precision and Recall scores.

The effectiveness of KGMatcher's hybrid strategy is evident from these results, but the nature of the dataset heavily influences its performance. The instance-based component of KGMatcher+, which relies on general pre-trained word embedding models, shows good results when complex, feature-rich instances are compared. On the other hand, in the Conference track KGMatcher scored much weaker results.

Lily

Lily is a comprehensive ontology alignment system ([220]), which integrates a variety of mapping techniques, including Generic Ontology Matching (GOM), the Large Scale Ontology Matching (LOM), which builds upon GOM for handling large-scale ontologies, the Instance Ontology Matching (IOM), and incorporates additional functionalities for Ontology Mapping Debugging and Ontology Matching Tuning. Collectively, these components aim to validate and refine the Precision of initial ontology alignments.

Lily's general procedure is structured around three primary phases. Initially, it undertakes preprocessing to structure the ontologies. Subsequently, it employs a method of enriching ontology concepts with contextual information through semantic subgraphs ([205]). For every concept, Lily creates a Semantic Description Document (SDD) that outlines its labels, place within the taxonomy, attributes, relationships to other concepts, and instance values. To augment these SDDs, Lily integrates external knowledge bases, such as WordNet, and domain-specific ontologies, notably UBERON ([142]), thereby enhancing the semantic depth of the ontology matching. The final stage involves computing similarities between concepts using terminological and structural approaches, integrated through similarity propagation techniques ([204]).

Lily's effectiveness has been demonstrated in its participation in various Ontology Alignment Evaluation Initiative (OAEI) campaigns, with the latest participation recorded in 2021. With notable Precision and Recall scores, it showcased remarkable performance across multiple tracks, including Anatomy, Conference, and Large Biomedical Ontologies. In the Anatomy track, Lily achieved a Precision of 0.901 and a Recall of 0.902. In the Large Biomedical Ontologies track, it recorded a Precision of 0.905 and a Recall of 0.828, attributing this success to the utilization of the UBERON ontology, a comprehensive multi-species anatomy resource. Conversely, in the Conference track, Lily's performance dipped to a Precision of 0.65 and a Recall of 0.48, highlighting the critical role of external knowledge sources in optimizing ontology alignment outcomes.

LogMap

LogMap([99]) is an advanced ontology alignment system tailored for efficiently matching large-scale ontologies while incorporating reasoning and repair strategies to minimize logical inconsistencies within mappings. The process within LogMap involves multiple steps, starting with lexical indexation to create an initial manageable set of mappings through an inverted index of the ontologies' lexical content. Recognizing the computational intensity of unsatisfiability detection and ontology alignment repair, LogMap applies logic-based module extraction for ontology modularization, resulting in smaller, semantically dense ontology modules. The system then employs propositional Horn reasoning, utilizing a Horn representation for ontology modules and candidate mappings, incorporating the Dowling-Gallier algorithm to identify unsatisfiable classes, albeit with acknowledged limitations. LogMap has been further enhanced with machine learning techniques and ontology embeddings ([20]), notably adopting the OWL2Vec approach to improve its alignment capabilities ([19]).

Participating annually in the Ontology Alignment Evaluation Initiative (OAEI) since 2011 ([100], [98]), LogMap has consistently been a top contender across various tracks, distinguished for its repair techniques and the coherence of its mappings. In the latest OAEI campaign in 2023 ([165]), LogMap demonstrated its robustness and maturity, achieving notable Precision and Recall scores across several tracks. It showed exceptional performance in the Anatomy track with a Precision of 0.92 and a Recall of 0.85, and it maintained strong results in other tracks such as Conference, Bio-ML, Knowledge Graph, and Common Knowledge Graphs, with Precision reaching as high as 1.00 in some cases.

Despite its strengths, LogMap's primary limitation lies in its dependency on lexical similarities for generating candidate mappings, a method that may falter with lexically varied and sparse ontologies. The observed high Precision but moderate Recall across its applications indicate a tendency towards accuracy over completeness, making it highly suitable for contexts where the correctness of mappings takes precedence over identifying all possible alignments. This characteristic underscores the importance of selecting ontology alignment systems based on the specific needs and characteristics of the matched ontologies.

LSMatch

LSMatch (Large Scale Ontology Matching System) is an ontology alignment system which uses terminological comparisons to find correspondences between concepts ([180]). The implemented method utilizes the Levenshtein string similarity metric in conjunction with a synonyms matcher. This matcher leverages background knowledge sources that include synonyms, facilitating the identification of concepts that share analogous semantics despite having different lexical representations. LSMatch can also find mappings of elements from monolingual and multilingual ontologies.

Initially, LSMatch preprocesses input ontologies. It extracts concepts, relations, and instances and then performs stemming and removing stopwords and non-alphabetic characters. The last step includes normalizing letters. Subsequently, the Levenshtein and synonyms matcher modules are incorporated. The former is a straightforward utilization of Levenshtein distance. The latter fetches synonyms from WordNet ([138]) and employs a synonym matcher. Support for multilingual ontologies is ensured by using MyMemory online translator [2]. Eventually, all the partial comparisons yield a number from the range [0, 1]. The final selection of alignments is based on a combined score exceeding the threshold equal to 0.95.

---

[2]https://mymemory.translated.net/

In 2023, LSMatch participated for the third time in the OAEI campaign ([179]). In the Anatomy track, it achieved an average Precision of 0.95 and an average Recall of 0.63. In the Conference track, the average Precision was 0.87, with an average Recall of 0.48. The Common KG Track displayed high performance with an average Precision of 0.97 and an average Recall of 0.69. In the Knowledge Graph Track, the system achieved an average Precision of 0.83 and an average Recall of 0.66. Finally, the Multifarm track yielded an average Precision of 0.68 and an average Recall of 0.36. In summary, LSMatch demonstrated notably high Precision across all tracks, yet it fell short in terms of Recall.

Matcha

Matcha, as described in [55], is a multi-strategy ontology alignment system comprising various independent matching modules, each adopting a distinct approach to processing ontologies and their content. These modules are broadly categorized into two groups: those that generate concept mappings and those that produce instance mappings.

Matcha includes specialized concept matching modules for concept mapping, with instance-based class matching as a key component. This module detects class overlaps through shared instances. The Lexical Matcher, another essential component, matches ontologies by finding literal full-name matches in their lexicons, considering the origins of these names for a detailed similarity evaluation. The String Matcher module contributes by determining ontologies' similarity based on the highest string similarity, utilizing one of four string similarity measures. The LLM Matcher, another advanced feature, computes the cosine similarity between the embeddings of ontology lexicons. The Mediating XRef Matcher is also utilized, leveraging cross-references and exact lexical matches between ontologies and a third-party proxy ontology. The Word Matcher module uses a weighted Jaccard index to assess ontologies' similarity and considers shared words for a semantic viewpoint on similarity.

For mapping instances, Matcha integrates three more modules: the Attribute Matcher for precise attribute value matches, the Attribute String Matcher using the ISub string similarity metric [54], and the Attribute to Lexicon Matcher for mapping instances by comparing external lexicon entries and attribute values.

Matcha's performance in the 2023 campaign showed varying results across different tracks. In the Anatomy track, it achieved an average Precision of 0.951 and a Recall of 0.93. The Biodiversity and Ecology track's Precision was 0.569, and the Recall was 0.93. In Common Knowledge Graphs, it attained perfect Precision (0.99) and a Recall of 0.89. In the Conference track, Matcha obtained an average Precision and Recall of 0.62. The Knowledge Graph track recorded an average Precision of 0.55 and Recall of 0.84, while Material Sciences and Engineering had an average Precision of 0.66 and Recall of 0.55. The Multifarm track results were 0.37 for Precision and 0.04 for Recall. Lastly, in the Food Nutritional Composition track, Matcha achieved a Precision of 0.0656 and Recall of 0.30, indicating that despite several participations in OAEI campaigns, Matcha is still in the early stages of development.

OTMapOnto

OTMapOnto ([6]) is an ontology alignment system based on optimal transport problem. It leverages the techniques developed in computational optimal transport to match concepts from input ontologies ([127]).

The noteworthy aspect of OTMapOnto is the fact that it is one of the few ontology alignment systems built upon robust formal foundations and mathematical definitions. Unlike approaches solely relying on syntactic analysis of OWL-expressed ontologies, OTMapOnto goes beyond pure implementation, leveraging a foundation grounded in formal methods and mathematical principles.

The process begins by transforming ontology elements into embedding vectors encompassing terminological, structural, and semantic content. Subsequently, the system employs optimal transport to transfer masses from the source embedding space to the target embedding space. The optimal transport solution involves a shape-based Wasserstein distance and a coupling matrix, which establishes connections between the embeddings of the source and target ontologies. This coupling matrix generates a collection of initial candidate matchings, subject to further refinement in subsequent steps.

In the Conference track, during the 2021 OAEI campaign, OTMapOnto achieved a Precision of 0.23 and a Recall of 0.73, surpassing the Recall of most systems that participated in the earlier edition of the OAEI campaign. For the Common Knowledge Graphs track, OTMapOnto demonstrated an overall Precision of 0.9 and a Recall of 0.84. In the Disease and Phenotype track, OTMapOnto achieved an average Precision of approximately 0.14 and an average Recall of 0.99 across the two tasks. In the Large Biomedical Ontologies track, OTMapOnto achieved an average Precision of approximately 0.415 and an average Recall of approximately 0.755. Thus, OTMapOnto demonstrated notable performance in the OAEI evaluation, particularly in the Disease and Phenotype track.

OLaLa

OLaLa ([80]) is an ontology alignment system which utilizes one of the Large Language Models (LLM), namely LLaMa [196], in order to decide whether or not two entities from two ontologies share a common semantics.

At first, the system retrieves all textual content associated with specific concepts from processed ontologies. Subsequently, a well-known Sentence BERT model is employed. The texts linked to each concept undergo embedding, and a semantic search is initiated. The source ontology is initially treated as a query, seeking the best matches among embeddings generated from the target ontology. The roles of ontologies are then swapped, with target ontology serving as the query space.

Next, the candidates are incorporated into the user-defined prompt and fed into the integrated LLM, resulting in the initial set of mappings. This alignment undergoes additional processing through a cardinality filter, ensuring only one-to-one mappings in the output and a confidence filter, eliminating correspondences with confidence values below a predefined threshold.

In the 2023 OAEI campaign ([81]), OLaLa participated in multiple tracks. In the Conference track, it achieved a Precision of 0.59 and a Recall of 0.7. In the Anatomy track, OLaLa demonstrated a Precision of 0.92 and a Recall of 0.89. The BioML track yielded lower average values, with Precision at 0.37 and Recall at 0.44. Conversely, in the Biodiv track, OLaLa obtained Precision and Recall values of 0.71 and 0.87, respectively. These results indicate that OLaLa is constructed upon a robust approach for extracting textual information from ontologies, showcasing its capability to generate high-quality mappings.

PropMatch

PropMatch is an ontology alignment system that incorporates the straightforward TF-IDF measures with Word and Sentence Embeddings to measure similarities between relations, based on the approach presented in [185] and [184]. As pointed out in [16], finding correspondences of properties is a frequently omitted aspect of ontology alignment, and PropMatch is the only solution which directly addresses this issue.

PropMatch utilizes four primary techniques. The first stage employs the TF-IDF and Soft TF-IDF models, which were prepared before the alignment process. Each entity from the input ontologies represents a virtual document in this stage. Documents associated with concepts are constructed using the labels and comments of the concepts, while virtual documents for relations are created from the labels and virtual documents of domains and ranges. The system then converts the documents to lowercase and tokenizes them. After constructing the TF-IDF models, it calculates the similarity score for each relation pair. This stage aims to find pairs of properties with low similarity that will be excluded from further processing.

Subsequently, PropMatch uses pre-trained models for word embeddings to assess domain similarity and sentence embeddings to evaluate relation label similarity. This process generates an initial set of candidate mappings. Following this, PropMatch follows the locality principle ([99]), borrowed from the competitive solution LogMap. The principle asserts that new correspondences are often found among previously aligned entities or entities from their close neighbourhood. As a result, the alignment includes the inverses of mapped relations. Eventually, the system repeats the entire procedure, passing candidate alignments as a parameter. This iterative approach allows the system to increase its confidence in computed similarity measures based on previously discovered correspondences.

PropMatch participated in the OAEI campaign in the most recent (at the moment of writing) installment in 2023 in the Conference track ([186]). It achieved the best results among all of the competitors in all metrics. The obtained Precision was equal to 0.83, while the Recall was equal to 0.54.

SORBETMatcher

SORBETMatcher, previously known as SEBMather, is an ontology alignment system designed to identify equivalence and subsumption mappings between concepts. It leverages the innovative SORBET Embeddings, which utilize large language models for ontology embedding ([65]).

The process within SORBETMatcher begins by narrowing down potential concept matches. Given the extensive time required to generate SORBET Embeddings for large ontologies, limiting the pool of concept correspondences is essential early in the process. To achieve this, SORBETMatcher integrates a string-matching algorithm to identify and preliminarily match concepts with similar or synonymous labels, thereby streamlining the candidate set. This step is followed by additional, track-specific candidate selection methods within the Ontology Alignment Evaluation Initiative (OAEI), although these methods are tailored rather than universally applicable.

The core of SORBETMatcher's methodology involves the application of SentenceBERT, a variant of the BERT model specifically adapted for generating sentence embeddings. This model produces the SORBET embeddings, encapsulating the semantic essence of ontology concepts. The model operates on input derived from random walks that articulate the context of each class, factoring in hierarchical and associative relationships. This approach facilitates the placement of analogous concepts from disparate ontologies into proximal regions within the latent space, mirroring the ontology structure and enhancing alignment precision. The final step in SORBETMatcher's process is the calculation of cosine similarities between concept pairs, forming a similarity matrix from which final mappings are derived based on a predefined similarity threshold.

SORBETMatcher is a newcomer to OAEI campaigns. In the most recent campaign from 2023, it showcased its versatility and robust outcomes ([165]). The Anatomy track it demonstrated a Precision score of 0.923 and a Recall of 0.895. Transitioning to the Conference track, SORBETMatcher achieved a Precision of 0.78 and a Recall of 0.75. In the Bio-ML track, the system acquired a Precision of 0.772 and a Recall of 0.699 ([66]). These outcomes highlight SORBETMatcher's adaptability and the effectiveness of its embedding-based approach in facilitating ontology alignment across varied domains.

TOM

TOM (Transformers for Ontology Matching) is an ontology alignment system which is built on top of a transformer-based language model incorporated to calculate a similarity between concepts ([113]).

The process begins with analyzing input ontologies using terminological methods to identify evident correspondences, aiming to alleviate the transformer matcher from evaluating straightforward pairs of concepts, which can be resource-intensive. Additionally, pairs of concepts that are clearly not alignable are identified. Subsequently, the Candidate Generator is employed to construct an input alignment for the transformer matcher. This alignment comprises the cartesian product of concepts from both ontologies, excluding the previously identified obvious correspondences and non-correspondences.

Following this, TOM iterates over the alignment and submits each pair of elements to the BERT-based model, which assigns a confidence value. The threshold filter is then applied to eliminate correspondences with low confidence. Finally, the max-weight bipartite extractor is integrated to fine-tune the output, removing redundant mappings and enhancing the overall alignment Precision.

In the 2022 OAEI campaign, TOM demonstrated moderate performance ([164]). In the Anatomy track, TOM achieved a Precision value of 0.93 and a Recall value of 0.808. It is noteworthy that, similar to other alignment systems utilizing terminological comparison, TOM delivered generally favourable results in the Anatomy track. Conversely, in the Conference track, TOM achieved a Precision score of 0.69 and a Recall of 0.48. Thus, while TOM demonstrated effectiveness in specific contexts, there is room for improvement in achieving more robust results across different ontology alignment tasks.

TOMATO

TOMATO (TOolkit for MATching Ontologies) is a system designed to align ontologies using machine learning techniques, with a focus on terminological comparisons ([171]). The implemented matching process is divided into two phases, leveraging traditional string similarity metrics to evaluate the relationships between ontology concepts.

In the initial stage, TOMATO takes two input ontologies and preprocesses their contents. This preprocessing involves removing stopwords, normalizing camelCase words into separate terms, and applying stemming to reduce words to their base or root form, standard practices in text processing to ensure consistency and improve the matching quality. Following this, it calculates similarities between pairs of concepts across the ontologies using various string similarity measures, such as the Levenshtein distance, Jaro-Winkler score, ISUB, and 3-gram similarity. These measures are applied to the concept names and their attributes and relations, generating a comprehensive vector of scores that reflect the degree of similarity between each concept pair. The subsequent stage involves training a machine learning classifier using these vectors alongside reference alignments provided by the Ontology Alignment Evaluation Initiative (OAEI)

The effectiveness of TOMATO's implementation, as demonstrated in its performance during the 2023 OAEI campaign, appears to be limited ([165]). In its participation, specifically within the Conference track, TOMATO achieved a precision of 0.09 and a recall of 0.6. These results indicate a high level of recall, suggesting TOMATO could identify a broad set of potential correspondences but with very low precision, indicating that many of these identified correspondences were inaccurate. This disparity highlights a significant challenge for TOMATO in balancing precision and recall, suggesting that while it can generate numerous potential alignments, enhancing the accuracy of these alignments remains an area for improvement.

Wiktionary Matcher

Wiktionary Matcher ([160]), also referred to as WktMtchr, is a label-based ontology alignment system, which uses Wiktionary – alternative to WordNet, online lexical resource ([178]). This system initiates the alignment process by using multiple string-matching techniques. Subsequently, the synonym matcher module establishes connections between concept labels and labels in the Wiktionary mentioned above. Such an approach resembles an upper ontology matching strategy, where correspondence is added to the final alignment solely based on the synonymy relation, without considering the specific word sense ([131]). If a label cannot be located, the system attempts to find matches by iteratively truncating labels consisting of multiple word tokens, enabling the detection of long sub-concepts even when the entire string is not found.

Wiktionary Matcher can also find mappings of instances using a string index., which is performed after aligning concepts. Instances belonging to classes that were previously matched receive a higher confidence. If one instance corresponds to multiple others, priority is given to correspondences where both concepts were matched before. Additionally, unlike other ontology alignment systems, Wiktionary Matcher provides a human-readable explanation for adding correspondences to the final alignment, enhancing interpretability and transparency in the alignment results.

In 2021, Wiktionary Matcher achieved moderate results in the OAEI campaign ([162]). In the anatomy track, it obtained a Precision equal to 0.956 and a Recall equal to 0.753. In the Common Knowledge track, it scored Precision and Recall, respectively, equal to 1.0 and 0.8. However, in the Conference track, the obtained value of Precision is equal to 0.66, while Recall is equal to 0.53. Such results allow drawing similar conclusions about Wiktionary Matchar as for GMap. Both systems can align ontologies with very specific terminologies, as shown by good results in the Anatomy track. However, if the labelling of concepts becomes vague, Wiktionary Matcher is more prone to errors.

WomboCombo

WomboCombo (Word Meaning-based Matcher Over Combinations) is a multi-stage ontology alignment system that uses terminological methods to find the equivalent entities in two ontologies ([104]). The initial stages are based on a simple pairing process based on exact string similarity. Subsequent steps use the pre-trained language model BERT to identify entities with equivalent meanings but different lexical representations. Each stage produces its own output, and these outputs are then combined to create a final alignment.

The combination step is the most resource-intensive element of WomboCombo. It is based on a classifier that distinguishes between nodes representing the same concept and those only similar. The process includes generating a training dataset with two classes, "same" and "similar," and training a Language Model-based classifier. Using a candidate pair pool, the trained model discerns and eliminates pairs predicted to be only similar, eventually returning pairs identified as semantically equivalent. The final alignment is yielded based on a simple voting process, which selects mappings chosen through the procedure by the majority of matching stages.

The system participated in the OAEI campaign 2022 ([164]) in the Knowledge Graph Matching track, showing that WomboCombo can only provide mappings of instances. Thus, comparing WomboCombo with more holistic solutions for the ontology alignment task is challenging. Moreover, due to several implementation errors, WomboCombo was excluded from the campaign.

One thing to note is that in contrast to the methods presented in this book, the authors did not provide any mathematical foundations or formal descriptions of the proposed process. WomboCombo can only be analyzed based on its implementation, and the authors did no further research (since no additional articles about WomboCombo were published at the time of writing).

3.1.2   Discussion

The provided overview of ontology alignment techniques highlights broad research in the field. The outline of 25 systems which participated in OAEI in the 2021,2022, and 2023 campaigns showcases a range of methodologies and approaches (that cannot be classified into a single comparison category, as provided in Figure 3.1), each with its unique strengths and limitations. The situation also showcases a significant gap in the field: most solutions lack a robust mathematical foundation.

The development of different approaches to the ontology alignment task has been mainly motivated by practical requirements entailed by reliance on the OWL standard. In other words, even very sophisticated solutions are inspired not by finding alignments of ontologies treated as knowledge representation method but by finding alignments of ontologies treated as OWL files. Approaching the topic from this perspective allows us to claim that the achievements in the field are significant. For example, AgreementMaker and its derivatives demonstrate the effectiveness of multi-strategy approaches, integrating terminological, structural, and semantic comparisons to achieve comprehensive ontology alignments. Incorporating association rule mining in AROA shows the benefits of integrating data mining techniques to find more nuanced correspondences. Similarly, systems like GraphMatcher or SORBETMatcher leverage advanced techniques like graph attention networks and large language models to enhance their mapping capabilities.

The review also demonstrates a trend towards integrating machine learning techniques as a solution's backbone (like ALOD2Vec, OLaLa, or TOM). However, their effectiveness varies significantly across different contexts, with some excelling in specific areas like Anatomy but showing limitations in more diverse settings like Conference tracks. These characteristics are caused by the fact that large language models, despite being very sophisticated tools, often operate as 'black boxes' and thus do not address the interpretation of textual representation of elements extracted from ontologies. Although there exist methods for explaining the outcomes of large language models ([218]), they have not been applied in the context of ontology alignment.

The inconsistent performance of many machine-learning-based systems (such as CIDER-LM, based on BERT) across different tracks in the OAEI campaigns suggests a lack of generalizability. Systems that excel in one context may show only moderate results in others, indicating a potential gap in their ability to adapt to varying ontological structures and requirements.

Therefore, the absence of a solid mathematical foundation in these systems raises questions about their theoretical robustness, generalizability, and transparency. Systems like OTMapOnto stand out for using formal methods; however, they should be treated as exceptions. Most systems, like LSMatch, prioritize practical effectiveness over theoretical clarity, often treating ontological elements as raw strings or using heuristic approaches without a clear mathematical rationale.

Moreover, many systems (like A-LIOn, TOMATO, and Wiktionary Matcher) focus only on finding mappings of concepts, neglecting the search for mappings of relations and instances. This shortback impacts the comprehensiveness of alignments. On the other hand, solutions like DLinker can only provide mappings of instances, treating them as vectors of values and discarding the fact that instances can be assigned to particular concepts, giving them explicitly expressed semantics, thus adding interpretability to otherwise raw values.

In conclusion, the practical effectiveness of the ontology alignment techniques described in the current section of the book is evident. However, it is mainly visible only in the performance in OAEI campaigns. Some of the systems' performances show a range of effectiveness, with some excelling in certain tracks but not others. This variability is caused by the approaches being tailored explicitly for different ontology alignment scenarios appearing in certain OAEI tracks and the difficulty in creating universally effective systems.

Therefore, there is a clear need for more research focused on grounding these solutions in solid mathematical theories. Such a foundation would not only enhance the theoretical robustness but also allow for more explicit approaches for their evaluation and eventual improvement. Additionally, a purely formal approach to ontology alignment would yield a framework that can be independent of ontology representation, thus discarding the reliance on OWL standard without the possibility of being adapted to be used within a solution that requires it.

3.2 Managing ontology evolution and maintaining ontology alignments over time

3.2.1 Problem overview

Ontologies, as adaptable methods for knowledge representation, play a crucial role in various applications by allowing for capturing complex properties of chosen domains, including relationships, hierarchies, and other interdependencies among various entities. Nonetheless, the dynamic nature of real-world domains often necessitates updates and modifications in the content of these ontologies. Effective management and modification strategies are essential to ensure that ontologies accurately reflect these changes, which becomes even more critical when an ontology is aligned with another. As one evolves, the inter-ontology mappings may no longer be valid, necessitating reevaluation of established correspondences. While designating the alignment from the ground up is one option, a more efficient strategy might involve analyzing the changes made to the ontologies and adjusting only the impacted mappings accordingly. The feasibility of such an approach relies on robust methods for managing the evolution of ontologies. Therefore, this book section is devoted to an overview of two related topics: strategies for managing the process of ontology evolution and techniques for maintaining the alignment between evolving ontologies.

A prime example of an application where the management of ontology evolution is essential is the organization and structuring of genomic data. The Gene Ontology Consortium conducts research on this topic by developing the Gene Ontology ([25], [26]), frequently referred to as GO. Initially, it was created to address the need for consistent descriptions of gene products in different databases. The maintained ontology is used in a wide range of biological and genomic research, and it covers three specific domains: molecular functions, biological processes, and cellular components. The GO is continuously updated and refined as new biological data is discovered, highlighting the need for precise descriptions of applied changes.

[183] describes a methodology for managing collaborative efforts on ontologies and overseeing their modifications over time. The discussed strategies, however, do not consider the historical record of changes made to the ontologies. The authors of [90] discuss various scenarios where changes to the Gene Ontology could occur. These modifications are critical for all GO users to consider, as they can affect the functional characterization of these gene products and, consequently, the interpretation of any analyses conducted using GO datasets. The research, however, lacks the formal definition of "a change" and focuses entirely on empirical descriptions in the specific ontology.

In the article[58], a more generic, domain-independent methodology for categorizing changes in ontologies is presented, which serves as foundational work for analyzing the evolution of both ontologies and their alignments. This approach provides a comprehensive framework for understanding and documenting alterations in ontologies. It lays the groundwork for subsequent studies focusing on the dynamics of ontology evolution and the implications these changes have on their alignments with other ontologies.

The research provided in [112] proposes an automatic detection method of ontology changes and, subsequently, a method for rewriting queries that can be executed against the evolving ontologies. The developed solution automates the process by detecting and describing changes between ontology versions using a high-level language and then interpreting these changes as Global-as-View (GAV) mappings, which allows for generating query rewritings compatible with different ontology versions. In cases where exact query rewritings are not possible, the proposed solution offers assistance in redefining queries or providing the best over-approximations, which include minimally-containing and minimally-generalized rewritings.

The method discussed in [176] adopts an alternative approach to handling ontology evolution. Instead of focusing on the chronological progression of ontology versions, it utilizes the modifications made in successive versions to construct a relevance graph. This graph arranges ontology versions based on relevance rather than chronological order. The relevance itself is determined by evaluating four key criteria: the level of conceptualization, frequency of usage, degree of abstraction, and the completeness of the ontology.

The $\tau - OWL$ framework, as introduced in [215], presents a comprehensive solution for managing temporal aspects in Semantic Web documents, mainly focusing on OWL ontologies. This framework is significant because it can incorporate time-varying elements into standard OWL ontologies without necessitating changes to the OWL framework itself. It achieves this through the innovative use of logic and physical annotations, which add temporal dimensions to conventional OWL ontologies. This approach maintains data independence and simplifies the validation process for schema and instances, enabling advanced temporal semantic tools to be applied.

Building on this, the authors in their later work [216] expanded the τ-OWL framework to support temporal schema versioning. This enhancement enables the framework to handle instances that vary over time and the evolution of the ontology schema itself. They introduced a set of primitives designed for updating the standard and temporal aspects of ontology schemas, complete with detailed operational semantics. This systematic method is crucial for managing large datasets and maintaining consistency across different versions of an ontology schema. Such schema versioning is particularly important in areas where ontology schemas need to adapt and evolve in response to changes in the real world. The extended $\tau - OWL$ framework ensures that historical and current data are retained within the same system, making it highly valuable for Semantic Web applications that require a complete historical record of ontology changes, even in big data environments.

A method for managing the evolution of ontologies which diverges from conventional versioning techniques can be found in [14]. Instead of creating distinct versions for each ontology update, this approach involves the creation of a Historical Knowledge Graph. This graph amalgamates information from all ontology versions into a single, unified structure. This strategy streamlines maintenance by eliminating the need to individually analyze and monitor changes across different versions. It facilitates more straightforward access to the entirety of the knowledge base, enhancing the efficiency of inference processes. However, this method comes with its challenges, primarily the need to store and manage an ever-expanding ontology, which, over time, could become increasingly complex and resource-intensive.

A groundwork for analyzing the impact of ontology evolution on established alignments is provided in [72] and its continuation [71]. The authors developed a formal, domain-independent framework, COnto-Diff, for analyzing the evolution of ontologies and their mappings. The proposed approach begins by matching different versions of an ontology to form an initial evolution mapping consisting of basic change operations such as insert, update, and delete. It then uses a rule-based approach to transform these basic operations into a more compact set of complex change operations. These complex operations include merging, splitting, or modifying entire subgraphs. The approach is evaluated using large life science ontologies, including the Gene Ontology and the NCI Thesaurus, and is compared with PromptDiff, another ontology evolution tool – the results demonstrate the practicality of COnto-Diff in ontology version management.

The most simplistic approach to the given topic is provided in [211]. It discusses a method for refining established mappings in biomedical ontologies by identifying correspondences with the updated ontology versions without necessitating a matching operation for the entire set of ontology entities. The described approach, however, is limited to mapping newly introduced concepts to the managed ontologies and does not undertake revalidation of mappings linked to modified concepts.

Much broader research can be found in [68], where authors investigate the evolution of ontology mappings in the life sciences domain, focusing on how changes in ontologies trigger adjustments in these mappings. The study encompasses three life science mappings and examines the impact of three matching strategies. It particularly emphasizes the role of naming and synonym information in these strategies and observes that, except for anatomy ontologies, mappings based on these common strategies often undergo significant changes. The research reveals a notable correlation between changes in ontologies and the resultant mapping modifications. The findings highlight the dynamic nature of ontology mappings and the necessity of considering matching strategy and ongoing ontology evolution for accurate and reliable data interpretation in life sciences. By providing formal definitions of versioning schemes, change models, and the change impact ratio, it is very close to the work found later in this book; however, it focuses only on the level of concepts.

A different approach to the considered topic can be found in [38], where authors analyze information about ontology evolution, but instead of revalidating existing alignments in light of ontology changes, they utilize this evolutionary information to refine and enhance concept mappings. This refined approach enables us to find connections between concepts, not only equivalency. The practical application of this methodology was demonstrated using the Logic Observation Identifiers Names and Codes (LOINC) ontology on its English and Spanish versions. It is important to note that the evaluation of this approach was somewhat limited, as it primarily concentrated on a handful of newly added mappings without an extensive analysis of their overall quality.

To the best of the author's knowledge, the most comprehensive approach to tracking ontology evolution while maintaining valid alignments is provided in [109] and [110]. The research addresses the complexities of managing changes in evolving web ontologies. It acknowledges the challenges posed by the dynamic nature of web ontologies, emphasizing the need to manage changes to maintain consistency and reliability effectively. The proposed approach contrasts with traditional methods requiring complete remapping, thus saving significant time and resources.

The papers introduce a framework for managing changes in evolving ontologies, such as versioning, consistency, recovery, and visualizing changes. Central to this framework is the Change History Log (CHL), which plays a crucial role in recording ontology changes in a coherent manner – the methodology includes various components such as change detection, inconsistencies detection, implementation and verification of changes, and ontology recovery. [109] provides a set of recovery and roll-back algorithms, while in [110] describes mapping reconciliation algorithms that use the change history log to update pre-established alignments that require revalidation. The proposed system's effectiveness is shown by comparisons with existing systems and evaluations using standard data sets.

The discussed research is similar to the one presented in this book. However, it has some limitations. Primarily, in our work, we have separated algorithms that process changes in concepts, instances, and relations, while in [109] and [110], ontologies are always treated as a whole structure. Despite its holistic nature, such an integrated solution is complicated to deploy in any distributed environment, because ontologies must always be treated as indivisible wholes. Therefore, even minimal changes in ontologies cannot be quickly processed, but the comprehensive procedure must be executed every time.

On the other hand, there is very little research devoted to measuring the impact of ontology evolution and methods of recognizing that not all modifications to an ontology hold equal importance, which implies that minor alterations in the ontology do not need to be followed by a revalidation of their alignments. Only in [153] have we found similar research devoted to knowledge graphs, which should not be treated as ontologies.

3.2.2 Discussion

Ontologies facilitate capturing complex properties of chosen domains, and the current state of the literature discussed in this section emphasizes their dynamic nature and applicability as methods for knowledge representation. The equally dynamic nature of real-world domains, notably in genomics and biomedicine, frequently require updates to the ontologies that have been developed and maintained.

The evolution of ontologies, exemplified by Gene Ontology, underscores the necessity for accurate methodologies to manage these changes effectively. Despite considerable efforts to comprehend and document changes in ontologies, as evidenced by works like [58] and [112], there is a notable deficiency in formalizing these processes, especially concerning ontology versioning and the revalidation of alignments.

A significant limitation identified in current research is the lack of formal frameworks for processing ontologies and their mappings across various abstraction levels, including concepts, relations, and instances. This deficiency leads to two primary issues. Firstly, ontologies are often confined to being perceived not as flexible tools for knowledge representation but as rigid structures expressed in formats like OWL, with analysis limited to what these formats permit. Secondly, treating ontologies as indivisible wholes poses a significant challenge in efficiently managing updates and changes. The absence of distinction among abstraction levels curtails the adaptability and precision needed to modify and align ontologies effectively.

The split algorithms, which would operate separately on the level of concepts, relations, and instances, could handle different types of ontology changes independently from each other. Those changes will still be tracked and resolved even if they affect one another. However, if they do not affect each other, the proposed decoupling entails higher flexibility.

Another notable gap in the literature is the absence of established criteria for evaluating the significance of changes within ontologies. This shortcoming implies that alterations are frequently treated uniformly, with the same level of importance. Such an approach can lead to the inefficient allocation of resources, as not all changes necessitate a comprehensive revalidation of ontology alignments.

The framework equipped with change significance measures could be used to track how many and how extensive changes have been applied to ontologies. With such functions, comparing their outcomes with some assumed significance threshold value would be easy, making it easy to decide if the designated alignment between the maintained ontologies needs revalidation. In other words, such functions would allow to trigger further actions.

In conclusion, the literature surveyed in this book section presents an array of methodologies for managing ontology evolution and maintaining alignment between evolving ontologies. While the field has progressed considerably, some open questions should be addressed. They include issues concerning formal foundations for processing changes at different levels of abstraction (that respect the distinct nature of concepts, relations, and instances), establishing criteria for assessing the significance of ontology changes, and differentiated versioning strategies.

3.3   Evaluating the quality of ontology alignments

3.3.1   Problem overview

Evaluating ontology alignment solutions is a crucial part of their development process, ensuring that the systems utilizing these approaches yield precise and dependable outcomes. This chapter offers an insight into the commonly used methods for assessing the performance of ontology alignment systems. It begins with exploring classic evaluation metrics from the information retrieval field ([130]). Due to the fact that, in essence, ontology alignment is the problem of determining a set of pairs of corresponding elements from two different ontologies, they can be confronted with mappings prepared beforehand containing all and only correct correspondences. Those prepared mappings form a benchmark dataset, which can be used to compare several different ontology alignment solutions using a structured and repeatable methodology.

Following the Definition 2.14 introduced in Chapter 2 let's assume that for two ontologies O_1 and O_2 the evaluated alignment is the one created for the concept level and is denoted as $Align_C(O_1, O_2)$. The given reference alignment is denoted as $Align_C^{ref}(O_1, O_2)$. It is straightforward to define two metrics that can characterize the quality of $Align_C(O_1, O_2)$.

The first one is called Precision and is calculated according to the following equation:

$$Pr(Align_C(O_1, O_2), Align_C^{ref}(O_1, O_2)) = \frac{|Align_C^{ref}(O_1, O_2) \cap Align_C(O_1, O_2)|}{|Align_C(O_1, O_2)|} \quad (3.1)$$

The above metric measures how well the evaluated solution retrieves relevant items and is defined as the ratio of true positive results to the total number of positive results returned by the system. In other words, the Precision answers the question, "Out of all the items the system identified as relevant, how many are actually relevant?". In the context of ontology alignment, Precision would measure how many of the identified correspondences are correct (in comparison with the reference alignment), and the system which output achieved high Precision returned more relevant results than irrelevant ones.

The second metric is called Recall and is calculated as follows:

$$Re(Align_C(O_1, O_2), Align_C^{ref}(O_1, O_2)) = \frac{|Align_C^{ref}(O_1, O_2) \cap Align_C(O_1, O_2)|}{|Align_C^{ref}(O_1, O_2)|}. \quad (3.2)$$

This metric measures the system's ability to retrieve all relevant items. It is the ratio of true positive results to the total number of relevant items that should have been retrieved. Recall answers the question, "Out of all the relevant items that there are, how many did the system successfully identify?". In the context of ontology alignment, Recall measures how many of the correct correspondences were identified by the system, and a high Recall indicates that the system returned most of the relevant results.

There exists the F-measure, which is a harmonic mean of Precision and Recall:

$$F(Align_C(O_1, O_2), Align_C^{ref}(O_1, O_2)) = (1 + \beta^2) \times$$

$$\frac{Pr(Align_C(O_1, O_2), Align_C^{ref}(O_1, O_2)) \times Re(Align_C(O_1, O_2), Align_C^{ref}(O_1, O_2))}{\beta^2 \times Pr(Align_C(O_1, O_2), Align_C^{ref}(O_1, O_2)) + Re(Align_C(O_1, O_2), Align_C^{ref}(O_1, O_2))} \tag{3.3}$$

where $\beta \in [0, \infty)$ is a parameter that controls the balance between Precision and Recall. For $\beta > 1$, Recall has a higher priority, while for $\beta < 1$, Precision significantly influences the F-measure. If $\beta = 1$, the F-measure treats both components equally. This variant (referred to as the F1 measure or, for the sake of simplicity, frequently just as F-measure), as aforementioned in Section 3.1, is used by OAEI organizers:

$$F1(Align_C(O_1, O_2), Align_C^{ref}(O_1, O_2)) =$$

$$2 * \frac{Pr(Align_C(O_1, O_2), Align_C^{ref}(O_1, O_2)) * Re(Align_C(O_1, O_2), Align_C^{ref}(O_1, O_2))}{Pr(Align_C(O_1, O_2), Align_C^{ref}(O_1, O_2)) + Re(Align_C(O_1, O_2), Align_C^{ref}(O_1, O_2))} \tag{3.4}$$

The F-measure is beneficial when a balance between Precision and Recall must be considered. It provides a way to consider both these aspects simultaneously, offering a more comprehensive view of the solutions's overall quality in a bird's eye view manner.

Obviously, Equations 3.1, 3.2, 3.3, and 3.4 can be adapted to assess alignments at both the instance and relation levels. However, for the sake of readability and conciseness, these modified versions are not presented as they do not offer substantial new content beyond the swapping of input parameters.

However, these fundamental measures have shortcomings when applied in the context of ontology alignment. A key issue is their binary nature and, more precisely, the impossibility of calculating the closeness of the solution ([44]). In other words, the strict definitions of Precision and Recall overlook partially correct alignments.

To illustrate this limitation, consider two different alignments two of the same set of ontologies. Let us assume that the first one is largely inaccurate, containing a majority of incorrect mappings. Contrastingly, the second alignment, while also incorrect, features mappings that are semantically closer to the correct ones. For example, it might include mappings of concepts that are either ancestors or descendants of those in the reference alignment. Standard Precision and Recall metrics would rate both alignments similarly low, failing to distinguish the relative quality of the second alignment, which is, in essence, closer to being correct. Addressing this issue led to the introduction of the relaxed Precision (Pr_ϑ) and relaxed Recall (Re_ϑ):

$$Pr_\vartheta(A, R) = \frac{\vartheta(Align_C(O_1, O_2), Align_C^{ref}(O_1, O_2))}{|Align_C(O_1, O_2)|}, \tag{3.5}$$

$$Re_\vartheta(A, R) = \frac{\vartheta(Align_C(O_1, O_2), Align_C^{ref}(O_1, O_2))}{|Align_C^{ref}(O_1, O_2)|} \tag{3.6}$$

where ϑ represents a function that measures the closeness between two sets of mappings. Following the assumption from Section 2.3 that the set $\widetilde{AL}$ contains all possible alignments of ontologies O_1 and O_2, the function ϑ adheres to the following conditions:

- $\forall AL_1, AL_2 \in \widetilde{AL} : \vartheta(AL_1, AL_2) \geq 0$

- $\forall AL_1, AL_2 \in \widetilde{AL} : \vartheta(AL_1, AL_2) \leq min(|AL_1|, |AL_2|)$

- $\forall AL_1, AL_2 \in \widetilde{AL} : \vartheta(AL_1, AL_2) \geq |AL_1 \cap AL_1|$

The function ϑ can be any kind of closeness function. Notably, if $\vartheta(AL_1, AL_2) = |AL_1 \cap AL_2|$, the relaxed versions of Precision and Recall reduce to their base definitions, making both Pr_ϑ and Re_ϑ generalizations of the classical metrics.

By handling near-misses and partial matches, introducing the relaxed versions of the classical measure allows for a more comprehensive and realistic evaluation of ontology alignment systems. Such an approach acknowledges the complexity of ontologies and the often granular, incomplete, and entirely subjective nature of reference alignments.

The most elaborate adaptation of classic measures, building upon the relaxed Precision and Recall from Equations 3.5 and 3.6 are their semantic counterparts ([45], [89]). The main goal was to create an evaluation method that would fully use the knowledge contained in the mapped ontologies. Therefore, the assumed ϑ was based on model theory. Conducted verification [57]) yielded positive results, showing that semantic measures reflected better the subjective nature of the correctness of mappings.

However, a subsequent paper ([34]) showed that the semantic Precision and Recall depend on the mapping structure and can assign different values to semantically equivalent solutions. Therefore, an extension to correct this flaw was proposed, which entailed further complications – the new measures could not verify overlapping true-positive mappings. The most recent article ([217]) devoted to the topic comes from 2008. However, the developed modifications of the original solution have not been experimentally verified. Therefore, their applicability is questionable; consequently, they have not been widely adopted. Thus, the Ontology Alignment Evaluation Initiative (OAEI) continues to rely on the standard versions of Precision and Recall for evaluation purposes, and the research of their semantic versions seems abandoned.

Two approaches that should be treated as a complementary extension of evaluation methods proposed by OAEI can be found in [139] and [140]. In the first article, the author critiques the traditional evaluation methods for providing limited information about the overall performance's uncertainty and for simplistic comparisons based on score juxtaposition. The paper proposes treating the evaluation of alignment systems as a statistical inference problem. It introduces the concept of 'risk' associated with alignment systems, where risk is defined as the complement of a performance score and follows a binomial distribution. The paper shows that the maximum likelihood estimation (MLE) used in traditional evaluations is equivalent to this risk-based approach. The paper's main contribution is a Bayesian model for estimating the performance score as a probability distribution based on the ontology alignment system's performance across multiple benchmarks. The proposed model was applied to the OAEI anatomy and conference tracks, and the collected were confronted with traditional evaluation methods, illustrating its potential for more meaningful comparisons in ontology alignment system evaluations.

The second extension (as presented in [140]) proposes to treat the evaluation and comparison of alignment systems as a multi-criteria decision-making (MCDM) problem, where performance metrics and alignment systems served as the criteria and alternatives, respectively. The authors engaged ontology alignment experts to determine their preferences regarding these performance metrics for different OAEI tracks. This process involved calibrating the significance of each metric and the degree to which one metric is favoured over another. Based on this expert input, the authors developed the Expert-Based Collective Performance (ECP) metric. This metric incorporates multiple performance scores to evaluate and compare alignment systems. It was observed that the rankings of alignment systems based on the ECP metric differed from those obtained using the F-measure, which only considers Precision and Recall. The study focused on experiments conducted on the OAEI tracks to demonstrate the effectiveness of MCDM-based methods. However, the authors highlight that their approach is versatile and can be applied to evaluate and compare ontology alignment systems using any benchmark dataset.

Another limitation of the approach used by OAEI is that the provided benchmark mappings mostly contain only simple alignments built from pairs of elements from two ontologies. Authors of [193] claim that systems which yield complex alignments have emerged in recent years. There is a lack of complex reference alignments on which these approaches can be systematically evaluated. Therefore, the authors proposed two sets of complex alignments between 10 pairs of ontologies from the well-known OAEI conference track. The remark has been noticed by OAEI organizers who, since 2018, provided a specific track dedicated solely to evaluating systems capable of finding complex mappings.

3.3.2 Discussion

Evaluating ontology alignment solutions is crucial in their development, ensuring these systems produce accurate and reliable outcomes. This section of the book overviews commonly used methods for assessing the performance of ontology alignment systems, starting with classic metrics such as Precision and Recall, borrowed from the field of information retrieval, which provide a structured and repeatable methodology to assess a system's performance by comparing its output against a predefined reference alignment.

In this context, the Ontology Alignment Evaluation Initiative (OAEI) has played a pivotal role in advancing the field of ontology alignment and ontology alignment evaluation by providing a standardized framework for evaluating alignment systems along with an extensive benchmark dataset containing a large set of ontologies and reference alignments between them. However, like any evaluation methodology, the OAEI's procedure has limitations.

The most prominent one is the dependence on reference alignments. Beyond the fact that such reference alignments are required to calculate Precision and Recall, there are two additional concerns: the potential limitations of the reference alignments themselves and the lack of such alignments in real-world scenarios. Additionally, domain experts might have varying opinions on what constitutes a 'correct' alignment.

OAEI evaluations also presume that the reference alignments are both comprehensive and accurate. This is a critical assumption, as the quality of these reference alignments directly impacts the reliability of the evaluation results. Suppose the reference alignments are incomplete or contain inaccuracies. In that case, they may not effectively represent the full range of potential correct alignments. As a result, alignment systems might be incorrectly assessed, either penalized for missing alignments that are not part of the incomplete reference set or inaccurately rewarded for aligning entities that are incorrectly aligned in the reference.

More importantly, reference alignments are often unavailable in practical applications outside controlled evaluation environments like the one utilized by OAEI. Real-world ontologies may not have a 'gold standard' alignment, especially in specialized or emerging domains. This lack of benchmarks renders the OAEI's approach impractical for real-world applications.

Additionally, the benchmark datasets do not change over time. Therefore, in subsequent years, competing systems may be tailored to find good mappings but only for the datasets provided by OAEI, which is especially visible in the systems that utilize Machine Learning approaches. Thus, OAEI evaluates the quality of alignment systems only in the context of benchmarks, which is not useful in real-world ontology alignment requirements. Moreover, the proposed evaluation tools cannot be used outside the competition.

Although several advances in evaluating ontology alignments exist, their achievements have not been widely accepted. To this date, the most frequently used ontology alignments evaluation method is the one used by OAEI. Therefore, it is essential to develop evaluation strategies that are not solely dependent on reference alignments and assess the quality of the evaluated alignments using methods that extend beyond traditional approaches.

3.4 Conclusions

The chapter explores the field of ontology alignment by providing the classification of basic and advanced approaches to the considered task, a selection of related problems, and practical challenges. It is a foundational resource for understanding the subject and gives theoretical and practical perspectives.

The first section, dedicated to the classification of ontology alignment techniques **how can ontology alignments be designated**, emphasizes the complexity of the task. At the most fundamental level, each category of the overviewed approaches to the task (linguistic, structural, semantic, and instance-based methods) has its own strengths and, at the same time, its own limitations. Recent literature showcased the inclusion of machine learning methodologies, particularly those based on large language models, which indicates a shift towards more modern, purely data-driven approaches. However, these advancements introduce new issues, particularly the interpretability of the obtained results. In other words- although good alignments may be found using those novel solutions, the reasons why machine learning methods yielded such outcomes cannot be deterministically provided.

The section emphasized the need to use diverse strategies to achieve effective ontology alignment, thus directly inspiring the methods provided in Chapter 4. We claim that relying solely on individual methods of designating ontology alignments and using them in isolation may not yield satisfactory results. Therefore, we propose introducing an additional layer of expert knowledge – incorporating fuzzy logic and fuzzy inference rules allows us to build a multistrategy solution to the problem of finding ontology mappings.

The subsequent section was focused on answering a question about **the methods for managing ontology evolution and maintaining ontology alignments over time**, which showed that the management of ontology evolution presents its unique set of challenges. The dynamic nature of knowledge domains and their modern applications necessitates robust strategies for tracking changes that may be introduced to the underlying ontologies and threats to the alignment integrity that may appear in the results.

The performed literature review proves the need for more formalized approaches to managing ontology evolution, particularly in distinguishing changes at different abstraction levels (concepts, relations, and instances) and establishing criteria for assessing change significance. Therefore, the finding presented in this section of the book served as a direct justification of the research provided in Chapter 5, which describes a complete formal framework for maintaining ontologies and their alignments over a period of time. The presented approach saves computational resources by avoiding restarting the alignment process from the beginning after even minor ontology changes have been applied.

The last section of the chapter was dedicated to describing **the approaches to evaluating the quality of ontology alignments**, which is crucial for validating the effectiveness of alignment systems. While the Ontology Alignment Evaluation Initiative (OAEI) provides a standardized framework for assessment, the reliance on reference alignments and benchmark datasets poses limitations in real-world applicability. The research on the relaxed and semantic versions of traditional metrics like Precision or Recall, and the introduction of risk-based and multi-criteria decision-making approaches indicates an ongoing effort to refine evaluation methodologies. However, the dependency on reference alignments and the challenges posed by real-world applications without such benchmarks emphasizes the need for more sophisticated and context-aware evaluation strategies.

The section highlights the most significant limitation of the traditional evaluation metrics, underlining the need for strategies that extend beyond common approaches. Chapter 6 describes an author's novel approach to the topic and provides an evaluation framework that uses only the content of the aligned ontologies. The developed methods surpass the found limitations of classical metrics such as Precision and Recall, filling the identified gap in the field of ontology alignment.

In conclusion, this chapter thoroughly examines ontology alignment techniques, shedding light on theoretical concepts, practical applications, and current challenges. It reviews the state of the art and identifies unanswered pressing questions, making it an invaluable resource for academics and practitioners in knowledge engineering and semantic technologies. Furthermore, it lays the groundwork for the author's research contributions, detailed in the following chapters.

4

Fuzzy logic framework for ontology alignment

Chapter 3 has shed light on the topic of ontology alignment, which continues to receive significant attention despite being somewhat overshadowed by other knowledge-processing approaches in recent years. The chapter explores various techniques proposed to address the challenge of aligning ontologies, often involving the evaluation of similarities between elements within the ontologies, such as concepts or relations. These similarities can be determined in multiple ways, e.g., based on the concepts' names, hierarchical relationships, instances, and attributes.

However, relying solely on individual methods may not yield satisfactory results. The author claims that only treating those values collectively and taking all of them during the decision-making process can lead to promising outcomes. One of the methods that could be used to introduce an additional layer of expert knowledge in the process of designating ontology alignment is fuzzy logic, and the main contribution of this chapter is a presentation of a novel, fuzzy-logic-based framework for ontology alignment.

The main contribution of this chapter is the set of algorithms for ontology alignment that incorporate fuzzy logic and fuzzy inference rules. The developed procedures follow the formal definitions presented in Chapter 2 and, thus, can be divided into the level of concepts, relations, and instances. The presented approach has been experimentally verified using state-of-the-art benchmark data provided by the Ontology Alignment Evaluation Initiative.

4.1 Introduction

The chapter introduces a fuzzy framework for ontology alignment, organized into concepts, relations, and instances. This tiered structure allows producing different types of alignments across different levels. Despite its specific focus, each alignment method adheres to a uniform methodology, represented in Figure 4.1.

The alignment process begins by extracting elements that can potentially be aligned (such as concepts, relations, or instances) from the input ontologies, denoted as O_1 and O_2. The next step is a core element of the framework, which is used to designate ontologies' alignments. At this point, additional input data can be provided, which may refer to the configuration settings and inference rules that guide the behaviour of the alignment algorithm, threshold values, weights, or any other tuning parameters.

Central to the proposed framework is utilizing similarity functions specifically designed to assess the similarity between the extracted elements. These functions are designed to accommodate different element types, transitioning their outputs into fuzzy variables through precise membership functions. This transition facilitates a linguistic representation of degrees of similarity between ontology elements.

DOI: 10.1201/9781003437888-4

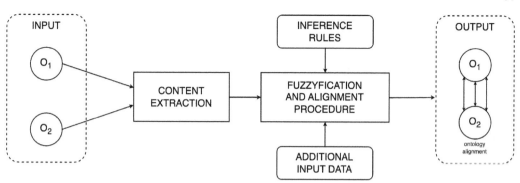

FIGURE 4.1

General architecture of fuzzy alignment framework

It is essential to highlight the flexibility of the membership functions used to transform similarity measurements into fuzzy variables. These membership functions can adopt many forms, each capable of encapsulating different characteristics of similarity between ontology elements. The ones presented in Sections 4.2, 4.3, and 4.4 and used within delivered algorithms were accepted based on the performed experimental evaluations which results can also be found in the remainder of this chapter. However, the proposed selection is by no means exclusive or exhaustive. The versatility of the proposed framework allows for the incorporation of alternative membership functions, each potentially tailored to specific alignment scenarios in certain applications.

Having the fuzzy representation of similarity degrees between ontology elements allows the use of fuzzy inference rules in the process. These rules are derived from the values of the generated fuzzy variables and consist of an "IF-THEN" statement, where the IF part (the antecedent) describes a condition in terms of fuzzy logic. The THEN part (the consequent) specifies the outcome. Such an approach embeds an additional layer of expert knowledge in finding ontology alignments. In sections 4.2, 4.3, and 4.4, similarly to the membership functions described earlier, we provide three rulesets (one of each ontology level, namely concepts, relations, and instances, provided in Tables 4.2, 4.8, and 4.14 respectively) proven useful during experimental verifications. Following [17] and [133], in the developed framework, the Mamdani model is used, with the minimum rule for the conjunction, the maximum rule for aggregation, and the maximum operator to accumulate the activated terms.

The main goal is to provide a value for the fuzzy output variable, denoted as *connection*. This variable serves as a determinant of alignment suitability, with its values indicating the strength of a potential alignment of two elements from different ontologies. For different levels of alignment (e.g., concepts, relations, and instances), the fuzzy output variable *connection* may take values from distinct sets of terms. For example, at the concept level, the set of possible values could be *independent, related, equivalent*, while at the instance level, it might be reduced to *independent, equivalent*. As a result, the final alignment includes only pairs of elements from the ontologies for which the fuzzy output variable *connection* obtains some selected values, signifying a solid alignment between those elements. Elements with other values for *connection* are not included in the alignment, as they do not exhibit the required level of similarity to be considered a proper match.

In most situations, the defuzzification of the *connection* variable is unnecessary, as the algorithms usually yield unequivocal outcomes. However, suppose there are several competitive pairs of elements to compare them. In that case, the defuzzification must be performed to produce a crisp value describing the degree to which the considered elements are related and, consequently, decide which should be added to the alignment. For this purpose, the centre of gravity method is used.

All developed methods presented in this chapter have been experimentally verified and implemented using the jFuzzyLogic library ([23]). We used a benchmark dataset of ontologies and their alignments provided by the Ontology Alignment Evaluation Initiative[1] (*OAEI*), which is a non-profit organization that since 2004 organizes annual campaigns where researchers and developers can evaluate their solutions and compare them with others accomplishments in the field.

The methodology involves providing a benchmark dataset (prepared by OAEI organizers) consisting of ontology pairs grouped into thematic sets or "tracks". Each ontology pair is accompanied by pre-prepared reference alignments, which are considered correct. Participants submit their alignments for ontology pairs, which are then compared to the given reference alignments. The evaluation metrics used in OAEI include Precision, Recall, and F1-measure, which measure the accuracy and completeness of the provided mappings ([35]). Other quality measures (such as the time required to designate an alignment) are also calculated. The dataset provided by OAEI is highly regarded in the literature as a state-of-the-art benchmark for ontology alignment evaluations.

In the conducted experiments, for the level of concepts and relations (presented in Sections 4.2 and 4.3) we decided to use *the Conference track*[2] from OAEI campaign from 2022. These ontologies are well suited for evaluating ontology-matching solutions due to their heterogeneous origins and comprehensible topics concerning organizing conferences.

For the instance level (presented in Section 4.4) we decided to use the most recent version of the IIMB dataset from *the Instance matching track* ([33]), which contains eighty ontologies about movies, each created by systematically applying a set of transformations to the selected origin ontology. Among others, the transformations include data value, structure, and semantics transformations.

The outcomes of the conducted experiments across all three levels—concepts, relations, and instances—demonstrate the efficacy of the proposed fuzzy framework for ontology alignment, showcasing its robustness and adaptability. These results are not only promising, but, in numerous instances, they highlight the superiority of the framework over alternative ontology alignment solutions.

4.2 Aligning ontologies on the concept level

This chapter focuses on concept alignment, which involves identifying semantically similar concepts across different ontologies. Formally, it can be defined as follows: *For a given two (A, V)-based ontologies $O_1 = (C_1, H_1, R^{C_1}, I_1, R^{I_1})$ and $O_2 = (C_2, H_2, R^{C_2}, I_2, R^{I_2})$, one should determine the alignment $Align_C(O_1, O_2)$ on the level of concepts, which follows the definition from Equation 2.31.*

4.2.1 Method overview

Researchers have explored various approaches to aligning ontologies on the concept level ([126]), including string-based matching, linguistic analysis, or machine learning algorithms. Many methods often form the foundation of various alignment systems and tools used in practice. They have been thoroughly tested, evaluated, and benchmarked against standard datasets and real-world ontologies, contributing to their reliability and robustness.

---

[1]https://oaei.ontologymatching.org/
[2]https://oaei.ontologymatching.org/2022/conference/index.html

The main objective of this chapter is not to present a solution that outperforms other existing methods in the literature. Instead, it serves two distinct purposes. Firstly, it offers a general exploration of how fuzzy logic can be effectively integrated into the task of ontology alignment.

Secondly, the chapter is included for completeness, forming one of the parts of a broader fuzzy-based framework for ontology alignment alongside the methods discussed in the two subsequent sections of the book. Combining these methods provides a complete, solid, fuzzy-based framework for ontology alignment.

The solution is based on the procedure presented in Algorithm 7. As its input it accepts two (A, V)-based ontologies $O_1 = (C_1, H_1, R^{C_1}, I_1, R^{I_1})$ and $O_2 = (C_2, H_2, R^{C_2}, I_2, R^{I_2})$ and takes the following steps:

- The alignment $Align_C(O_1, O_2)$ is initialized as an empty set.

- The algorithm iterates over all possible pairs of concepts (c_1, c_2) from the cartesian product $C_1 \times C_2$.

- For each pair of concepts, four similarity scores are calculated: sim_{attr}, sim_{jw}, sim_{lv}, and sim_{wn} using functions from Table 4.1. The similarity scores are then fuzzified based on accepted membership functions.

- The procedure determines the value of the fuzzy output variable *connection*, which represents the alignment decision, which is done by using fuzzy inference rules, which combine the fuzzified similarity scores using predefined rules to determine the degree of alignment between the two concepts.

- If the value of *connection* is determined to be "equivalent", the pair of concepts (c_1, c_2) is added to the alignment $Align_C(O_1, O_2)$.

- Finally, the alignment between concepts $Align_C(O_1, O_2)$ is returned.

Algorithm 7 Fuzzy-based approach for concept alignment

Input: O_1, O_2
Output: $Align_C(O_1, O_2)$
1: $Align_C(O_1, O_2) = \emptyset$
2: **for all** $(c_1, c_2) \in C_1 \times C_2$ **do**
3:     $sim_{attr} := sim_{attr}(c_1, c_2)$
4:     $sim_{jw} := sim_{jw}(c_1, c_2)$
5:     $sim_{lv} := sim_{lv}(c_1, c_2)$
6:     $sim_{wn} := sim_{wn}(c_1, c_2)$
7:     fuzzify sim_{attr} based on the accepted membership function
8:     fuzzify sim_{jw} based on the accepted membership function
9:     fuzzify sim_{lv} based on the accepted membership function
10:     fuzzify sim_{wn} based on the accepted membership function
11:     designate the value of *connection* using fuzzified values of $sim_{attr}, sim_{jv}, sim_{lv}$ and sim_{wn} and accepted inference rules
12:     **if** *connection* == *equivalent* **then**
13:         $Align_C(O_1, O_2) = Align_C(O_1, O_2) \cup \{(c_1, c_2)\};$
14:     **end if**
15: **end for**
16: **return** $Align_C(O_1, O_2)$

TABLE 4.1
Similarity functions for the concept level

Symbol	Explanation
$sim_{attr}(c_1, c_2)$	The value of similarity between concepts' attributes defined as the Jaccard index between sets A^{c_1} and A^{c_2}: $$sim_{attr}(c_1, c_2) = \frac{|A^{c_1} \cap A^{c_2}|}{|A^{c_1} \cup A^{c_2}|}$$ This function is plausible to calculate due to the fact that both O_1 and O_2 are both (A, V)-based, thus they share the same pool of attributes' names.
$sim_{jw}(c_1, c_2)$	The value of similarity between id^{c_1} and id^{c_2} calculated using Jaro-Winkler similarity ([64]). It is assumed that concepts' identifiers id^c from Equation 2.3 can be treated as text values.
$sim_{lv}(c_1, c_2)$	The value of similarity between id^{c_1} and id^{c_2} calculated using Levenshtein similarity function ([214])
$sim_{wn}(c_1, c_2)$	The value of Wu-Palmer similarity ([136] between preprocessed concepts' identifiers using *tokenize_and_tag* function defined in Equation 2.26. It is calculated as: $$sim_{wn}(c_1, c_2) = sup(\{sim_{Wu-Palmer}(t_1, t_2) \mid$$ $$(t_1, t_2) \in tokenize\_and\_tag(id^{c_1}) \times tokenize\_and\_tag(id^{c_1})\})$$

Table 4.1 provides an overview of similarity functions used to calculate the degree of relatedness of the given concepts $c_1 \in C_1$ and $c_2 \in C_2$. All of the presented functions may seem like oversimplification; however, a plethora of similar approaches to concept matching ([75], [106], [145], [206]) can be found in the literature.

In this section, we have overviewed a fuzzy logic-based framework for aligning ontologies at the concept level, leveraging similarity functions and adaptable inference rules, which sets the stage for the next section, where we will detail specific membership functions and inference ruleset, enabling a comprehensive experimental verification of the proposed solution.

4.2.2   Experimental evaluation

The developed approach has been implemented and experimentally verified. As described in Section 4.1 each similarity function must be accompanied with a dedicated method of fuzzifying values it returns, thus Figures 4.2, 4.3, 4.4, and 4.5 provide membership functions used during the experiment for sim_{attr}, sim_{jw}, sim_{lv}, and sim_{wn} respectively.

Table 4.2 contains a set of fuzzy inference rules used in the experiment. They have been formulated for fuzzy variables corresponding with similarity functions from Table 4.1.

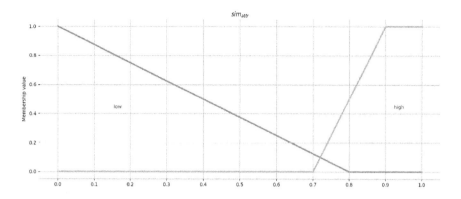

FIGURE 4.2
Fuzzy membership function for sim_{attr}

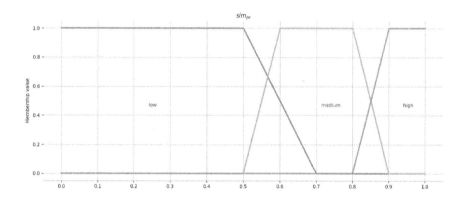

FIGURE 4.3
Fuzzy membership function for sim_{jw}

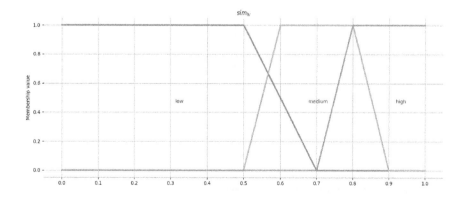

FIGURE 4.4
Fuzzy membership function for sim_{lv}

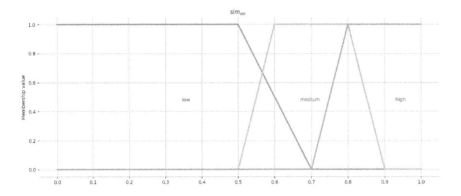

FIGURE 4.5
Fuzzy membership function for sim_{wn}

TABLE 4.2
Fuzzy inference rules on ontology alignment on the concept level

No	Rule
1	IF sim_{jw} IS high AND sim_{lv} IS high AND sim_{wn} IS high THEN *connection* IS equivalent
2	IF sim_{jw} IS high AND sim_{lv} IS high AND sim_{wn} IS high AND sim_{attr} IS high THEN *connection* IS equivalent
3	IF sim_{jw} IS high AND sim_{lv} IS high THEN *connection* IS equivalent
4	IF sim_{jw} IS high AND sim_{wn} IS high THEN *connection* IS equivalent
5	IF sim_{lv} IS high AND sim_{wn} IS high THEN *connection* IS equivalent
6	IF sim_{jw} IS medium AND levenshteinSim IS medium AND sim_{wn} IS medium THEN *connection* IS related
7	IF (sim_{jw} IS medium AND sim_{lv} IS medium) OR (sim_{jw} IS medium AND sim_{wn} IS medium) THEN *connection* IS related
8	IF sim_{jw} IS low AND sim_{lv} IS low AND sim_{wn} IS low THEN *connection* IS independent
9	IF (sim_{jw} IS low AND sim_{lv} IS medium) OR (sim_{jw} IS medium AND sim_{lv} IS low) AND sim_{wn} IS low THEN *connection* IS independent
10	IF sim_{jw} IS low AND sim_{lv} IS low AND sim_{wn} IS low AND sim_{attr} IS low THEN *connection* IS independent
11	IF sim_{attr} IS high THEN *connection* IS equivalent
12	IF sim_{attr} IS high AND (sim_{jw} IS low OR sim_{jw} is medium) THEN *connection* IS independent

In order to defuzzify the eventual degree of connection between two concepts, a membership function from Figure 4.6 can be used.

For the purpose of the experiment we used *the Conference track*[3] from Ontology Alignment Evaluation Initiative campaign. OAEI provided reference alignments for only

---

[3]https://oaei.ontologymatching.org/2022/conference/index.html

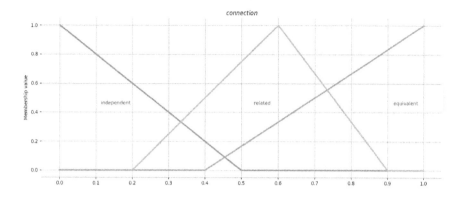

FIGURE 4.6
Fuzzy membership function for *connection* on the concept level

seven ontologies (cmt, confOf, edas, ekaw, iasted, sigkdd, sofsem), which yields twenty-one reference pairs, with which we can confront the outputs provided by the developed fuzzy-based ontology alignment framework. We generated an alignment for each pair and compared it with an appropriate reference. Subsequently, for each result, we calculated Precision, Recall, and F1-measure values. The outcomes of the conducted experiments can be found in Table 4.3.

TABLE 4.3
Results of fuzzy-based concept alignment framework

Source ontology	Target ontology	Precision	Recall	F1-measure
cmt	conference	0.71	0.45	0.55
cmt	confOf	0.80	0.40	0.53
cmt	edas	1.00	1.00	1.00
cmt	ekaw	1.00	0.63	0.77
cmt	iasted	0.80	1.00	0.89
cmt	sigkdd	1.00	0.80	0.89
conference	confOf	0.88	0.64	0.74
conference	edas	0.88	0.50	0.64
conference	ekaw	0.69	0.39	0.50
conference	iasted	0.80	0.31	0.44
conference	sigkdd	0.89	0.67	0.76
confOf	edas	0.90	0.64	0.75
confOf	ekaw	0.90	0.45	0.60
confOf	iasted	1.00	0.44	0.61
confOf	sigkdd	1.00	0.67	0.80
edas	ekaw	0.62	0.50	0.55
edas	iasted	0.78	0.39	0.52
edas	sigkdd	1.00	0.64	0.78
ekaw	iasted	0.83	0.56	0.67
ekaw	sigkdd	0.86	0.60	0.71
iasted	sigkdd	0.92	0.73	0.81

TABLE 4.4
Average Precision results for the conference track

Alignment tool	Average Precision
edna	0.88
StringEquiv	0.88
Fuzzy-based framework	**0.87**
DOME	0.87
ALIN	0.87
LogMap	0.84
LogMapLt	0.84
AML	0.83
ONTMAT1	0.82
Wiktionary	0.80
SANOM	0.78
Lily	0.59

Unfortunately, the OAEI organization has provided only a summary of the average values for the whole dataset and not the partial results obtained on specific pairs of ontologies by individual tools that competed during the 2022 campaign. Therefore, we decided to follow the method and calculate the average values of Precision, Recall, and F1-measure obtained for individual pairs of ontologies from the dataset to compare the developed method with the others.

Table 4.4 presents the results of an experiment that compares the performance of the proposed solution with other existing methods documented in the literature in terms of average Precision.

Among the tools evaluated, the top performers are edna and StringEquiv, scoring 0.88. Notably, the proposed solution also exhibits strong performance, achieving an average Precision of 0.87. This places it in the same rank as other competitive tools like DOME and ALIN, achieving an average Precision of 0.87. These values indicate a relatively high rate of correctly identified matches. Slightly below, we find LogMap and LogMapLt with average Precision values of 0.84, followed by AML with a score of 0.83. ONTMAT1" and Wiktionary achieve average Precision values of 0.82 and 0.80, respectively. SANOM follows with a Precision value of 0.78. Lastly, Lily demonstrates a lower average Precision value of 0.59.

Table 4.5 contains the results of an experiment comparing the performance of different alignment tools on average recall. SANOM is at the top of the list, with an average recall of 0.76. AML closely follows it with an average recall of 0.70 and Lily with 0.63. LogMap achieves an average recall of 0.64, placing it at the top of the results. The proposed solution achieves an average recall of 0.59, which places it above Wiktionary, which achieves an average recall of 0.58. DOME, edna, and LogMapLt all achieve an average recall of 0.54. ALIN follows with an average recall of 0.52, while StringEquiv is slightly behind with 0.50. Finally, ONTMAT1 achieves an average recall value of 0.49.

The average recall value of 0.59 achieved by the proposed solution reveals its capacity to identify a portion of the correct matches between ontologies successfully. While this suggests that the solution captures many relevant mappings, it also implies room for further enhancement.

It is important to note that the recall measure quantifies explicitly the number of concept mappings discovered from the reference alignment. In evaluating the solution's

TABLE 4.5

Average Recall results for the conference track

Alignment tool	Average Recall
SANOM	0.76
AML	0.70
Lily	0.63
LogMap	0.64
Fuzzy-based framework	**0.59**
Wiktionary	0.58
DOME	0.54
edna	0.54
LogMapLt	0.54
ALIN	0.52
StringEquiv	0.50
ONTMAT1	0.49

practicality, we underscore the crucial significance of the Precision measure. Precision gauges the accuracy of the identified mappings, reflecting the ratio of correctly predicted matches to the total predicted matches. The reasoning behind this approach is that maintaining high precision minimizes the risk of introducing incorrect concept mappings into the alignment, ensuring the quality and reliability of the alignment outcomes. This principle is fundamental when the solution is applied in real-world scenarios.

Table 4.6 summarizes average scores of F1-measures obtained by ontology alignment tools participating in the OAEI'2022 campaign and the proposed fuzzy solution. F1-measure shows how well an alignment system can identify relevant mappings while avoiding incorrect ones. The proposed solution obtained a fourth score, allowing us to draw conclusions similar to those from Tables 4.4 and 4.5.

In summary, the contents of Tables 4.4, 4.5, and 4.6 shed light on the effectiveness of the proposed solution. Although the fuzzy approach described in this section of the book did

TABLE 4.6

Average F1-measure results for the conference track

Alignment tool	Average F1-measure
SANOM	0.77
AML	0.76
LogMap	0.73
Fuzzy-based framework	**0.69**
Wiktionary	0.68
DOME	0.67
edna	0.67
LogMapLt	0.66
ALIN	0.65
StringEquiv	0.64
ONTMAT1	0.61
Lily	0.61

not achieve the best results, it showed its potential in comparison to well-known ontology alignment methods found in the literature, aligning it with some of the best-performing solutions.

4.3   Aligning ontologies on the relation level

This chapter focuses on ontology alignment on the relation level, which involves identifying semantically similar definitions of connections between concepts. Formally, it can be defined as follows: *For given two (A, V)-based ontologies $O_1 = (C_1, H_1, R^{C_1}, I_1, R^{I_1})$ and $O_2 = (C_2, H_2, R^{C_2}, I_2, R^{I_2})$, one should determine the alignment $Align_R(O_1, O_2)$ on the level of concepts, which follows the definition from Equation 2.34.*

4.3.1   Method overview

Designating ontology alignment on the level of relations is a difficult task for several reasons. According to [16], the empirical analysis of existing ontologies unveiled diverse naming conventions used to define relations in ontologies. For example, relations tend to be named with verbs (e.g., plays, uses) or end with prepositions (e.g., friendOf, partOf). Additionally, it is not uncommon that active and passive forms of the same verb are used (e.g., wrote and written) or names contain words encapsulated within auxiliary words (e.g., memberOf and member).

Secondly, the OWL format categorizes attributes and relations under a single group called "properties," blurring the boundaries between different types of entities within ontologies. Different design decisions (some ontologies adopt a class-centric approach, while others prioritize an attribute-centric perspective) made during ontology creation further complicate the alignment and matching of relations within ontologies.

This chapter provides a solution that takes into consideration the issues described above. It is based on comparing domains and ranges of relations (using Equations 2.19 and 2.20 and the semantics of relations defined in Equation 2.16. The solution's core is presented in Algorithm 8. As its input it accepts two (A, V)-based ontologies $O_1 = (C_1, H_1, R^{C_1}, I_1, R^{I_1})$ and $O_2 = (C_2, H_2, R^{C_2}, I_2, R^{I_2})$ and their alignment on the concept level $Align_C(O_1, O_2)$. It takes the following steps:

- It initializes an empty set $Align_R(O_1, O_2)$.

- The algorithm iterates over all relations from the set R^{C_1}.

- For each relation r_1 in R^{C_1} it initializes an empty set of candidates $candidates = \emptyset$ and extracts a domain and a range of r_1 using Equations 2.19 and 2.20. Functions dom and rng are part of a general, formal framework (with foundations described in Chapter 2), and they both return sets of concepts. However, in practical applications, a concept relation from the set R^C contains only one pair of concepts. Thus, to extract those two concepts (a domain and a range of a relation), a square bracket notation is used to denote the first (and usually the only) element of a set.

- For every pair c_1 and c_1' the algorithm creates two auxilliary sets f_{c_1} and $f_{c_1'}$ for their ancestors or descendants.

- For each pair (p, q) in the cartesian product $f_{c_1} \times f_{c_1'}$ it retrieves sets of connected concepts (c_2 and c_2') using concepts p and q and the given ontology alignment on the concept level.

Algorithm 8 Fuzzy-based approach to ontology alignment on relation level

---

Input: $O_1, O_2, Align_C(O_1, O_2)$
Output: $Align_R(O_1, O_2)$

1: $Align_R(O_1, O_2) := \emptyset$
2: **for all** $r_1 \in R^{C_1}$ **do**
3:      $candidates = \emptyset$
4:      $c_1 := dom(r_1)[0];$
5:      $c_1' := rng(r_1)[0];$
6:      $f_{c_1} := \{c_1\} \cup \{y \in C_1 | (c_1, y) \in H \vee (y, c_1) \in H\}$
7:      $f_{c_1'} := \{c_1'\} \cup \{y \in C_1 | (c_1', y) \in H \vee (y, c_1') \in H\}$
8:      **for all** $(p, q) \in f_{c_1} \times f_{c_1'}$ **do**
9:          $c_2 := \{c_2 \in C_2 | (p, c_2) \in Align_C(O_1, O_2)\};$
10:          $c_2' := \{c_2' \in C_2 | (q, c_2') \in Align_C(O_1, O_2)\};$
11:          **for all** $r_2 \in \{r_2 \in R_2^C | c_2 \times c_2' \subseteq r_2\}$ **do**
12:              $sim_{dm} := \max_{\tilde{c}_2 \in c_2} sim_C(c_1, \tilde{c}_2)$
13:              $sim_{rn} := \max_{\tilde{c}_2' \in c_2'} sim_C(c_1', \tilde{c}_2')$
14:              $sim_R := sim_R(r_1, r_2)$
15:              fuzzify sim_{dm} based on the accepted membership function
16:              fuzzify sim_{rn} based on the accepted membership function
17:              fuzzify sim_{dm} based on the accepted membership function
18:              designate the value of *connection* using fuzzified values of sim_{dm}, sim_{rn}, and sim_R and fuzzy inference rules
19:              **if** *connection* $\in \{equivalent, closely\_related\}$ **then**
20:                  add $(r_1, r_2, connection)$ to *candidates*;
21:              **end if**
22:          **end for**
23:      **end for**
24:      add the best (r_1, r_2) from *candidates* to $Align_R(O_1, O_2)$;
25: **end for**
26: **return** $Align_R(O_1, O_2)$

- For each relation r_2 in R_2^C which connects at least one pair from the cartesian product $c_2 \times c_2'$ it calculates the value of sim_{dm} as the highest similarity between c_1 and the best-matching concept in c_2, the value of sim_{rn} as the highest similarity between c_1' and the best-matching concept in c_2', and the similarity sim_R between semantics of r_1 and r_2. Table 4.7 overviews similarity functions sim_C and sim_R used in Algorithm 8.

- It converts the similarity scores sim_{dm}, sim_{rn}, and sim_R into fuzzy values using accepted membership functions.

- It designates the value of *connection* using fuzzified values of sim_{dm}, sim_{rn}, and sim_R and accepted inference ruleset. If the designated value of *connection* is either *equivalent* or *closely_related*, a triple $(r_1, r_2, connection)$ is added to the set *candidates*.

- It chooses the best (r_1, r_2) pair from *candidates* set based on the assumption that the connection *equivalent* is better than *closesly_related*, and adds it to $Align_R(O_1, O_2)$.

- Finally, the alignment on the relation level $Align_R(O_1, O_2)$ is returned.

Detailed explanations and formal definitions of the functions used in Algorithm 8, specifically sim_C and sim_R, can be found in Table 4.7. This table provides an in-depth

TABLE 4.7
Similarity functions for the relation level

Symbol	Explanation

hline

$sim_C(c_1, c_2)$ — The value of the degree to which two concepts can be aligned with each other, which is used to calculate the similarity of concepts participating in relation from two ontologies. In other words – it allows for comparison of structural context that some relation put on concepts. It can be any kind of similarity function found in the literature, for example, in order to utilize the notion of attributes semantics (defined in Equation 2.7) sim_C can be defined as:

$$sim_C(c_1, c_2) = 1 - d_s(ctx(c_1), ctx(c_2))$$

$sim_R(r_1, r_2)$ — The value of similarity between two relations' semantics (from Equation 2.16), defined as:

$$sim_R(r_1, r_2) = 1 - d_s(S_R(r_1), S_R(r_2))$$

description of how these functions function and what their roles are in the proposed procedure of ontology alignment on the relation level.

Both functions from Table 4.7 use a function d_s to measure the distance between two logic formulas. This function initially transforms the input formulas into the disjunctive standard form (DNF), allowing them to be treated as sets of grouped symbols. Subsequently, the Cartesian product of groups from both input expressions is created, and the Jaccard distance is used to determine the distance for each pair. Finally, the function calculates the average of partial distances.

It is worth noting that since d_s operates as a distance metric, while both sim_C and sim_R function as similarity measures, the value obtained from d_s is subtracted from 1. This yields a value that can be interpreted as a similarity score. For more information on d_s, please refer to [157].

Within Algorithm 8 sim_C is used twice to produce values sim_{dm} and sim_{rn}. The former is the value to which the relation's domains can be aligned, while the latter represents the alignment degree of the relation's range. The idea behind using sim_{dm} and sim_{rn} is to consider both the source and target concepts of relations when assessing their potential alignment. It is illustrated in Figure 4.7. These two values serve distinct purposes:

- sim_{dm} (Domain Alignment Similarity): This similarity value, calculated using sim_C, represents the degree to which the domains of two relations can be aligned. In other words, it quantifies how similar the two relations' source concepts (domain) are. If sim_{dm} is high, it implies that the domains of the two relations are similar or equivalent, making them good candidates for alignment. On the contrary, a low sim_{dm} indicates dissimilarity between the domains, suggesting that aligning these relations based on their domains may not be suitable.

- Similar to sim_{dm}, this similarity measure, also computed using sim_C, represents the degree of alignment between the ranges of two relations. It assesses how similar or equivalent the two relations' target concepts (range) are. A high sim_{rn} indicates that the

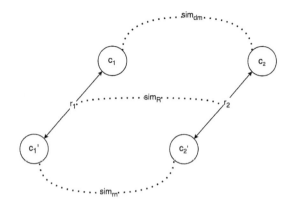

FIGURE 4.7
Fuzzy variables in relation alignment

ranges of the two relations are similar or equivalent, making them potential alignment candidates based on their ranges. Conversely, a low sim_{rn} implies that the ranges are dissimilar, and alignment based on ranges may not be appropriate.

In this section, we have described a fuzzy framework for ontology relation alignment. The forthcoming section contains specific membership functions and inference rulesets used during the experimental verification of the proposed solution.

4.3.2 Experimental evaluation

In order to experimentally verify the developed approach to ontology relation alignment, its implementation must contain specific membership functions accompanying each similarity function overviewed in Section 4.3.1. Therefore, Figures 4.8, 4.9, and 4.10 provide such specific functions for sim_{rn}, sim_{dm}, and sim_R respectively.

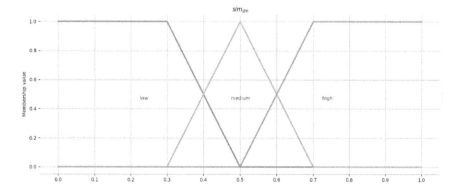

FIGURE 4.8
Fuzzy membership function for sim_{dm}

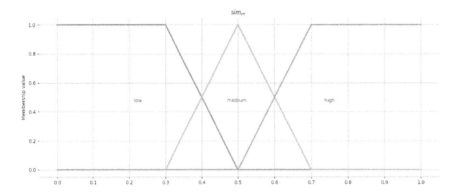

FIGURE 4.9

Fuzzy membership function for sim_{rn}

Having fuzzified values sim_{dm}, sim_{rn}, and sim_R, it is possible to perform fuzzy reasoning using a set of predefined inference rules presented in Table 4.8, which in consequence allows to produce the outcome of Algorithm 8.

As described in earlier sections of this chapter, to get the degree to which two relations can be aligned, the *connection* variable must be de-fuzzified. In order to achieve this goal during the planned experiment the function depicted in Figure 4.11 has been developed.

Conducting an experimental evaluation focused solely on the level of relations presents challenges due to the nature of the benchmark dataset provided by the Ontology Alignment Evaluation Initiative. While the dataset includes a plethora of diverse ontologies and their reference alignments, these alignments often predominantly involve mappings of concepts, with relations receiving comparatively less attention.

One of the reasons for this situation is the utilization of OWL[4] language, which is the most common method of representing ontologies. In relations, its primary restriction incorporates the idea of properties, which entails grouping attributes and relations. This approach significantly complicates establishing robust alignments between ontologies, particularly concerning relations.

This is why many alignment solutions in the literature overlook this aspect of ontologies, concentrating on either the concept level or the instance level, the latter benefiting from a separate dataset provided by the Ontology Alignment Evaluation Initiative prepared only for evaluating instance matching solutions. supports this observation citecheatham2018properties – the analysis indicated that top-ranked alignment systems (as ranked by OAEI) achieved an average precision of 0.36, an average recall of 0.18, and an average F1-measure of 0.21 for property matching. While individual results showed slight enhancements, overall system performance remained notably higher for concept matching.

To assess the effectiveness of the fuzzy framework for relation alignment presented in this chapter, we selected *the Conference track* from the OAEI campaign conducted in 2016. This track is the only non-synthetic track within the OAEI dataset that encompasses property mappings. Consequently, it provides a unique opportunity to filter and evaluate mappings related to"object properties," which represent relations between concepts in the context of

---

[4]https://www.w3.org/OWL/

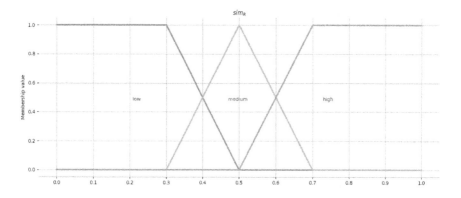

FIGURE 4.10
Fuzzy membership function for sim_R

OWL. Additionally, we decided to check two different approaches to providing values of similarity functions from Table 4.7. Thus, the experiment consisted of two parts:

- **Experiment 1** involved reusing OAEI's provided reference alignments. The similarity between two concepts, denoted as c_1 and c_2 and extracted from the reference alignment (sim_{ref}), was adapted by considering the inheritance relationship between the mapped concept and the domain/range of the currently processed relation. The adaptation was formulated as follows:

$$sim(c_1, c_2, v) = \frac{sim_{ref}(c_1, c_2)}{(x \cdot len(path(c_2, v)) + 1)} \tag{4.1}$$

Here, v signifies the domain/range of the processed relation, *path* signifies the inheritance path between c_2 and v, and *len* represents the length of this path. The additional variable

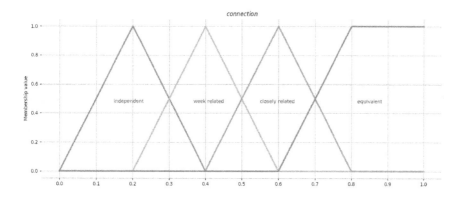

FIGURE 4.11
Fuzzy membership function for *connection* variable on the relation level

TABLE 4.8

Fuzzy Rules for ontology relation alignment

No	Rule
1	IF sim_{dm} is high AND sim_{rn} is high AND sim_R is high THEN *connection* is equivalent.
2	IF sim_{dm} is high AND sim_{rn} is high AND sim_R is medium THEN *connection* is equivalent.
3	IF sim_{dm} is high AND sim_{rn} is high AND sim_R is low THEN *connection* is weak related.
4	IF sim_{dm} is high AND sim_{rn} is medium AND sim_R is high THEN *connection* is equivalent.
5	IF sim_{dm} is high AND sim_{rn} is low AND sim_R is high THEN *connection* is closely related.
6	IF sim_{dm} is medium AND sim_{rn} is high AND sim_R is high THEN *connection* is equivalent.
7	IF sim_{dm} is low AND sim_{rn} is high AND sim_R is high THEN *connection* is closely related.
8	IF sim_{dm} is medium AND sim_{rn} is medium AND sim_R is medium THEN *connection* is weak related.
9	IF sim_{dm} is medium AND sim_{rn} is medium AND sim_R is low THEN *connection* is weak related.
10	IF sim_{dm} is medium AND sim_{rn} is medium AND sim_R is high THEN *connection* is closely related.
11	IF sim_{dm} is medium AND sim_{rn} is low AND sim_R is medium THEN *connection* is weak related.
12	IF sim_{dm} is medium AND sim_{rn} is high AND sim_R is medium THEN *connection* is closely related.
13	IF sim_{dm} is low AND sim_{rn} is medium AND sim_R is medium THEN *connection* is weak related.
14	IF sim_{dm} is high AND sim_{rn} is medium AND sim_R is medium THEN *connection* is closely related.
15	IF sim_{dm} is low AND sim_{rn} is low AND sim_R is low THEN *connection* is independent.
16	IF sim_{dm} is low AND sim_{rn} is low AND sim_R is medium THEN *connection* is independent.
17	IF sim_{dm} is low AND sim_{rn} is low AND sim_R is high THEN *connection* is weak related.
18	IF sim_{dm} is low AND sim_{rn} is medium AND sim_R is low THEN *connection* is independent.
19	IF sim_{dm} is low AND sim_{rn} is high AND sim_R is low THEN *connection* is independent.
20	IF sim_{dm} is medium AND sim_{rn} is low AND sim_R is low THEN *connection* is independent.
21	IF sim_{dm} is high AND sim_{rn} is low AND sim_R is low THEN *connection* is independent.

TABLE 4.9
Results of Experiment 1

Ontology 1	Ontology 2	Precision	Recall	F1-measure
cmt	sofsem	0	0	N/A
cmt	confOf	1.00	0.25	0.40
cmt	edas	1.00	0.40	0.57
cmt	ekaw	N/A	0	N/A
cmt	sigkdd	1.00	1.00	1.00
sofsem	confOf	1.00	1.00	1.00
sofsem	edas	N/A	0	N/A
sofsem	ekaw	0.20	0.50	0.29
sofsem	sigkdd	N/A	0	N/A
confOf	edas	1.00	0.33	0.50
confOf	ekaw	0	N/A	N/A
confOf	sigkdd	N/A	N/A	N/A
edas	ekaw	1.00	0.33	0.40
edas	sigkdd	N/A	N/A	N/A
ekaw	sigkdd	N/A	N/A	N/A

x takes a value of 1 if v equals c_2 or if it is a descendant of c_2, and 2 in other cases. This experiment aimed to evaluate our solution's efficacy in identifying relation alignments. The results are presented in Table 4.9. The value "N/A" in this and further tables represents the fact that the selected measure couldn't be calculated.

- **Experiment 2** involved employing an external ontology alignment system named LogMap [95] as a tool for computing the similarity between two concepts. LogMap is a prominent ontology alignment solution known for its high performance across multiple OAEI evaluation campaigns. This experiment sought to emulate automatic concept matching. The results collected during the second part of the experiment can be found in Table 4.10.

In both experiments, the sim_R function has been calculated as described in Table 4.7. The necessary semantics of relations from Equation 2.16 were supplied using the method from Section 2.2.2.

The chosen dataset (*the Conference track*) comprises six ontologies (*cmt, conference, confOf, edas, ekaw, sighdd*), yielding a total of 15 ontology pairs. In both experiments, an alignment on the relation level (following the definition from Equation 2.34) was generated for each ontology pair using Algorithm 8. Subsequently, each obtained alignment was compared to the reference alignment, leading to the calculation of standard metrics Precision, Recall, and F1-measure.

Table 4.11 summarizes the average results obtained from both experiments and the average performance of participants in the OAEI campaigns from 2013 and 2016 (taken from [16]). Comparing the results, it is clear that the approach to relation alignment presented in this chapter achieved higher precision and recall values than the average participant in the OAEI campaigns. However, it is essential to note that competitive systems in these campaigns attempt to establish mappings for both attributes (data properties) and relations (object properties), whereas our approach exclusively focuses on relations. This distinction makes direct comparisons impossible, making it difficult to assert whether our proposed

TABLE 4.10
Results of Experiment 2

Ontology 1	Ontology 2	Precision	Recall	F1-measure
cmt	sofsem	0	0	N/A
cmt	confOf	1.00	0.25	0.40
cmt	edas	1.00	0.20	0.33
cmt	ekaw	1.00	0.33	0.50
cmt	sigkdd	1.00	1.00	1.00
sofsem	confOf	1.00	1.00	1.00
sofsem	edas	N/A	0	N/A
sofsem	ekaw	0.50	0.50	0.50
sofsem	sigkdd	N/A	0	N/A
confOf	edas	1.00	0.33	0.50
confOf	ekaw	0	N/A	N/A
confOf	sigkdd	N/A	N/A	N/A
edas	ekaw	0	0	N/A
edas	sigkdd	N/A	N/A	N/A
ekaw	sigkdd	N/A	N/A	N/A

solution is better than competitive solutions from the literature. Nevertheless, the collected outcomes strongly indicate that our method produces sound alignments with good precision.

To further support this observation, Table 4.12 presents relation mappings extracted from reference alignments provided by OAEI. They are confronted with information on whether they have been found during Experiment 1 or Experiment 2 and whether they have been found by LogMap, which is one of the most prominent ontology alignments solutions ([96], [97], [95]). Our approach successfully identified 8 out of 28 relation mappings in the first experiment and 7 out of 28 in the second. This performance surpasses the LogMap tool, which identified only 6 out of 28 relation mappings.

In summary, the experimental verification yields promising results, with several prominent ontology alignment systems performing worse than the approach presented in this chapter. As mentioned, direct performance comparison with existing solutions is impossible. Nonetheless, overall evaluation shows that the developed method is effective.

TABLE 4.11
Comparison of average results

	Precision	Recall	F1-measure
Experiment 1	0.53	0.29	0.37
Experiment 2	0.63	0.25	0.36
OAEI data from 2013	0.36	0.18	0.21
OAEI data from 2016	0.45	0.17	0.23

TABLE 4.12
Comparison with LogMap

Relation 1	Relation 2	Experiment 1	Experiment 2	LogMap
cmt#assignedByReviewer	conference#invited_by	-	-	-
cmt#assignExternalReviewer	conference#invites_co-reviewers	-	-	-
cmt#writePaper	confOf#writes	+	+	-
cmt#hasBeenAssigned	confOf#reviewes	-	-	-
cmt#hasAuthor	confOf#writtenBy	-	-	-
cmt#hasSubjectArea	confOf#dealsWith	+	-	-
cmt#memberOfConference	edas#isMemberOf	+	+	-
cmt#hasConferenceMember	edas#hasMember	+	+	-
cmt#hasAuthor	edas#isWrittenBy	-	-	-
cmt#hasBeenAssigned	edas#isReviewing	-	-	-
cmt#assignedTo	edas#isReviewedBy	-	-	-
cmt#writtenBy	ekaw#reviewWrittenBy	-	+	-
cmt#hasBeenAssigned	ekaw#reviewerOfPaper	-	-	-
cmt#assignedTo	ekaw#hasReviewer	-	-	-
cmt#submitPaper	sigkdd#submit	+	+	+
conference#has_a_track-workshop-tutorial-topic	confOf#hasTopic	+	+	-
conference#has_a_review_expertise	edas#hasRating	-	-	-
conference#has_a_review	ekaw#hasReview	+	+	+
conference#contributes	ekaw#authorOf	-	-	-
conference#is-given_by	sigkdd#presentationed_by	-	-	+
conference#gives_presentations	sigkdd#presentation	-	-	+
confOf#reviewes	edas#isReviewing	-	-	-
confOf#writtenBy	edas#isWrittenBy	+	+	+
confOf#writes	edas#hasRelatedPaper	-	-	+
edas#isReviewedBy	ekaw#hasReviewer	-	-	-
edas#isReviewing	ekaw#reviewerOfPaper	-	-	-
edas#isLocationOf	ekaw#locationOf	+	-	-
edas#hasLocation	ekaw#heldIn	-	-	-
TOTAL		8/28	7/28	6/28

4.4 Aligning ontologies on the instance level

This chapter focuses on ontology alignment on the instance level. Formally, it can be defined as follows: *For given two (A, V)-based ontologies $O_1 = (C_1, H_1, R^{C_1}, I_1, R^{I_1})$ and $O_2 = (C_2, H_2, R^{C_2}, I_2, R^{I_2})$, one should determine the alignment $Align_I(O_1, O_2)$ on the level of instances, which follows the definition from Equation 2.32.*

4.4.1 Method overview

Ontologies are pivotal in structuring and organizing information in various domains, enabling knowledge sharing and interoperability among systems. Even though recent advances in the field have slowed down compared to research done between 2005 and 2015, the emergence of Knowledge Graphs ([88]) shows that there are still open challenges to address.

The idea of Knowledge Graphs originates from the Semantic Web, databases, knowledge representation, natural language processing, and machine learning. They utilize a graph-oriented approach to structuring data and describing relations within its content, eventually enriching it with semantics (hence, they are referred to as knowledge graphs, not data graphs).

Contrary to the research devoted to the semantic web, which primarily focuses on semantics on the schema level of knowledge representation, knowledge graphs are solely devoted to describing and expressing facts about the real world. In other words, Knowledge Graphs focus on instances.

In the context of ontologies (which are the main topic of this book), instances are concrete, individual objects or entities that are classified under specific concepts. They represent the individual elements or entities within a domain, grounding abstract concepts in real-world objects. For example, if we have a concept "Movie" in ontology devoted to cinema, instances of this concept could be "Interstellar" or "Dune".

Therefore, while ontology alignment at the concept and relation level focuses on aligning the high-level structure and taxonomies, instance-level alignment addresses matching individual instances across ontologies. Finding mappings of instances defined in two independent ontologies is the last step of designating ontology alignments in the fuzzy framework presented in this chapter.

The most significant difficulty when designating ontology alignment on the instance level is addressing semantic ambiguity and contextual interpretation – instances can have multiple meanings or interpretations depending on the context in which they are used. This context is formally expressed by concepts to which particular instances are assigned because instances may be included within several different concepts (according to Definitions 2.2 and 2.5). Therefore, the approach proposed in this chapter explicitly addresses this issue and enforces that before aligning instances, we need to clearly understand how the concepts and relations from the source ontology relate to those in the target ontology. Thus, we assume the existence of ontology alignment on the level of concepts and relations beforehand. Such alignment can be provided by methods described in Sections 4.2 and 4.3 or some external tools found in the literature.

The most significant difficulty in the latter approach is that many ontology alignments generated by methods which only process ontologies expressed in OWL format often include mappings between heterogeneous ontology elements. For example, they may include mappings of attributes to relations or relations to attributes. This situation treats attributes and relations as properties of concepts, which rejects the strict separation of abstraction levels described in Chapter 2.

In order to further increase the flexibility of the presented framework and to facilitate the bidirectional compatibility between it and any external tool, we introduce a notion of ontology alignment universe.

Definition 4.1 *An ontology alignment universe* , denoted as A_{AR}, encompasses the full spectrum of possible correspondences between concepts, attributes and relations from two *(A, V)* based ontologies O_1 and O_2. This set consists of all conceivable mappings, formally defined as the sum of Cartesian products of various elements taken from O_1 and O_2:

$$A_{AR} = 2^{C_1 \times C_2 \cup A \times R^{C_1} \cup A \times R^{C_2} \cup A \times A \cup R^{C_1} \times R^{C_2}} \tag{4.2}$$

Its elements represent different types of connections established between two ontologies on a level of concepts, concepts' structures, and relations; thus, along straightforward mappings of concepts, they include attribute-attribute mappings, attribute-relation mappings, relation-attribute mappings, and relation-relation mappings. As easily seen, the discussed definition does not follow the strict alignment definition from Equation 2.30 used in the book. It is introduced to express alignments provided by some external tools that freely approach the definition of ontology alignment and allow for mapping elements with different characteristics.

Definition 4.2 A set of mappings of attributes and relations from O_1 and O_2 designated by some external ontology alignment method will be denoted as $A_{ext}(O_1, O_2)$ (obviously $A_{ext}(O_1, O_2) \in A_{AR}$). To evaluate the quality of the mapping, we assume that the accepted external ontology alignment tools also provide a function ω with a signature $\omega : A_{AR} \to [0, 1]$ which assigns to each element of A_{ext} an actual number from range [0,1] which can be interpreted as scoring of the particular mapping from $A_{ext}(O_1, O_2)$.

Definition 4.3 By C_{max}, we will denote a function that takes two instances as input and returns a pair of concepts to which those instances belong and have the highest alignment scoring ω. It has a signature $C_{max} : I_1 \times I_2 \to C_1 \times C_2$ and can be formally defined as:

$$C_{max}(i_1, i_2) = \underset{(c_1, c_2) \in Ins^{-1}(i_1) \times Ins^{-1}(i_2)}{\text{argmax}} \omega(c_1, c_2) \tag{4.3}$$

To process two instances in the context of the alignment of their shared properties (both attributes and relations), we introduce a family of filtering functions: f_{AR}, f_A and f_R, along with their modifications f_{AR}^C, f_A^C and f_R^C. Their purpose is to filter the content of given $A_{ext}(O_1, O_2)$ and to pick only alignments associated with the provided instances.

Definition 4.4 The filtering function f_{AR}, with a signature $f_{AR} : I_1 \times I_2 \times A_{AR} \to A_{AR}$, provides the most general filtering, which only extracts alignments associated with given instances:

$$
\begin{aligned}
f_{AR}(i_1, i_2, A_{ext}(O_1, O_2)) = & \\
\bigcup_{c_1 \in Ins^{-1}(i_1)} & \{(a_1, r^{C_2}) | (a_1, r^{C_2}) \in A_{ext}(O_1, O_2), a_1 \in A^{c_1}, i_2 \in r^{C_2}\} \cup \\
\bigcup_{c_2 \in Ins^{-1}(i_2)} & \{(r^{C_1}, a_2) | (r^{C_1}, a_2) \in A_{ext}(O_1, O_2), i_1 \in r^{C_1}, a_2 \in A^{c_2}\} \cup \\
\bigcup_{(c_1, c_2) \in Ins^{-1}(i_1) \times Ins^{-1}(i_2)} & \{(a_1, a_2) | (a_1, a_2) \in A_{ext}(O_1, O_2), a_1 \in A^{c_1}, a_2 \in A^{c_2}\} \cup \\
& \{(r^{C_1}, r^{C_2}) | (r^{C_1}, r^{C_2}) \in A_{ext}(O_1, O_2), i_1 \in r^{C_1}, i_2 \in r^{C_2}\}
\end{aligned}
\tag{4.4}
$$

In the equation above, the notation $i \in r^C$ denotes a situation in which an instance i participates (obviously with some other instance) in a relation $r^I \in R^I$ which is a complementary relation to r^C (according to Definition 2.9. Formally, it can be defined as $i \in r^C \implies \exists i' \in I : (i, i') \in r^I \vee (i', i) \in r^I$.

Definition 4.5 The filtering function f_{AR}^C, with a signature $f_{AR} : I_1 \times I_2 \times C_1 \times C_2 \times A_{AR} \to A_{AR}$ is a modification of the base function f_{AR} which narrows its results to the given concepts. Formally, it is defined as:

$$
\begin{aligned}
f_{AR}^C(i_1, i_2, c_1, c_2, A_{ext}(O_1, O_2)) = \\
\{(a_1, r^{C_2})|(a_1, r^{C_2}) \in A_{ext}(O_1, O_2), a_1 \in A^{c_1}, i_2 \in r^{C_2}\}\cup \\
\{(r^{C_1}, a_2)|(r^{C_1}, a_2) \in A_{ext}(O_1, O_2), i_1 \in r^{C_1}, a_2 \in A^{c_2}\}\cup \\
\{(a_1, a_2)|(a_1, a_2) \in A_{ext}(O_1, O_2), a_1 \in A^{c_1}, a_2 \in A^{c_2}\}\cup \\
\{(r^{C_1}, r^{C_2})|(r^{C_1}, r^{C_2}) \in A_{ext}(O_1, O_2), i_1 \in r^{C_1}, i_2 \in r^{C_2}\}
\end{aligned}
\tag{4.5}
$$

Definition 4.6 The filtering function f_A, with a signature $f_A : I_1 \times I_2 \times A_{AR} \to A_{AR}$, extracts alignments of attributes associated with given instances:

$$
\begin{aligned}
f_A(i_1, i_2, A_{ext}(O_1, O_2)) = \\
\bigcup_{(c_1,c_2)\in Ins^{-1}(i_1)\times Ins^{-1}(i_2)} \{(a_1, a_2)|(a_1, a_2) \in A_{ext}(O_1, O_2), a_1 \in A^{c_1}, a_2 \in A^{c_2}\}
\end{aligned}
\tag{4.6}
$$

Definition 4.7 The filtering function f_A^C, with a signature $f_A : I_1 \times I_2 \times C_1 \times C_2 \times A_{AR} \to A_{AR}$, is a modification of the base function f_A^C which narrows its results to the given concepts:

$$
\begin{aligned}
f_A^C(i_1, i_2, c_1, c_2, A_{ext}(O_1, O_2)) = \\
\{(a_1, a_2)|(a_1, a_2) \in A_{ext}(O_1, O_2), a_1 \in A^{c_1}, a_2 \in A^{c_2}\}
\end{aligned}
\tag{4.7}
$$

Definition 4.8 The filtering function f_R, with a signature $f_R : I_1 \times I_2 \times A_{AR} \to A_{AR}$, extracts alignments of relations associated with given instances:

$$
\begin{aligned}
f_R(i_1, i_2, A_{ext}(O_1, O_2)) = \\
\{(r^{C_1}, r^{C_2})|(r^{C_1}, r^{C_2}) \in A_{ext}(O_1, O_2), i_1 \in r^{C_1}, i_2 \in r^{C_2}\}
\end{aligned}
\tag{4.8}
$$

The set of definitions above helps to bridge the primary distinction between the formal definitions of ontologies and their alignments given in Chapter 2 and methods based on OWL format. Consequently, it is possible to formulate the fuzzy-based method for ontology alignment on the instance level. Its core is presented in Algorithm 9. As its input the procedure accepts two (A, V)-based ontologies $O_1 = (C_1, H_1, R^{C_1}, I_1, R^{I_1})$ and $O_2 = (C_2, H_2, R^{C_2}, I_2, R^{I_2})$ and the alignment $A_{ext}(O_1, O_2)$ provided by some external tool. It takes the following steps:

- It initializes two empty sets: *candidates* to store potential instance alignments and $Align_I(O_1, O_2)$ to store the final instance-level alignments.

- For each pair of concepts (c_1, c_2) from the cartesian product of sets C_1 and C_2 it the algorithm checks if (c_1, c_2) is in the provided external alignment set $A_{ext}(O_1, O_2)$. If this condition is met, the procedure initializes an empty set $AL_{O_1,O_2}(c_1, c_2)$ and adds it to $Align_I(O_1, O_2)$.

Algorithm 9 Fuzzy-based approach to ontology alignment on instance level

---

Input: O_1, O_2, $A_{ext}(O_1, O_2)$
Output: $Align_I(O_1, O_2)$
1: $candidates := \emptyset$
2: $Align_I(O_1, O_2) := \emptyset$
3: **for all** $(c_1, c_2) \in C_1 \times C_2$ **do**
4:      **if** $(c_1, c_2) \in A_{ext}(O_1, O_2)$ **then**
5:          $AL_{O_1, O_2}(c_1, c_2) := \emptyset$
6:          $Align_I(O_1, O_2) := Align_I(O_1, O_2) \cup \{AL_{O_1, O_2}(c_1, c_2)\}$
7:      **end if**
8: **end for**
9: **for all** $i_1, i_2 \in I_1 \times I_2$ **do**
10:      $sim_{PR} := sim_{PR}(i_1, i_2)$
11:      $sim_{AS} := sim_{AS}(i_1, i_2)$
12:      $sim_{RS} := sim_{RS}(i_1, i_2)$
13:      $sim_{PC} := sim_{PC}(i_1, i_2)$
14:      $sim_{CC} := sim_{CC}(i_1, i_2)$
15:      $sim_{MS} := sim_{MS}(i_1, i_2)$
16:      $sim_{PS} := sim_{PS}(i_1, i_2)$
17:      fuzzify sim_{PR} based on the accepted membership function
18:      fuzzify sim_{AS} based on the accepted membership function
19:      fuzzify sim_{RS} based on the accepted membership function
20:      fuzzify sim_{PC} based on the accepted membership function
21:      fuzzify sim_{CC} based on the accepted membership function
22:      fuzzify sim_{MS} based on the accepted membership function
23:      fuzzify sim_{PS} based on the accepted membership function
24:      designate the value of *connection* using fuzzified values of sim_{PR}, sim_{AS}, sim_{RS}, sim_{PC}, sim_{CC}, sim_{MS}, and sim_{PS} and fuzzy inference rules
25:      **if** $connection = equivalent$ **then**
26:          $candidates := candidates \cup \{(i_1, i_2)\}$;
27:      **end if**
28: **end for**
29: **for all** $(i_1, i_2) \in candidates$ **do**
30:      **for all** $(c_1, c_2) \in Ins^{-1}(i_1) \times Ins^{-1}(i_2)$ **do**
31:          $AL_{O_1, O_2}(c_1, c_2) := AL_{O_1, O_2}(c_1, c_2) \cup \{(i_1, i_2)\}$
32:      **end for**
33: **end for**
34: **return** $Align_I(O_1, O_2)$

- For each pair of instances i_1 and i_2 from the cartesian product of sets I_1 and I_2 the procedure calculates seven similarity scores, denoted as sim_{PR}, sim_{AS}, sim_{RS}, sim_{PC}, sim_{CC}, sim_{MS}, and sim_{PS}.

- It applies fuzzification to these similarity scores based on predefined membership functions.

- It determines the value of the *connection* variable using the fuzzified values of the similarity scores and a set of accepted fuzzy inference rules. If the *connection* is equal to *"equivalent,"* the procedure adds the instance pair (i_1, i_2) to the *candidates* set.

- For each instance pair (i_1, i_2) in the *candidates* set the procedure generates the cartesian product of sets $Ins^{-1}(i_1)$ and $Ins^{-1}(i_2)$ (a set of pairs of concepts to which instances i_1 and i_2 belong). Then it it adds the pair (i_1, i_2) to the apriopriate set $AL_{O_1,O_2}(c_1, c_2)$.

- Finally, the instance-level alignment set $Align_I(O_1, O_2)$ is returned as the result of the algorithm.

Table 4.13 provides a detailed explanations and formal definitions of functions used in Algorithm 9, namely sim_{PR}, sim_{AS}, sim_{RS}, sim_{PC}, sim_{CC}, sim_{MS}, and sim_{PS}. It offers a comprehensive understanding of how these functions operate and contribute to the overall instance alignment process.

The functions sim_{PR}, sim_{AS}, and sim_{RS} from Table 4.13 are based on the auxiliary function $prsim$ calculates a property-relatedness similarity of two instances. It has a signature $prsim : I_1 \times I_2 \times A_{AR} \rightarrow [0,1]$, thus as its input it accepts two instances, i_1 and i_2, and a set $align$ of mappings between elements from two ontologies O_1 and O_2, such that $align \subseteq A_{ext}(O_1, O_2)$. In this context the main distinction between sim_{PR}, sim_{AS} and sim_{RS} from is the usage of filtering functions f_{AR}, f_A and f_R from definitions 4.4, 4.7 and 4.8.

In order to define $prsim$, it is necessary first to introduce two helper functions λ_{value} and $to\_value\_representation$. The function λ_{value} operates on two input sets, denoted as x and y, which consist of elementary values such as strings or numbers. It employs a similarity function, denoted as $sim\_function$, to perform pairwise comparisons between atomic values within these sets. $sim\_function$ can be any arbitrary given similarity function for a particular datatype; for example, the Longest Common Subsequence similarity can be used to calculate similarities between strings. The main purpose of this function is to reflect the overall similarity between the provided sets. Formally, λ_{value} is defined as:

$$\lambda_{value}(x, y) = \frac{\sum_{v \in x} \max_{v' \in y} sim\_function(v, v') + \sum_{v \in y} \max_{v' \in x} sim\_function(v, v')}{|x| + |y|} \quad (4.9)$$

By $to\_value\_representation$, we denote a function that accepts an instance as its input and transforms this instance into a set consisting of values of its attributes. If the given instance lacks any attributes, the function produces a set containing only one element – the identifier of that instance:

$$to\_value\_representation(i) = \begin{cases} \bigcup_{c \in Ins^{-1}(i)} \bigcup_{a \in A^c} \{v_c^i(a)\} & \text{if } A^c \neq \emptyset \\ \{id^i\} & \text{otherwise} \end{cases} \quad (4.10)$$

The final method that computes a property-relatedness similarity score ($prsim$) is given in Algorithm 10. It takes the following steps to produce the end value:

- If the set of alignments, denoted as $align$, is empty, the algorithm terminates and returns the value 0 since there are no alignments to compute similarity.

- It initializes a variable called *partial* to 0. This variable will accumulate partial similarity scores during the calculation.

- It iterates over each pair of aligned elements, denoted as (e_1, e_2), in the set $align$. These aligned elements represent correspondences between elements from the two ontologies.

- For each pair of concepts (c_1, c_2) to which i_1 and i_2 belong (obtained through the cartesian product of sets returned by the function Ins^{-1}), the procedure checks the type of elements e_1 and e_2 to determine their nature within the ontology.

TABLE 4.13
Similarity functions for the instance level

Symbol	Explanation

$sim_{PR}(i_1, i_2)$ The value of similarity of properties calculated according to the procedure from Algorithm 10:

$$sim_{PR}(i_1, i_2) = prsim(i_1, i_2, f_{AR}(i_1, i_2, A_{ext}(O_1, O_2)))$$

$sim_{AS}(i_1, i_2)$ The value of similarity of properties calculated according to the procedure from Algorithm 10 narrowed only to attributes:

$$sim_{AS}(i_1, i_2) = prsim(i_1, i_2, f_A(i_1, i_2, A_{ext}(O_1, O_2)))$$

$sim_{RS}(i_1, i_2)$ The value of similarity of properties calculated according to the procedure from Algorithm 10 narrowed only to relations:

$$sim_{RS}(i_1, i_2) = prsim(i_1, i_2, f_R(i_1, i_2, A_{ext}(O_1, O_2)))$$

$sim_{PC}(i_1, i_2)$ The ratio of properties (understood as both relations and attributes) that have been successfully matched between instances i_1 and i_2, to the total number of properties associated with these instances within concepts c_1 and c_2 such that $(c_1, c_2) = C_{max}(i_1, i_2)$:

$$sim_{PC}(i_1, i_2) = \frac{|f_{AR}^C(i_1, i_2, c_1, c_2, A_{ext}(O_1, O_2))|}{|rel(i_1)| + |rel(i_2)| + |A^{c_1}| + |A^{c_2}|}$$

In the denominator of the above expression we utilize the *rel* function defined on Equation 2.23.

$sim_{CC}(i_1, i_2)$ The ratio of concepts that i_1 and i_2 belong to which have been successfully mapped to the total number of those concepts:

$$sim_{CC}(i_1, i_2) = \frac{|(Ins^{-1}(i_1) \times Ins^{-1}(i_2)) \cap A_{ext}(O_1, O_2)|}{|Ins^{-1}(i_1) \times Ins^{-1}(i_2)|}$$

$sim_{MS}(i_1, i_2)$ The number of relations connecting instances i_1 and i_2 mapped with the maximal scoring value ω divided by the number of all relations associated with i_1 and i_2:

$$sim_{MS}(i_1, i_2) = \frac{|\{(r_1, r_2) \in f_R(i_1, i_2, A_{ext}(O_1, O_2)) \mid \omega(r_1, r_2) = 1\}|}{|rel(i_1)| + |rel(i_2)|}$$

$sim_{PS}(i_1, i_2)$ The number of attributes used in instances i_1 and i_2 mapped with the maximal scoring value ω divided by the number of all attributes ever used in i_1 and i_2 in all conceptss:

$$sim_{PS}(i_1, i_2) = \frac{|\{(a_1, a_2) \in f_A(i_1, i_2, A_{ext}(O_1, O_2)) \mid \omega(a_1, a_2) = 1\}|}{\sum\limits_{c_1 \in Ins^{-1}(i_1)} |A^{c_1}| + \sum\limits_{c_2 \in Ins^{-1}(i_2)} |A^{c_2}|}$$

Algorithm 10 Calculating $prsim$

Input: $i_1 \in I_1$, $i_2 \in I_2$, $align \subseteq A_{ext}(O_1, O_2)$
Output: $prsim(i_1, i_2) \in [0, 1]$

1: **if** $align == \emptyset$ **then**
2:     **return** 0
3: **end if**
4: $partial := 0$
5: **for all** $(e_1, e_2) \in align$ **do**
6:     **for all** $(c_1, c_2) \in Ins^{-1}(i_1) \times Ins^{-1}(i_2)$ **do**
7:         **if** $e_1 \in A \wedge e_2 \in A$ **then**
8:             $v := v_{c_1}^i(e_1)$
9:             $v' := v_{c_2}^i(e_2)$
10:         **else if** $e_1 \in R^{C_1} \wedge e_2 \in R^{C_2}$ **then**
11:             $v := \bigcup_{i \in rng(i_1, e_1)} to\_value\_representation(i)$
12:             $v' := \bigcup_{i' \in rng(i_2, e_2)} to\_value\_representation(i')$
13:         **else if** $e_1 \in A \wedge e_2 \in R^{C_2}$ **then**
14:             $v := v_{c_1}^i(e_1)$
15:             $v' := \bigcup_{i' \in rng(i_2, e_2)} to\_value\_representation(i')$
16:         **else if** $e_1 \in R^{C_1} \wedge e_2 \in A$ **then**
17:             $v := \bigcup_{i \in rng(i_1, e_1)} to\_value\_representation(i)$
18:             $v' := v_{c_2}^i(e_2)$
19:         **end if**
20:         $partial = partial + \lambda_{value}(v, v')$
21:     **end for**
22: **end for**
23: **return** $\frac{partial}{|align|}$

- If either e_1 or e_2 is a relation, the algorithm iterates over instances from its range (using function rng from Equation 2.22). It produces a sum of value representations (using function $to\_value\_representation$ from Equation 4.10). It stores the result as v or v'.

- If e_1 or e_2 is an attribute, the algorithm extracts the value of this attribute in the instance belonging to the concept from the current iteration. It stores the result as v or v'.

- The procedure calculates a partial similarity score using a similarity function denoted as λ_{value} (from Equation 4.9) applied to v and v'. This partial score represents the similarity between e_1 and e_2 in the context of the instances i_1 and i_2. It adds the calculated partial similarity score to the variable *partial*.

- After processing all aligned elements and concept pairs, the algorithm calculates the final similarity score; it is calculated as the average similarity score by dividing the accumulated partial similarity scores in the variable *partial* by the cardinality of the set *align*. It is then returned as the final output of the algorithm.

This section provided a third and final element of a fuzzy-logic-based framework for ontology alignment. In the subsequent section, we will present the results of experimental

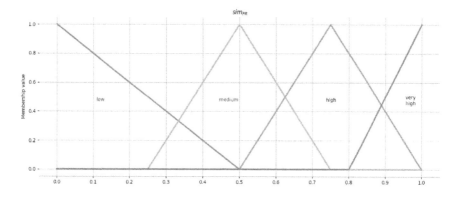

FIGURE 4.12
Fuzzy membership function for sim_{PR}

verification of the developed solution using specific membership functions and inference rules tailored specifically for this purpose.

4.4.2 Experimental evaluation

In order to conduct exprimental verification of the proposed fuzzy framework for instance alignment, in a similar manner to the procedures discussed in Sections 4.2.2 and 4.3.2, to convert incorporated similarity functions described in Table 4.13 into their linguistic representation we must equip them with appropriate membership functions. Figures 4.12, 4.13, 4.14, 4.15, 4.16, 4.17, and 4.18 show such functions for sim_{PR}, sim_{AS}, sim_{RS}, sim_{PC}, sim_{PC}, sim_{CC}, sim_{MS}, and sim_{PS} respectively.

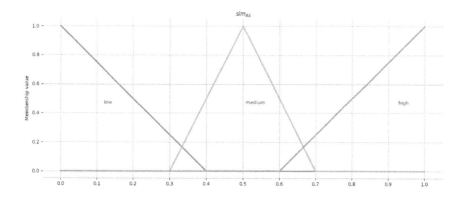

FIGURE 4.13
Fuzzy membership function for sim_{AS}

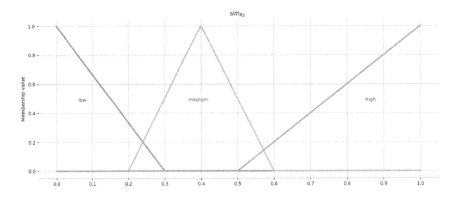

FIGURE 4.14
Fuzzy membership function for sim_{sRS}

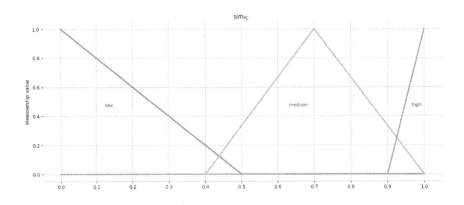

FIGURE 4.15
Fuzzy membership function for sim_{PC}

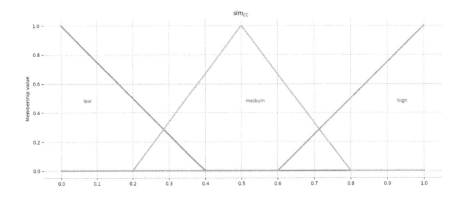

FIGURE 4.16
Fuzzy membership function for sim_{CC}

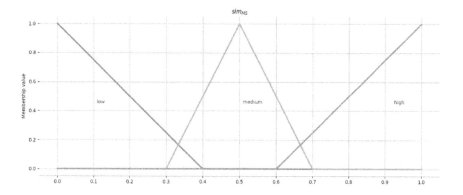

FIGURE 4.17
Fuzzy membership function for sim_{MS}

Having fuzzified values sim_{PR}, sim_{AS}, sim_{RS}, sim_{PC}, sim_{PC}, sim_{CC}, sim_{MS}, and sim_{PS}, it is possible to perform fuzzy reasoning using a set of predefined inference rules. The ruleset used in the conducted experiments are presented in Table 4.14.

Eventually, to get the degree of connection between two relations, de-fuzzifying the *connection* variable can be de-fuzzified by using a membership function from Figure 4.19.

The performed evaluation of the fuzzy-based ontology alignment at the instance level relied on utilizing a dataset provided by the Ontology Alignment Evaluation Initiative (OAEI). However, there is a notable difference between these earlier experiments and the one described in the current chapter, primarily related to selecting a specific track for evaluation. For verifying instance-level alignments, we opted to utilize the ISLab Instance Matching Benchmark (IIMB), a dedicated benchmark designed explicitly for this particular task ([3]).

The chosen dataset comprises 80 ontologies, with the first serving as the source ontology, while the remaining 79 are distinct versions generated automatically using the Semantic Web

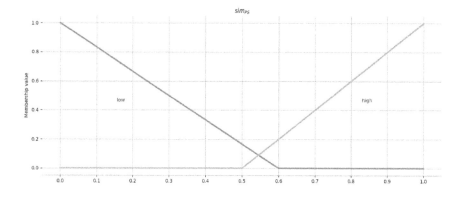

FIGURE 4.18
Fuzzy membership function for sim_{PS}

TABLE 4.14
Fuzzy Rules for ontology instance alignment

No	Rule
1	IF sim_{PR} IS very high AND sim_{PC} IS high AND sim_{CC} IS high THEN *connection* IS equivalent
2	IF sim_{PR} IS very high AND sim_{CC} IS high AND (sim_{PS} IS high OR sim_{MS} IS high) THEN *connection* IS equivalent
3	IF sim_{PR} IS high AND sim_{CC} IS high AND sim_{MS} IS high THEN *connection* IS equivalent
4	IF sim_{MS} IS high AND sim_{AS} IS high THEN *connection* is equivalent
5	IF sim_{AS} IS high AND sim_{RS} IS high THEN *connection* is equivalent
6	IF sim_{CC} IS high AND (sim_{MS} IS high AND sim_{AS} IS high) THEN *connection* is equivalent
7	IF sim_{PR} IS medium AND (NOT sim_{MS} IS high AND NOT sim_{PC} IS high) THEN *connection* IS independent
8	IF sim_{PR} IS medium AND (NOT sim_{CC} IS high AND (NOT sim_{RS} IS high OR NOT sim_{AS} IS high)) THEN *connection* IS independent

INstance Generation (SWING) framework ([56]). These transformations can be broadly categorized into three main groups:

- *Data Value Transformations (DVL).* These alterations focus on changes in the cardinality and content of property values within instance descriptions. Examples include value deletions and modifications through the insertion or substitution of random characters.

- *Data Structure Transformations (DST).* This category encompasses changes to property names and structures within instance descriptions. Examples include splitting string values and modifying property names.

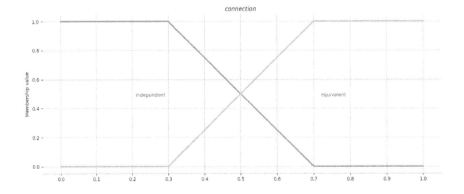

FIGURE 4.19
Fuzzy membership function for *connection* for instance level

- *Data Semantics Transformations (DSS).* These transformations involve modifications to class or type properties within instance descriptions, such as property type deletions or modifications.

Consequently, the set as mentioned above of 80 ontologies forms 80 distinct alignment tasks organized into four key categories:

- Tasks Cases 01-20: Data Value transformations

- Tasks Cases 21-40: Data Structure transformations

- Tasks Cases 41-60: Data Semantics transformations

- Tasks Cases 61-80: Mixed Transformations (which comprises all previous types of transformations)

For each of the 80 tasks, we employed a fuzzy-based instance-matching approach, which was implemented using the jFuzzyLogic library ([23]) library [23]. This approach was utilized to generate alignments for each task. Given that each task was supplied with a reference alignment, enabling a comparison between the results obtained from our tested solution and the reference, we conducted this comparison. Subsequently, we computed fundamental evaluation metrics, namely Precision, Recall, and F1-measure.

The collected results for tasks from the "Data Value Transformations" category are presented in Table 4.15. Similarly, for tasks categorized as "Data Structure Transformations," the evaluation outcomes can be found in Table 4.16. Tasks from the "Data Semantics Transformations" group are summarized in Table 4.17, and the results of the evaluation of tasks involving "Mixed Transformations" can be found in Table 4.18.

TABLE 4.15
Results of Data Value Transformation (Test Cases 01-20)

Test Case ID	Precision	Recall	F1-measure
1	0.909	0.962	0.935
2	1.000	0.405	0.577
3	1.000	0.214	0.352
4	0.982	0.584	0.732
5	1.000	0.318	0.482
6	0.956	0.721	0.822
7	0.893	0.367	0.520
8	0.919	0.992	0.954
9	1.000	0.189	0.318
10	0.987	0.211	0.348
11	0.990	0.545	0.703
12	0.944	0.877	0.909
13	0.913	0.803	0.854
14	0.978	0.718	0.828
15	1.000	0.211	0.348
16	0.959	0.323	0.484
17	0.931	0.956	0.943
18	1.000	0.110	0.198
19	0.984	0.685	0.808
20	0.894	0.370	0.523

TABLE 4.16

Results of Data Structure Transformation (Test Cases 21-40)

Test Case ID	Precision	Recall	F1-measure
21	0.892	0.997	0.942
22	0.924	0.400	0.558
23	1.000	0.003	0.005
24	0.886	0.997	0.938
25	1.000	0.003	0.005
26	0.880	0.682	0.769
27	0.875	0.997	0.932
28	1.000	0.003	0.005
29	0.878	0.830	0.854
30	0.891	0.674	0.768
31	0.769	0.027	0.053
32	0.942	0.671	0.784
33	1.000	0.003	0.005
34	1.000	0.003	0.005
35	1.000	0.003	0.005
36	0.871	0.852	0.861
37	0.893	0.822	0.856
38	0.888	0.997	0.939
39	0.892	0.203	0.330
40	1.000	0.003	0.005

Table 4.15 reveals noticeable variability in performance across different test cases. For instance, Test Case 2 demonstrates an exceptionally high Precision (1.00), showing that all identified correspondences were correct, yet the Recall is relatively low (0.405), revealing that many accurate correspondences were missed. Similar patterns emerge in several other test cases, such as Test Cases 1, 3, 5, and 7, where Precision is relatively high, but Recall is lower. This pattern indicates that our approach tends to generate alignments with a higher proportion of true positives but may overlook some correct correspondences.

However, the considered task category involves alterations of data values used within compared instances and all of the ontologies are results of the modification process (conducted according to the SWING framework ([56])). Such an approach to creating benchmark datasets and reference alignments raises some doubts. For example, if an instance in which all of its values have been changed still represents the same object from the real world, is its alignment still sound?

Similarlt to the Data Value Transformation experiments, Table 4.16 shows considerable diversity in the performance across different test cases. Structural transformations introduce complexities, as shown by the results of Test Cases with low Recall values (e.g., Test Cases 23, 25, 28, and 33), which indicates that the approach struggles when ontologies undergo structural changes that make it challenging to identify correspondences. However, also similarly to results from Table 4.15, the obtained values of Precision are high, which unequivocally proves that the proposed approach favours finding true positive instance mappings, which may be more valuable in the practical applications.

Table 4.17 shows the results of the experiments from the Data Semantics Transformation category. The Precision scores across all test cases (41-60) are consistently high, ranging from 0.933 to a perfect score of 1. This signifies that the system appropriately deals with correctly identifying correct correspondences. Like Precision, the Recall scores are uniformly high, ranging from approximately 0.994 to 0.997, which indicates that the system

TABLE 4.17

Results of Data Semantics Transformation (Test Cases 41-60)

Test Case ID	Precision	Recall	F1-measure
41	0.941	0.997	0.968
42	0.943	0.997	0.969
43	0.933	0.997	0.964
44	0.938	0.997	0.967
45	0.948	0.997	0.972
46	0.941	0.997	0.968
47	0.961	0.994	0.977
48	0.936	0.997	0.966
49	1.000	0.500	0.667
50	1.000	0.500	0.667
51	0.948	0.997	0.972
52	0.931	0.997	0.963
53	0.965	0.994	0.979
54	0.943	0.997	0.969
55	0.958	0.995	0.976
56	0.938	0.997	0.967
57	0.938	0.997	0.967
58	0.941	0.997	0.968
59	0.930	0.994	0.961
60	0.943	0.997	0.969

captures the majority of relevant correspondences during the data semantics transformation process. The consistently high Precision, Recall, and F1-measure values allow us to claim that the developed framework perfectly deals with data semantics transformation and it's effectiveness remains stable across various data semantics transformation scenarios.

The final set of ontology alignment tasks encompasses various transformation scenarios that combine structural, semantic, and value-based alterations. In simpler terms, it includes modifications from all three previously mentioned categories. Table 4.18 illustrates that Precision scores consistently exhibit high values within this task group, with several cases achieving a perfect score of 1. Unfortunately, the Recall results are relatively low, which was expected due to the presence of the same type of modification seen in the Data Value Transformation category. This similarity in modifications affects the overall performance of the framework.

Mixed transformations can pose particular challenges because they involve modifications of multiple aspects of data. Precision is a metric for identifying how many detected correspondences are true positives. In applications where false positives can lead to significant repercussions, such as in medical diagnoses, achieving high Precision is more crucial than achieving high Recall. Moreover, the lower value of Recall is caused by the non-uniform quality of reference correspondence, which was automatically generated and not verified afterwards.

The primary objective of this experiment was to verify a hypothesis that the performance of the fuzzy-based instance matching approach, as described in this chapter, is either superior or, at the very least, not worse than existing alignment systems documented in the literature. To achieve this, we concurrently used the LogMap tool ([99]) and the AML tool ([52]) to generate alignments and subsequently evaluate their quality using measures like Precision, Recall, and F1-measure.

TABLE 4.18
Results of Mixed Transformation (Test Cases 61-80)

Test Case ID	Precision	Recall	F1-measure
61	1.000	0.003	0.005
62	1.000	0.003	0.005
63	1.000	0.117	0.210
64	1.000	0.003	0.005
65	0.709	0.107	0.186
66	0.775	0.201	0.320
67	0.857	0.033	0.063
68	0.929	0.073	0.135
69	0.778	0.019	0.037
70	1.000	0.006	0.011
71	0.957	0.123	0.218
72	1.000	0.030	0.057
73	0.667	0.005	0.011
74	0.939	0.085	0.156
75	1.000	0.003	0.005
76	1.000	0.003	0.005
77	1.000	0.500	0.667
78	1.000	0.006	0.011
79	1.000	0.003	0.005
80	0.875	0.038	0.073

Eventually, we collected samples of Precision, Recall, and F1-measure values for our framework, AML, and LogMap. These sets were then subjected to statistical analysis to assess the aforementioned hypothesis. Throughout all analyses, we maintained a significance level of $\alpha = 0.05$.

We initially examined the distribution of all these value sets utilizing the Shapiro-Wilk test to identify the most suitable statistical test for this analysis. None of the samples came from a normal distribution. Therefore, we chose the non-parametric Friedman ANOVA test for further examination.

During the analysis of Precision samples (summarized in Table 4.19), we obtained the Friedman value test is equal to 43.075, with a p-value less than 0.000001. Following the Friedman test, we proceeded with a Dunn Benferroni test, which is typically utilized to make pairwise comparisons between the different approaches and determine which one performs significantly better. The results indicated that our approach achieved the best results in terms of Precision. More specifically, when compared to LogMap, our framework demonstrated statistically superior performance. LogMap had a statistical value of 3.499 with a p-value of 0.002, signifying that it generated fewer correct correspondences than our framework. Similarly, AML also performed less effectively in Precision, with a statistical value of 6.56 and a p-value of less than 0.000001, which suggests that AML produced fewer correct correspondences than our approach.

During the analysis of Recall samples (which can be found in Table 4.20), the result of the Friedman test yielded a value of 59.299, with a p-value less than 0.000001. This result indicates that at least one of the systems being compared performs differently. Similar to the analysis of Precision, we then used Dunn Benferroni's post-hoc test. The results revealed that our approach demonstrated Recall performance that is not statistically worse than the

TABLE 4.19
Average precision values for different transformation types

Approach	Average Precision
Data value transformations	
Fuzzy-based framework	0.96
AML	0.89
LogMap	0.90
Data structure transformations	
Fuzzy-based framework	0.92
AML	0.42
LogMap	0.93
Data semantics transformations	
Fuzzy-based framework	0.95
AML	0.75
LogMap	0.85
Mixed Transformations	
Fuzzy-based framework	0.92
AML	0.33
LogMap	0.92

TABLE 4.20
Average recall values for different transformation types

Approach	Average Recall
Data value transformations	
Fuzzy-based framework	0.53
AML	0.79
LogMap	0.89
Data structure transformations	
Fuzzy-based framework	0.46
AML	0.43
LogMap	0.99
Data semantics transformations	
Fuzzy-based framework	0.95
AML	0.89
LogMap	0.95
Mixed Transformations	
Fuzzy-based framework	0.07
AML	0.29
LogMap	0.76

AML system. The statistical value was equal to 2.25, with a p-value of 0.073. This suggests that our approach and AML are comparable regarding Recall, with no significant difference.

On the other hand, there was a statistically significant difference in Recall values between our approach and the LogMap. The test value is equal to 5.23, with a p-value less than 0.000001, which shows that our approach achieved Recall performance significantly different and superior to the LogMap system.

The statistical analysis of F1-measure samples (which can be found in Table 4.21), led to a similar conclusion as with Precision and Recall. The Friedman test yielded a statistical value of 28.825, and the corresponding p-value was less than 0.000001. This outcome indicates a significant difference in performance among the systems being compared. Subsequently, Dunn Bonferroni's posthoc test was used. It indicated no significant difference between the F1-measure results obtained by our approach and the AML system. The statistical value for this comparison was equal to 0.533, with a p-value equal to 1. This suggests that our approach and AML perform similarly regarding F1-measure, with no statistically significant distinction between them.

The LogMap system performed better than both our approach and the AML system. The statistical value for the comparison between LogMap and our approach was equal to 4.348, with a p-value less than 0.000041. This indicates that LogMap achieved superior F1-measure performance compared to our approach and AML.

In summary, the results of the conducted experiments are promising. These experiments span diverse transformation scenarios, covering structural, semantic, and value-based alterations. Across these various tasks, our framework consistently demonstrated good Precision scores, highlighting its ability to identify correct mappings of instances. The Recall scores were lower, which is a reasonable trade-off given the potential consequences of false positives in practical applications. All of the above observations are supported by statistical

TABLE 4.21
Average F1-measure values for different transformation types

Approach	Average F1-measure
Data value transformations	
Fuzzy-based framework	0.63
AML	0.83
LogMap	0.89
Data structure transformations	
Fuzzy-based framework	0.48
AML	0.42
LogMap	0.96
Data semantics transformations	
Fuzzy-based framework	0.94
AML	0.80
LogMap	0.89
Mixed Transformations	
Fuzzy-based framework	0.11
AML	0.30
LogMap	0.82

analysis, which provided clear evidence to claim that the performance of the proposed solution is either superior or, at least, not worse than that of existing alignment systems.

4.5 Conclusions

This chapter presents a novel approach to ontology alignment, utilizing the flexibility of fuzzy logic. It provides insights into finding correspondences between elements from ontologies on the level of concepts, relations, and instances. While certain elements discussed in this chapter build upon prior work by the author, it also introduces new and original contributions:

- Section 4.2 focuses on aligning ontologies at the concept level. The research found in the literature primarily concentrates on this level, leaving little room for innovation in the field. Thus, this section demonstrates how fuzzy logic can be integrated into the ontology alignment task. The initial research was previously published in [121]. The chapter provides formal definitions thoroughly reviewed and consolidated in conjunction with other research by the author. Additionally, the chapter extends and comprehensively discusses the results of experimental validation.

- Section 4.3 explores methods for mapping relations. It highlights that providing correspondences for relations is often overlooked by researchers, resulting in a scarcity of capable tools and low-quality mappings. The developed fuzzy-based methods presented in this section have been proved useful during their experimental verification. The developed solution surpasses multiple solutions found in the literature – multiple leading ontology alignment solutions obtained worse results of ontology alignment on a relation level than the presented approach. The methods introduced in [84] form the basis for this section. The book delivers detailed, formal definitions of incorporated similarity function (consistent with the remainder of the book) and a much broader discussion of the results collected during the conducted experiment.

- Section 4.4 addresses the level of instances. Similar to Section 4.3, the presented methods have been experimentally verified, proving their usefulness and applicability. This chapter is a straight development of methods briefly presented in [85] – it provides the entirely overhauled formal definitions of similarity functions along with an extended presentation of experimental results.

In summary, the core of this chapter's contribution is a series of algorithms tailored for ontology alignment, seamlessly incorporating fuzzy logic and fuzzy inference rules. They all adhere to the formal definitions in Chapter 2. The practical viability of the presented approach has been evaluated through rigorous experimentation, employing state-of-the-art benchmark data provided by the Ontology Alignment Evaluation Initiative. The collected results showcase the potency of the fuzzy-logic-based framework in effectively providing ontology alignments on all considered levels, namely concepts, relations, and instances.

Part III

Maintenance and Evaluation

5

Ontology evolution and version management in ontology alignment

In Chapters 3 and 4, we have explored various approaches and solutions to the ontology alignment task. These techniques offer valuable means to establish alignments between ontologies, but it is important to note that they often come with significant computational costs. Processing large and complex knowledge structures and identifying similarities between them can be computationally intensive.

However, in real-world scenarios, ontologies are not static entities and may require modifications or updates due to unforeseen new requirements, prompting questions about the effects on the existing alignments between ontologies. If changes occur in one of the aligned ontologies, must we completely reestablish the alignment from scratch? Or can we revalidate and update the existing alignment to bypass the expensive computations associated with restarting the mapping procedures?

The main contribution of this chapter is introducing a set of formal tools that address these questions. Collectively, these tools provide a framework for the maintenance of ontologies and their alignments over a period of time. Utilizing them makes it possible to assess the effects of ontology changes on existing alignments and efficiently update them, therefore avoiding restarting the alignment process from the beginning.

5.1 Introduction

Consider a scenario presented in Figure 5.1 where two ontologies (O_1 and O_2) have been initially aligned at time t_0. As time progresses, O_2 changes in time t_1. Following this, O_1 changes twice, once at time t_2 and then again at time t_3. Eventually, at time t_4, O_2 goes through another round of changes. As a result, the alignment between O_1 at time t_3 and O_2 at time t_4 may differ significantly from the initially established alignment and obviously cannot be used to provide means of communication between knowledge-based systems which utilize ontologies O_1 and O_2. In this case, the procedure of designating the alignment may need to be executed again from scratch, incurring all the computational costs once more. However, if specific measures are taken, it may be possible to reduce the disadvantage of repeating the ontology alignment procedure.

To begin with, we need to understand how ontologies change over time. Thus, it is essential to clearly and precisely describe their modifications. A tool that can represent any possible ontological modification is necessary to enable efficient analysis of ontology changes. Furthermore, it is vital to organize the descriptions of these changes based on the time they occurred. As a solution, Section 5.2 introduces the concept of an Ontology Log. This formal structure can track the changes made to maintained ontologies over time. It records every change made to some ontology and the time at which it was made. The log serves as a historical record of all modifications made to an ontology.

DOI: 10.1201/9781003437888-5

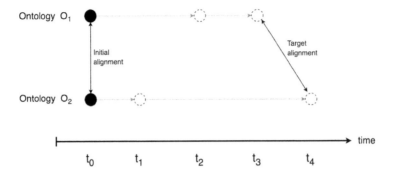

FIGURE 5.1
An example of the evolution of ontologies and the outdating of their alignment

Secondly, we claim that not all changes made to ontologies have the same level of importance or impact. While some changes, such as minor modifications to the label of a concept, may not have a substantial impact on the overall structure and meaning of the ontology, others, like significant updates to the relationships between concepts or changes to the definitions of core concepts' structures, may result in a significant shift in the ontology's meaning and structure. It is crucial to consider the extent and effect of the changes when assessing whether a previously established ontology alignment remains valid. This leads us to the essential question – how can we evaluate whether ontologies have evolved so their alignment may be invalidated? In Section 5.3, we provide three functions Ψ_C, Ψ_I, and Ψ_R (for the level of concepts, relations, and instances) that calculate the degree to which an ontology has changed. If a particular measure (Ψ_C, Ψ_I, or Ψ_R) surpasses an assumed threshold, then we can safely claim that the validity of the existing alignment is compromised.

At this point, alignment methods may be used again. However, an alternative approach is to use ontology alignment updating procedures, which take an initial alignment and the descriptions of the changes applied to the ontologies as input. As a result, the procedures update the alignment based solely on the ontologies' changes, which involves adding new mappings, removing invalid ones, and revalidating existing ones. Section 5.4 contains a detailed discussion of such algorithms.

5.2   Tracking changes in evolving ontologies

The universal timeline TL represents the temporal dimension of evolving ontologies. It consists of a set of distinct points in time denoted as t_n, where n is a natural number. Each point in time corresponds to a specific state or version of the evolving ontology. Formally, it can be defined as:

$$TL = \{t_n | n \in \mathbb{N}\} \tag{5.1}$$

To establish a strict partial order on TL, an ordering relation denoted as $\prec$ is defined. This relation represents the temporal sequence of the points in TL. The strict partial order $\langle TL, \prec \rangle$ satisfies three conditions:

1. **Irreflexivity**: This condition states that no element in TL can be related to itself. In other words, the ordering relation has no loops or self-relations. This condition ensures that each point in time is distinct and unique in the timeline.

2. **Transitivity**: The transitivity condition means that if one point in time is related to a second point, and the second point is related to a third point, then the first point is related to the third point. This condition ensures that the ordering relation consistently captures the evolving ontologies' temporal sequence.

3. **Antisymmetry**: The antisymmetry condition specifies that two points in time must be identical if they are related in both directions. Specifically, if $t_i \prec t_j$ and $t_j \prec t_i$, then t_i and t_j represent the same point in time. This condition guarantees the absence of conflicting or contradictory relations in the ordering, uniquely positioning each point in time in the timeline.

Defining the strict partial order on the universal timeline of evolving ontologies makes it possible to reason about the temporal aspects of ontology evolution. This temporal ordering can be utilized in various tasks, including ontology versioning, change management, and ontology alignment across different versions. The history of changes made to an ontology O can be represented using its timeline.

Definition 5.1 *The ontology timeline of ontology O, denoted as $TL(O)$ is a subset of the universal timeline TL ($TL(0) \subseteq TL$). It consists of a series of moments when the ontology was modified somehow. Each moment in $TL(O)$ corresponds to a specific modification or version of the ontology.*

Definition 5.2 *The ontology repository of ontology O, denoted as $Rep(O)$, is a set containing a collection of the various states of ontology O created over time. It is an ordered sequence of the ontology's different versions, where each version is represented as $O^{(m)}$. Formally it is defined below:*

$$Rep(O) = \left\{ O^{(m)} \mid m \in TL(O) \right\} \tag{5.2}$$

The notation $O^{(m)} = (C^{(m)}, H^{(m)}, R^{C(m)}, I^{(m)}, R^{I(m)})$ is used to refer to the ontology O at a specific moment in time t_m. It represents the state of the ontology at that particular moment, including its classes $C^{(m)}$, hierarchy $H^{(m)}$, concept relationships $R^{C(m)}$, instances $I^{(m)}$, and instance relationships $R^{I(m)}$. In this notation, the expression $O^{(m-1)} \prec O^{(m)}$ denotes that $O^{(m-1)}$ is an earlier version of the ontology O compared to the version $O^{(m)}$. This notation can also be applied to individual elements of the ontology. For example, $c^{(m-1)} \prec c^{(m)}$ indicates that $c^{(m-1)}$ is an earlier version of the concept $c^{(m)}$.

Additionally, every timeline $TL(O)$ has a starting point, denoted as 0, which marks the initiation of tracking the evolution of ontology O. At this initial moment, the ontology is represented as $O^{(0)} = (C^{(0)}, H^{(0)}, R^{C(0)}, I^{(0)}, R^{I(0)})$. Furthermore, the superscript notation can be applied to extend the alignment definitions from Section 2.3. For example, $Align(O_1^{(m)}, O_2^{(n)})$ denotes an alignment between ontologies O_1 and O_2 in their respective states at time m and n, where m and n are points in the universal timeline TL.

Obviously, indexing in the proposed notation can be substituted with timestamps articulated in a standardized date format. This alteration means that elements within the timeline set TL could, for instance, be denoted as $t_{2024.03.1313:24:48}$, representing precise moments in time. Consequently, to depict the state of an ontology O at a specific juncture, one would employ the notation $O^{(t_{2024.03.1313:24:48})}$. However, despite the precision provided by this approach, for the purposes of clarity and genericity throughout the remainder of the book, we opt to retain the original notation, which utilizes lowercase indices. Such conventional indexing facilitates a more streamlined discussion, avoiding the potential complexity and visual clutter associated with long timestamp strings.

In order to keep track of the changes that occur as ontologies evolve, we require a tool that can inform us of *what* changes were made and *when*. To accomplish this, we introduce the concept of the Ontology Log, which offers a comprehensive view of the modifications made to an ontology.

Definition 5.3 *The ontology log is a set of triples formed by using functions $diff_C, diff_R$, and $diff_I$, which can find changes applied to a given ontology O on the concepts, relations, and instances levels, respectively. When used for all subsequent pairs of neighbouring ontology versions in the timeline $TL(O)$, they create the final form of the log:*

$$Log(O) = \Big\{ \big\langle diff_C(O^{(m-1)}, O^{(m)}),$$
$$diff_I(O^{(m-1)}, O^{(m)}), \tag{5.3}$$
$$diff_{R^C}(O^{(m-1)}, O^{(m)}) \big\rangle \mid m \in TL(O) \setminus \{0\} \Big\}$$

The function $diff_C$ takes two versions of the set of ontology concepts, $C^{(m-1)}$ and $C^{(m)}$, as its input and produces three sets as its output: a set of concepts newly added to the ontology, a set of concepts removed from it, and a set of modified concepts, which includes pairs of the same concept in its earlier and later state. We define it formally as follows:

$$diff_C(C^{(m-1)}, C^{(m)}) = \Big\langle new_C(C^{(m-1)}, C^{(m)}),$$
$$del_C(C^{(m-1)}, C^{(m)}), \tag{5.4}$$
$$alt_C(C^{(m-1)}, C^{(m)}) \Big\rangle$$

where:

1. $new_C(C^{(m-1)}, C^{(m)}) = C^{(m)} \setminus C^{(m-1)}$

2. $del_C(C^{(m-1)}, C^{(m)}) = C^{(m-1)} \setminus C^{(m)}$

3. $alt_C(C^{(m-1)}, C^{(m)}) = \Big\{ (c^{(m-1)}, c^{(m)}) \mid c^{(m-1)} \in C^{(m-1)} \wedge c^{(m)} \in C^{(m)} \wedge ctx(c^{(m-1)}) \neq ctx(c^{(m)}) \Big\}$

The function $diff_{R^C}$ receives two versions of the set of concept relations R^C. Its output comprises three sets that respectively describe the added relations, removed relations, and relations of modified concepts. The formal definition is presented below:

$$diff_{R^C}(R^{C(m-1)}, R^{C(m)}) = \Big\langle new_{R^C}(R^{C(m-1)}, R^{C(m)}),$$
$$del_{R^C}(R^{C(m-1)}, R^{C(m)}), \tag{5.5}$$
$$alt_{R^C}(R^{C(m-1)}, R^{C(m)}) \Big\rangle$$

where:

1. $new_{R^C}(R^{C(m-1)}, R^{C(m)}) = R^{C(m)} \setminus R^{C(m-1)}$

2. $del_{R^C}(R^{C(m-1)}, R^{C(m)}) = R^{C(m-1)} \setminus R^{C(m)}$

3. $alt_{R^C}(R^{C(m-1)}, R^{C(m)}) = \Big\{ (r^{(m-1)}, r^{(m)}) \mid r^{(m-1)} \in R^{C(m-1)} \wedge r^{(m)} \in R^{C(m)} \wedge$
   $\frac{|r^{(m-1)} \cap r^{(m)}|}{|r^{(m-1)} \cup r^{(m)}|} \neq 1 \vee S_R(r^{(m-1)}) \neq S_R(r^{(m)})) \Big\}$

At the level of instances, the $diff_I$ function cannot rely solely on changes to the set of instances – the set of instances only contains instance identifiers, and the actual values of instances (which are specific materializations of particular concepts) are defined within the structures of concepts. Therefore, the $diff_I$ function needs to consider the ontology O more comprehensively. It takes as input two versions of sets of concepts and instances, and similarly to Equation 5.4, returns three sets. The first set contains instance identifiers that have been added to the ontology or newly assigned to some concept. The second set includes instance identifiers that have been removed from the ontology or whose assignments to some concept have been deleted. The third set comprises instance identifiers whose valuations in some concepts have been modified. Additionally, it provides the concepts to which such instances have been assigned in their earlier and later versions. The formal definition of $diff_I$ is provided as follows:

$$diff_I(O^{(m-1)}, O^{(m)}) = \Big\langle new_I(I^{(m-1)}, C^{(m-1)}, I^{(m)}, C^{(m)}),$$
$$del_I(I^{(m-1)}, C^{(m-1)}, I^{(m)}, C^{(m)}), \qquad (5.6)$$
$$alt_I(I^{(m-1)}, C^{(m-1)}, I^{(m)}, C^{(m)}) \Big\rangle$$

where:

1. $new_I(I^{(m-1)}, C^{(m-1)}, I^{(m)}, C^{(m)}) =$
   $\Big\{ i \mid (i \in I^{(m)} \wedge i \notin I^{(m-1)}) \vee (Ins^{-1}(i, C^{(m-1)}) = \emptyset \wedge Ins^{-1}(i, C^{(m)}) \neq \emptyset) \Big\}$

2. $del_I(I^{(m-1)}, C^{(m-1)}, I^{(m)}, C^{(m)}) =$
   $\Big\{ (i \mid i \in I^{(m-1)} \wedge i \notin I^{(m)}) \vee (Ins^{-1}(i, C^{(m-1)}) \neq \emptyset \wedge Ins^{-1}(i, C^{(m)}) = \emptyset) \Big\}$

3. $alt_I(I^{(m-1)}, C^{(m-1)}, I^{(m)}, C^{(m)}) =$
   $\Big\{ (i, c^{(m-1)}, c^{(m)}) \mid i \in c^{(m-1)} \wedge i \in c^{(m)} \wedge v^i_{c^{(m-1)}} \neq v^i_{c^{(m)}} \Big\}$

5.3 Assessing the significance of ontology modifications

To accurately track the evolution of an ontology and understand the significance of changes made, one must employ appropriate functions. However, functions like $diff_C$, $diff_R$, and $diff_I$ track changes do not reveal the extent of modifications to the ontology. In this chapter, we introduce three new functions, Ψ_C, Ψ_R, and Ψ_I, for calculating the degree of modification applied to concepts, relations, and instances in some given ontology.

Applying these functions to different ontology versions enables obtaining a real value representing the degree of modification. Suppose the degree of modification calculated by Ψ_C, Ψ_I, or Ψ_R exceeds a specific threshold due to significant changes in the aligned ontologies. In that case, one should implement appropriate procedures to ensure the alignment remains valid.

The choice of threshold values for these functions will depend on the specific application and the required level of sensitivity, which can vary depending on the domain. The availability of three different functions, each designed to capture different types of changes in the ontology and quantify their significance, provides flexibility and allows for a more nuanced understanding of the ontology's evolution.

5.3.1 For the concept level

On the level of concepts, the function Ψ_C must meet the following postulates:

- **P1.** $\Psi_C(C^{(m-1)}, C^{(m)}) \in [0, 1]$

- **P2.** $\Psi_C(C^{(m-1)}, C^{(m)}) = 0 \iff diff_C(C^{(m-1)}, C^{(m)}) = \langle \emptyset, \emptyset, \emptyset \rangle$

- **P3.** $\Psi_C(C^{(m-1)}, C^{(m)}) = 1 \iff diff_C(C^{(m-1)}, C^{(m)}) = \langle C^{(m)}, C^{(m-1)}, \emptyset \rangle$

The initial postulate **P1** states that the function Ψ_C must have values in the range of [0,1]. The following two postulates address edge cases. The second postulate **P2** pertains to a scenario where the significance of a change is minimal and equivalent to 0, which occurs when no modifications are made to the ontology at the concept level. That is, no new concepts are added, no concepts are removed, and no concepts are altered in any way.

P3 deals with the scenario opposite to **P2**. It states that the value of change significance should be the highest (equal to 1) only if the ontology has undergone a complete transformation. Such a situation occurs when all the previous concepts have been removed (which means the first part of $diff_C$ equals $C^{(m-1)}$) and all the current concepts are new (which means the second part of $diff_C$ equals $C^{(m)}$). If each concept from the previous state has been deleted and each concept from the new state is new, then no changes were made. As a result, the third component of $diff_C$ is an empty set.

The definition of a function Ψ_C which fulfils the developed postulates can be found below:

$$\Psi_C(C^{(m-1)}, C^{(m)}) = \frac{\mid new_C(C^{(m-1)}, C^{(m)}) \mid + \mid del_C(C^{(m-1)}, C^{(m)}) \mid}{\mid C^{(m)} \mid + \mid del_C(C^{(m-1)}, C^{(m)}) \mid} + \frac{\displaystyle\sum_{(c_1, c_2) \in alt_C(C^{(m-1)}, C^{(m)})} d_s(ctx(c_1), ctx(c_2))}{\mid C^{(m)} \mid + \mid del_C(C^{(m-1)}, C^{(m)}) \mid} \quad (5.7)$$

Equation 5.7 defines a function Ψ_C that calculates the significance of changes made to the set of concepts between two consecutive states of the ontology, represented by $C^{(m-1)}$ and $C^{(m)}$. The function consists of two components: ratios of the number of changes made to the concepts and the total number of concepts in the ontology.

The first component is the ratio of newly added and deleted concepts to the sum of the total number of concepts in the last state and the number of deleted concepts. This component measures the percentage of change made to the set of concepts.

The second component is the ratio of the sum of pairwise distances between all pairs of corresponding concepts in the past and current states that have been altered (e.g., renamed, had their hierarchy changed) to the sum of the total number of concepts in the last state and the number of deleted concepts. This component measures the extent to which the altered concepts have been modified.

Because both components of Equation 5.7 share the same denominator, they can be treated as one expression. The denominator will always be higher than the numerator, ensuring that the output of Ψ_C always falls within the range of $[0,1]$, which consequently meets the requirements enforced by postulate **P1**.

When no changes are made to the concepts in an ontology, the difference between the previous version $C^{(m-1)}$ and the current version $C^{(m)}$ will be an empty set. In this case, the numerator of Equation 5.7 will be equal to 0, resulting in the entire equation being equal to 0, which satisfies the postulate **P2** that requires that minimal changes should result in a change significance score of 0.

On the other hand, if every concept in the ontology is modified, the difference between $C^{(m-1)}$ and $C^{(m)}$ will contain all of the concepts in both sets. In this case, the numerator and denominator of Equation 5.7 will be equal, resulting in a value of 1, which satisfies the requirement of postulate **P3**, that specifies that the change significance score should be 1 when the ontology undergoes a complete modification at the level of concepts.

Equation 5.7 uses a function d_s with a signature $d_s : EXP_A \cup EXP_R \times EXP_A \cup EXP_R \rightarrow [0,1]$, which measures the distance between two logic expressions taken from either EXP_A (from Definition 2.3)or EXP_R (from Definition 2.8). It first converts the input expressions into the disjunctive normal form (DNF), allowing them to be treated as separate sets of symbols. Then, using the Jaccard distance measure, d_s calculates the distance between two sets of these symbol groups by creating a Cartesian product of the groups from both input expressions and calculates the distance between each pair. Finally, the function takes the average of these partial distance values to obtain the overall distance between the two expressions. For more information on how d_s operates, please refer to [157]. The discussed method will be used further in this chapter if a necessity for calculating a distance between two logic expressions emerges.

5.3.2 For the relation level

On the level of relations, to estimate the significance of changes made within ontologies, the function Ψ_R must satisfy the following postulates:

- **P1.** $\Psi_R(R^{C(m-1)}, R^{C(m)}) \in [0,1]$

- **P2.** $\Psi_R(R^{C(m-1)}, R^{C(m)}) = 0 \iff diff_{R^C}(R^{C(m-1)}, R^{C(m)}) = \left\langle \emptyset, \emptyset, \emptyset \right\rangle$

- **P3.** $\Psi_R(R^{C(m-1)}, R^{C(m)}) = 1 \iff diff_{R^C}(R^{C(m-1)}, R^{C(m)}) = \left\langle R^{C(m)}, R^{C(m-1)}, \emptyset \right\rangle$

Postulate **P1** is concerned with the output values of the function Ψ_R, which calculates the degree of change in an ontology after modifications. According to this postulate, the values produced by Ψ_R should always fall within the range of $[0,1]$. It is essential because it allows for the accurate quantification and comparison of changes made to different ontologies.

Postulate **P2** deals with a scenario where the degree of change in an ontology is minimal, meaning that no new relations were added, removed or altered. In this case, the value outputted by the function Ψ_R should be equal to 0, indicating that no significant change was made to the ontology.

Postulate **P3** applies to a situation where the ontology has undergone complete modification at the level of relations. In this case, the function output should be at its maximum value, equal to 1. This postulate ensures that the function Ψ_R can accurately reflect significant changes in an ontology.

The definition of the function Ψ_R fullfiling the given postulates can be found below:

$$\Psi_R(R^{C(m-1)}, R^{C(m)}) = \frac{\mid new_{R^C}(R^{C(m-1)}, R^{C(m)}) \mid}{\mid R^{C(m)} \mid + \mid del_{R^C}(R^{C(m-1)}, R^{C(m)}) \mid} +$$
$$\frac{\mid del_{R^C}(R^{C(m-1)}, R^{C(m)}) \mid}{\mid R^{C(m)} \mid + \mid del_{R^C}(R^{C(m-1)}, R^{C(m)}) \mid} +$$
$$\frac{\sum_{(r_1, r_2) \in alt_{R^C}(R^{C(m-1)}, R^{C(m)})} d_s(S_R(r_1), S_R(r_2))}{\mid R^{C(m)} \mid + \mid del_{R^C}(R^{C(m-1)}, R^{C(m)}) \mid} \quad (5.8)$$

Equation 5.8 comprises three components, each calculating a distinct aspect of change significance. The first component determines the ratio of new relations added to the ontology to the total number of relations after removing any that have been deleted. This component quantifies the proportion of new relations added and assesses the impact of these new relations.

The second component calculates the ratio of deleted relations to the total number of relations after deleting any that have been removed. This component represents the degree of impact of the deleted relations.

The third component calculates the sum of the semantic distance between pairs of related entities that have been altered or changed from version $m - 1$ to version m. The semantic distance is calculated using a distance function d_s, and the pairs of related entities are obtained from the set of alternated relations between the two ontology versions. This component represents the degree of influence of the changes made to the relations between concepts.

The denominator in all three components of Equation 5.8 is the same. It is calculated as the sum of the total number of relations in version m and the number of relations that have been deleted between versions $m - 1$ and m, which allows us to treat the whole expression as a sum of the numerators divided by the denominator, which is always greater than the numerator. It ensures that the function Ψ_R meets the requirements of postulate **P1**. Consequently, the output of Ψ_R will always fall within the range of [0,1], providing a reliable measure of change in the ontology.

If no changes have been made to the relations in the ontology, the difference between the previous version of the ontology $R^{C(m-1)}$ and the current version $R^{C(m)}$ will be an empty set. In this scenario, the numerator of Equation 5.8 will be equal to 0, resulting in the entire equation being equal to 0. It satisfies postulate **P2**, which requires that the change significance score be 0 when minimal changes are made to the ontology.

If all relations in the ontology have been modified, the difference between $R^{C(m-1)}$ and $R^{C(m)}$ will contain all of the relations in both sets. In this scenario, the numerator and denominator of Equation 5.8 will be equal, resulting in a value of 1. Thus, it meets the postulate **P3** requirement, which stipulates that the change significance score should be 1 when the ontology undergoes a complete modification at the level of relations.

5.3.3 For the instance level

The function Ψ_I is designed to evaluate the importance of changes made to instances, which can include adding or deleting instances and changes to their values. Thus, it must take as input two sets of concepts, $C^{(m-1)}$ and $C^{(m)}$, which is necessary because changes to instances are closely related to the definitions of the concepts that they belong to, specifically the values of v_c^i in Equation 2.10. It satisfies the following postulates:

- **P1.** $\Psi_I(I^{(m-1)}, C^{(m-1)}, I^{(m)}, C^{(m)}) \in [0, 1]$

- **P2.** $\Psi_I(I^{(m-1)}, C^{(m-1)}, I^{(m)}, C^{(m)}) = 0 \iff$
  $diff_I(I^{(m-1)}, C^{(m-1)}, I^{(m)}, C^{(m)}) = \left\langle \emptyset, \emptyset, \emptyset \right\rangle$

- **P3.** $\Psi_I(I^{(m-1)}, C^{(m-1)}, I^{(m)}, C^{(m)}) = 1 \iff$
  $diff_I(I^{(m-1)}, C^{(m-1)}, I^{(m)}, C^{(m)}) = \left\langle I^{(m)}, I^{(m-1)}, \emptyset \right\rangle$

The first postulate, **P1**, mandates that the function Ψ_I's output must fall within the 0 to 1 range. This specification ensures that the significance of instance-level changes is quantified as a fraction within this interval.

The second postulate, **P2**, addresses the situation where the ontology undergoes no modifications. Under these circumstances, the change significance is negligible, reflected by a score of 0.

The third postulate, **P3**, contrasts with **P2** by examining a scenario where all instances from the ontology's initial state are removed, and entirely new instances populate their latest state. This extreme transformation dictates that the significance of instance-level changes reaches its peak, signified by a score of 1.

A definition of Ψ_I that adheres to these postulates is presented below:

$$
\begin{aligned}
\Psi_I(&I^{(m-1)}, C^{(m-1)}, I^{(m)}, C^{(m)}) = \\
&\frac{\mid new_I(I^{(m-1)}, C^{(m-1)}, I^{(m)}, C^{(m)}) \mid}{\mid I^{(m)} \mid + \mid del_I(I^{(m-1)}, C^{(m-1)}, I^{(m)}, C^{(m)}) \mid} + \\
&\frac{\mid del_I(I^{(m-1)}, C^{(m-1)}, I^{(m)}, C^{(m)}) \mid}{\mid I^{(m)} \mid + \mid del_I(I^{(m-1)}, C^{(m-1)}, I^{(m)}, C^{(m)}) \mid} + \\
&\frac{\displaystyle\sum_{(i,c^{(m-1)},c^{(m)})\in alt_I(I^{(m-1)},C^{(m-1)},I^{(m)},C^{(m)})} dist(v^i_{c^{(m-1)}}, v^i_{c^{(m)}})}{\mid I^{(m)} \mid + \mid del_I(I^{(m-1)}, C^{(m-1)}, I^{(m)}, C^{(m)}) \mid}
\end{aligned}
\tag{5.9}
$$

Equation 5.9's function assesses the degree of change significance at the instance level by accounting for all possible types of changes. This function includes three terms, each corresponding to a different change type. The first term assesses the significance of newly added instances to the ontology by dividing the number of new instances by the total number of instances after implementing the changes, including the count of deleted instances. The second term evaluates the significance of instances deleted from the ontology, using the same denominator as the first term for its calculation.

Finally, the third term quantifies the significance of changes made to existing instances. It calculates the distance between the valuations of each instance before and after the changes have been made, sums up all instances that have been altered, and then divides that by the same denominator as the first two terms. For this purpose, the algorithm uses a function called *dist*, which is used to calculate the distance between two vectors of values that represent instances. These vectors may contain values from different domains, such as integers, captions, and decimals, and their contents are heterogeneous. As a result, there is no generic definition of *dist*, and it must be tailored for each concept structure in the ontology to compare instances of those concepts. Some examples of custom *dist* functions can be found in [85].

Equation 5.9 has three components, each of which calculates a different type of change significance. However, the denominators of all three components are the same. Therefore, we can treat the whole expression as a sum of their nominators divided by the denominator, which ensures that the output value of the function Ψ_I will always be a value between 0 and 1, which meets the first postulate **P1**.

When no changes have been made to the instances in the ontology, the difference between the sets of instances in the previous state and the current state will be an empty set, denoted as $\langle \emptyset, \emptyset, \emptyset \rangle$. In this case, the numerator of all three components in Equation 5.9 will be zero, which makes the whole expression equal to zero, fulfilling the second postulate **P2**.

Finally, in a situation where all instances in the ontology have either been altered or removed and replaced with new ones, the numerator and denominator of all three components will be equal, resulting in a value of 1 for the whole expression. Thus, it fulfils the third postulate **P3**.

5.4 Methods for updating ontology alignment

This section focuses on a series of algorithms that enable the revalidation and updating of ontology alignments in case one of the mapped ontologies changes. Using these methods ensures that the maintained alignment always remains relevant. All of the proposed procedures are based on detailed definitions of ontologies and their elements, which are presented in Section 2.1, as well as how to track changes that may be applied to them, presented in Section 5.2.

It is important to note that the primary goal of the procedures introduced in this book is not to surpass existing ontology alignment methods in the literature regarding mapping accuracy. Instead, these algorithms focus on addressing other issues – their principal objective is to update the previously established ontology alignment in light of new changes, relying solely on information about these modifications. The intention is to restore the alignments to a quality comparable to that achieved by analyzing all the ontologies from the beginning with standard ontology alignment systems based on certain predefined metrics.

5.4.1 Updating ontology alignment on the concept level

The changes in ontology concepts, encompassing additions, modifications, and deletions, are crucial in influencing the existing alignment between the source ontology (denoted as O_1) and the target ontology (O_2) on the concept level. Assuming that ontology O_1 has been altered, to ensure the alignment's validity, it is essential to process the sets of changes defined in Equation 5.4. The approach proposed in this section involves three concurrent sub-procedures that collectively contribute to the revalidation of the alignment $Align(O_1^{(m-1)}, O_2^{(n)})$ between ontologies $O_1^{(m-1)}$ and $O_2^{(n)}$ in their versions from $m-1$-th and n-th moments in time, respectively and eventually provide the alignment $Align(O_1^{(m)}, O_2^{(n)})$.

5.4.1.1 Adding new mappings on the concept level

The first of the three procedures, presented in Algorithm 11, focuses on new elements added to the source ontology. It takes as input the difference in concepts between two consecutive

---

Algorithm 11 Updating the existing alignment with new mappings

Input: $diff_C(O_1^{(m-1)}, O_1^{(m)}), Align_C(O_1^{(m-1)}, O_2^{(n)}), \tau$
Output: $Align_C(O_1^{(m)}, O_2^{(n)})$
 1: $adds = \{(c_1^{(m)}, c_2^{(n)}) \mid (c_1^{(m)}, c_2^{(n)}) \in new_C(C_1^{(m-1)}, C_1^{(m)}) \times C_2^{(n)} \wedge \lambda_C(c_1^{(m)}, c_2^{(n)}) \geq \tau\}$
 2: $Align_C(O_1^{(m)}, O_2^{(n)}) := Align_C(O_1^{(m-1)}, O_2^{(n)}) \cup adds;$
 3: **Return** $Align_C(O_1^{(m)}, O_2^{(n)});$

---

versions of the source ontology, the existing alignment between the previous version of the source ontology and the target ontology, and a threshold τ for the similarity score of the new mappings. The algorithm proceeds as follows:

1. It first generates a set of candidate mappings between the new concepts in $C_1^{(m)}$ and the existing concepts in $C_2^{(n)}$ using the function new_C. The set of candidate mappings is filtered based on a similarity score threshold τ using the function λ_C. The resulting set of candidate mappings is denoted as *adds*.

2. The algorithm updates the existing alignment by adding the new mappings in *adds* to it. Specifically, it performs the union of the sets $Align_C(O_1^{(m-1)}, O_2^{(n)})$ and *adds* and stores the result in $Align_C(O_1^{(m)}, O_2^{(n)})$.

3. Finally, the algorithm returns the updated alignment $Align_C(O_1^{(m)}, O_2^{(n)})$.

The algorithm incorporates the concept alignment degree function, denoted as λ_C (Line 2), which was previously developed by the author in a separate publication ([157]). However, it is essential to note that the algorithm is flexible in terms of the choice of ontology mapping tool and allows for the substitution of λ_C with any other suitable tool available in the literature (e.g., [194]). This flexibility enables researchers and practitioners to utilize different mapping approaches based on their specific requirements and preferences.

Regarding complexity, the algorithm's primary task involves comparing all the added concepts in the source ontology with those in the target ontology. This comparison process ensures that appropriate mappings are established between the two ontologies. However, the algorithm's final complexity remains no higher than polynomial despite the need to examine all the added concepts.

The size of the set $new_C(C_1^{(m-1)}, C_1^{(m)})$, which represents the added concepts, is typically smaller compared to the size of the target ontology's concept set, denoted as $C_2^{(n)}$. This observation contributes to the algorithm's efficiency, as the size of the target ontology mainly influences the computational burden. The relatively small size of the added concepts set allows for efficient processing and ensures that the algorithm remains viable for real-world applications.

In summary, the algorithm's utilization of the concept alignment degree function and its requirement to compare added concepts with target ontology concepts do not significantly impact its final complexity. With a complexity no higher than polynomial, the algorithm provides an acceptable efficiency level. The ability to substitute the alignment function with alternative mapping tools further enhances its flexibility and usability. Researchers and practitioners can leverage the algorithm's efficiency and adaptability to align and evolve ontologies while employing diverse ontology mapping techniques based on their specific needs and the availability of tools in the literature.

Algorithm 12 Updating alignments of modified concepts

Input: $diff_C(O_1^{(m-1)}, O_1^{(m)}), Align_C(O_1^{(m-1)}, O_2^{(n)}), \epsilon, \tau$

Output: $Align_C(O_1^{(m)}, O_2^{(n)})$

1: $Align_C(O_1^{(m)}, O_2^{(n)}) := Align_C(O_1^{(m-1)}, O_2^{(n)});$

2: **for all** $(c_1^{(m-1)}, c_1^{(m)}) \in alt_C(C_1^{(m-1)}, C_1^{(m)})$ **do**

3:      $dels := \{(c_1^{(m-1)}, c_2^{(n)}) \in Align_C(O_1^{(m-1)}, O_2^{(n)}) \mid \exists c_1^{(m)} \in C_1^{(m)} : (c_1^{(m-1)}, c_1^{(m)}) \in alt_C(C_1^{(m-1)}, C_1^{(m)}) \wedge \mid \lambda_C(c_1^{(m-1)}, c_2^{(n)}) - \lambda_C(c_1^{(m)}, c_2^{(n)}) \mid \geq \epsilon\};$

4:      $Align_C(O_1^{(m)}, O_2^{(n)}) := Align_C(O_1^{(m-1)}, O_2^{(n)}) \setminus dels$

5:      $\widetilde{C_2^{(n)}} := C_2^{(n)}$

6:      **if** $\exists (b^{(m)}, c_1^{(m)}) \in H_1^{(m)} \wedge \exists (c_1^{(m)}, c_2^{(n)}) \in Align_C(O_1^{(m)}, O_2^{(n)})$ **then**

7:         **if** $\neg\exists (b^{(m)}, c_1^{(m-1)}) \in H_1^{(m-1)}$ **then**

8:            $Align_C(O_1^{(m)}, O_2^{(n)}) := Align_C(O_1^{(m)}, O_2^{(n)}) \cup \{(b^{(m)}, c_2^{(n)})\}$

9:            $\widetilde{C_2^{(n)}} := \widetilde{C_2^{(n)}} \setminus \{c_2^{(n)}\}$

10:         **end if**

11:      **end if**

12:      **if** $\exists (b^{(m-1)}, c_1^{(m-1)}) \in H_1^{(m-1)} \wedge \neg\exists (b^{(m)}, c_1^{(m)}) \in H^{(m)} \wedge \exists (b^{(m)}, c_2^{(n)}) \in Align_C(O_1^{(m)}, O_2^{(n)})$ **then**

13:         $Align_C(O_1^{(m)}, O_2^{(n)}) := Align_C(O_1^{(m)}, O_2^{(n)}) \setminus \{(b^{(m)}, c_2^{(n)})\}$

14:         $\widetilde{C_2^{(n)}} := \widetilde{C_2^{(n)}} \setminus \{c_2^{(n)}\}$

15:      **end if**

16:      $Align_C(O_1^{(m)}, O_2^{(n)}) := Align_C(O_1^{(m)}, O_2^{(n)}) \cup \{(c_1^{(m)}, c_2^{(n)}) \mid (c_1^{(m)}, c_2^{(n)}) \in \{c_1^{(m)}\} \times \widetilde{C_2^{(n)}} \wedge \lambda_C(c_1^{(m)}, c_2^{(n)}) \geq \tau\}$

17: **end for**

18: **Return** $Align_C(O_1^{(m)}, O_2^{(n)});$

5.4.1.2 Revalidating mappings on the concept level

The second procedure, outlined in Algorithm 12, targets modified concepts. Like its predecessor, this algorithm requires the concept difference (Equation 5.4) between two successive versions of the source ontology, the current alignment between the source ontology's previous version and the target ontology, and two tuning parameters, ϵ and τ, as inputs. The algorithm operates in the following manner:

1. At first, it initializes the alignment between $O_1^{(m)}$ and $O_2^{(n)}$ as the alignment between $O_1^{(m-1)}$ and $O_2^{(n)}$.

2. The algorithm then iterates over all pairs of concepts $(c_1^{(m-1)}, c_1^{(m)})$ in $C_1^{(m-1)}$ and $C_1^{(m)}$ that have changed between the two-time steps.

3. For each such pair of concepts, the algorithm identifies all pairs $(c_1^{(m-1)}, c_2^{(n)})$ in the alignment between $O_1^{(m-1)}$ and $O_2^{(n)}$ where $c_1^{(m-1)}$ matches the first element of the pair $(c_1^{(m-1)}, c_1^{(m)})$, and the difference in the alignment score between $c_1^{(m-1)}$ and $c_2^{(n)}$ and the alignment score between $c_1^{(m)}$ and $c_2^{(n)}$ is greater than or equal to ϵ. These pairs are stored in a set called $dels$.

4. The algorithm then removes all pairs in $dels$ from the alignment between $O_1^{(m)}$ and $O_2^{(n)}$.

5. The algorithm then creates a copy of $C_2^{(n)}$ called $\widetilde{C_2^{(n)}}$.

6. If there exists a pair $(b^{(m)}, c_1^{(m)})$ in $H_1^{(m)}$ and a pair $(c_1^{(m)}, c_2^{(n)})$ in the alignment between $O_1^{(m)}$ and $O_2^{(n)}$, and there is no pair $(b^{(m)}, c_1^{(m-1)})$ in $H_1^{(m-1)}$, then the algorithm adds the pair $(b^{(m)}, c_2^{(n)})$ to the alignment between $O_1^{(m)}$ and $O_2^{(n)}$ and removes the concept $c_2^{(n)}$ from $\widetilde{C_2^{(n)}}$.

7. If there exists a pair of concepts $(b^{(m)}, c_1^{(m)})$ in the concept hierachy $H_1^{(m)}$ and $(c_1^{(m)}, c_2^{(n)})$ in the alignment $Align_C(O_1^{(m)}, O_2^{(n)})$, the algorithm checks if there exists no pair $(b^{(m)}, c_1^{(m-1)})$ in the hierachy $H_1^{(m-1)}$. If this is true, it adds the pair $(b^{(m)}, c_2^{(n)})$ to the alignment $Align_C(O_1^{(m)}, O_2^{(n)})$ and remove the concept $c_2^{(n)}$ from the set $\widetilde{C_2^{(n)}}$.

8. If there exists a pair $(b^{(m-1)}, c_1^{(m-1)})$ in the hierarchy $H_1^{(m-1)}$ and there is no pair $(b^{(m)}, c_1^{(m)})$ in the hierarchy $H^{(m)}$ but there exists a pair $(b^{(m)}, c_2^{(n)})$ in the alignment $Align_C(O_1^{(m)}, O_2^{(n)})$, then the algorithm removes the pair $(b^{(m)}, c_2^{(n)})$ from the alignment $Align_C(O_1^{(m)}, O_2^{(n)})$ and removes the concept $c_2^{(n)}$ from the set $\widetilde{C_2^{(n)}}$.

9. Next, it adds pairs of concepts $(c_1^{(m)}, c_2^{(n)})$ to the alignment $Align_C(O_1^{(m)}, O_2^{(n)})$ if they satisfy the following conditions:

   - the pair $(c_1^{(m)}, c_2^{(n)})$ belongs to the cartesian product $c_1^{(m)} \times \widetilde{C_2^{(n)}}$
   - the alignment score $\lambda_C(c_1^{(m)}, c_2^{(n)})$ is greater than or equal to a threshold value τ.

10. Finally, the algorithm returns the updated alignment $Align_C(O_1^{(m)}, O_2^{(n)})$.

The discussed procedure is the most complex among the discussed steps as it involves checking whether modified concepts in the source ontology can be matched with concepts in the target ontology. This checking process requires iterating over the set of concepts in the target ontology, resulting in a polynomial complexity with respect to the number of concepts in both ontologies.

Considering the steps allows us to claim that the overall complexity of the algorithm depends on three main factors: the size of $Align_C(O_1^{(m-1)}, O_2^{(n)})$, the size of $alt_C(C_1^{(m-1)}, C_1^{(m)})$, and the complexity of operations performed within specific loops. The time complexity of the algorithm can be approximated as $O(|alt_C(C_1^{(m-1)}, C_1^{(m)})| * |Align_C(O_1^{(m-1)}, O_2^{(n)})| + |dels|)$, where $|alt_C(C_1^{(m-1)}, C_1^{(m)})|$ represents the size of the set of altered concepts and $|dels|$ represents the size of the set of mappings to be deleted.

However, it is worth noting that the number of altered concepts in the source ontology is typically much smaller than the number of concepts in the target ontology. Consequently, the algorithm's performance is primarily determined by the number of concepts in the target ontology. This observation implies that the algorithm's complexity is polynomial but with a relatively lower degree, making it more manageable and efficient compared to exponential-time algorithms.

In practical terms, as the size of the target ontology increases, the algorithm's execution time may grow at a polynomial rate. The actual growth rate depends on the specific sizes of the altered concepts, alignment, and deletion sets. However, due to the relatively smaller size of the altered concepts set, the algorithm remains suitable for real-world applications, providing a reasonable balance between computational complexity and effectiveness in aligning and evolving ontologies.

Algorithm 13 Removing stale mappings of deleted concepts from the existing alignment

---

Input: $diff_C(O_1^{(m-1)}, O_1^{(m)}), Align_C(O_1^{(m-1)}, O_2^{(n)})$
Output: $Align_C(O_1^{(m)}, O_2^{(n)})$
  1: $del := \{(c_1^{(m-1)}, c_2^{(n)}) \in Align_C(O_1^{(m-1)}, O_2^{(n)}) \mid c_1^{(m-1)} \in del_C(C_1^{(m-1)}, C_1^{(m)})\};$
  2: $Align_C(O_1^{(m)}, O_2^{(n)}) := Align_C(O_1^{(m-1)}, O_2^{(n)}) \setminus del;$
  3: **Return** $Align_C(O_1^{(m)}, O_2^{(n)});$

5.4.1.3   Removing stale mappings on the concepts level

The last of the procedures, outlined in Algorithm 13, removes stale mappings of deleted concepts from an existing ontology alignment. The input to this algorithm includes the differences between two versions of the same ontology O_1 and an alignment between O_1 and another ontology O_2. The output of this algorithm is an updated alignment between O_1 and O_2, where stale mappings of deleted concepts have been removed. The following steps are taken:

1. It first identifies the set of mappings in the existing alignment that involves a concept deleted in the current version of O_1. Specifically, it identifies all mappings of the form $(c_1^{(m-1)}, c_2^{(n)}) \in Align_C(O_1^{(m-1)}, O_2^{(n)})$ where $c_1^{(m-1)}$ is a deleted concept in $O_1^{(m)}$. This set of mappings is denoted by del.

2. It then removes all mappings in del from the existing alignment $Align_C(O_1^{(m-1)}, O_2^{(n)})$, effectively updating the alignment to remove any stale mappings of deleted concepts.

3. Finally, the algorithm returns the updated alignment $Align_C(O_1^{(m)}, O_2^{(n)})$.

When considering the algorithm's steps individually, the overall complexity of the algorithm is determined by the sizes of two key components: $Align_C(O_1^{(m-1)}, O_2^{(n)})$ and del. The time complexity of the algorithm can be approximated as $O(|Align_C(O_1^{(m-1)}, O_2^{(n)})| + |del|)$, where $|Align_C(O_1^{(m-1)}, O_2^{(n)})|$ represents the size of the alignment set and del represents the size of the set of mappings that need to be deleted.

The first element, $|Align_C(O_1^{(m-1)}, O_2^{(n)})|$, represents the size of the alignment set. This set contains mappings between concepts from the source ontology $O_1^{(m-1)}$ and the target ontology $O_2^{(n)}$. The associated complexity depends on the number of mappings in the alignment set. Therefore, as the size of the alignment set increases, the algorithm's time complexity also increases. However, other factors within the algorithm's implementation may influence the actual complexity, such as the specific operations performed on the alignment set.

The second element, $|del|$, represents the size of the set of mappings to be deleted. This set contains mappings that need to be removed from the alignment set. Its complexity depends on the number of mappings in the deletion set. Removing mappings from the alignment set involves certain operations, such as set difference or membership checks. Assuming constant time operations for these set operations, the time complexity scales linearly with the size of the deletion set.

5.4.2   Updating ontology alignment on the relation level

Analogously to the modifications addressed at the ontology's concept level, changes at the relation level can also be effectively managed by breaking down the process into three distinct yet concurrently executable steps. These steps are specifically tailored to address various facets of the modification process: identifying opportunities to introduce new mappings, revalidating and updating current mappings in response to changes, and discarding mappings that have become obsolete. Each step of this algorithm interacts with the original state of the relation-level ontology alignment, represented as $Align_R(O_1^{(m-1)}, O_2^{(n)})$, while also considering the outcomes from the $diff_R(O_1^{(m-1)}, O_1^{(m)})$ operation.

5.4.2.1 Adding new mappings on the relation level

The first procedure in the context of relation-level alignment, outlined in Algorithm 14, is designed to handle newly added relations in the source ontology. It operates based on the existing alignment between the previous version of the source ontology and the target ontology, denoted as $Align_R(O_1^{(m-1)}, O_2^{(n)})$. The algorithm also takes into account the difference in relations between two consecutive versions of the source ontology, represented by $diff_R(O_1^{(m-1)}, O_1^{(m)})$. A similarity threshold ϵ is also provided to determine the minimum score required for accepting new mappings.

Algorithm 14 Adding new mappings on the level of relations

Input: $diff_R(O_1^{(m-1)}, O_1^{(m)}), Align_R(O_1^{(m-1)}, O_2^{(n)}), \epsilon$
Output: $Align_R(O_1^{(m)}, O_2^{(n)})$
1: $Align_R(O_1^{(m)}, O_2^{(n)}) := Align_R(O_1^{(m-1)}, O_2^{(n)})$;
2: **for all** $(r_1^{(m)}, r_2^{(n)}) \in new_{R^C}(R^{C_1(m-1)}, R^{C_1(m)}) \times R^{C_2(n)}$ **do**
3:     **if** $\lambda_R(r_1^{(m)}, r_2^{(n)}) \geq \epsilon$ **then**
4:         $Align_R(O_1^{(m)}, O_2^{(n)}) := Align_R(O_1^{(m)}, O_2^{(n)}) \cup \{(r_1^{(m)}, r_2^{(n)})\}$
5:         **if** $\exists r_1'^{(m)} \in R^{C_1(m)} : (r_1'^{(m)} \leftarrow r_1^{(m)})$ **then**
6:             $Align_R(O_1^{(m)}, O_2^{(n)}) := Align_R(O_1^{(m)}, O_2^{(n)}) \cup \{(r_1'^{(m)}, r_2^{(n)})\}$
7:         **end if**
8:     **end if**
9: **end for**
10: **return** $Align_R(O_1^{(m)}, O_2^{(n)})$;

The algorithm proceeds as follows:

1. The algorithm starts by initializing the alignment of relations between $O_1^{(m)}$ and $O_2^{(n)}$ using the previous alignment $Align_R(O_1^{(m-1)}, O_2^{(n)})$.

2. It then iterates through each pair $(r_1^{(m)}, r_2^{(n)})$ in the cartesian product of the set of new relations $new_{R^C}(R^{C_1(m-1)}, R^{C_1(m)})$ and relations from the target ontology $R^{C_2(n)}$. For each pair, it checks if the similarity measure $\lambda_R(r_1^{(m)}, r_2^{(n)})$ is greater than or equal to a specified threshold ϵ.

3. If the similarity is above the threshold, the pair $(r_1^{(m)}, r_2^{(n)})$ is added to the alignment $Align_R(O_1^{(m)}, O_2^{(n)})$ using the union operation.

4. Additionally, if there exists a relation $r_1'^{(m)}$ in $R^{C_1(m)}$ that can be considered a generalization of $r_1^{(m)}$, the pair $(r_1'^{(m)}, r_2^{(n)})$ is also included in the alignment.

5. After processing all new relations, the algorithm returns the updated alignment $Align_R(O_1^{(m)}, O_2^{(n)})$.

The provided algorithm is an initial step in handling relation-level alignment by incorporating newly added relations into the existing alignment. Its time complexity exhibits a linear growth rate, which is dependent on the size of the Cartesian product between the sets $new_{RC}(R^{C_1(m-1)}, R^{C_1(m)})$ and $R^{C_2(n)}$. It is important to note that the set $new_{RC}(R^{C_1(m-1)}, R^{C_1(m)})$ tends to be relatively small in real-world applications, thereby ensuring that the overall complexity remains acceptable and manageable for practical use cases.

This algorithm effectively integrates newly added relations by considering several factors. Firstly, it considers the existing alignment between the source and target ontologies, ensuring the new mappings align with the previously established correspondences. Additionally, it considers the differences in relations introduced during ontology evolution, allowing for incorporating these changes into the alignment process. Furthermore, the algorithm incorporates a similarity threshold, denoted as ϵ, which is crucial in filtering out mappings that do not meet the desired similarity level.

One notable advantage of this procedure is its ability to capture hierarchical connections between relations accurately. Utilizing the hierarchical structures of the ontologies ensures that the alignment remains consistent and reflects the new elements introduced. This hierarchical perspective enhances the alignment's overall quality by preserving the relationships between the relations and maintaining the coherence of the ontologies.

In practical terms, the algorithm's linear time complexity, influenced by the size of the Cartesian product, guarantees efficient execution even for moderately sized target ontologies. The relatively small size of the set $new_{RC}(R^{C_1(m-1)}, R^{C_1(m)})$ further contributes to its computational feasibility. As a result, this procedure is well-suited for real-world applications where new relations are introduced, enabling the alignment and evolution of ontologies with reasonable computational costs.

5.4.2.2 Revalidating mappings on the relation level

The procedure presented in Algorithm 15 is used to update and reevaluate relations alignment based on the source ontology changes. It takes as inputs the alignment $Align_R(O_1^{(m-1)}, O_2^{(n)})$ in its initial version, the differences in relations $diff_R(O_1^{(m-1)}, O_1^{(m)})$, and a similarity threshold ϵ.

To produce an updated version of the alignment $Align_R(O_1^{(m)}, O_2^{(n)})$ it takes the following steps:

1. It begins by initializing $Align_R(O_1^{(m)}, O_2^{(n)})$ with the previous alignment $Align_R(O_1^{(m-1)}, O_2^{(n)})$. This step ensures that the alignment initially includes the previously established mappings.

2. Next, it identifies the mappings that need to be revalidated. It creates a set alt that contains pairs of relations $(r_1^{(m-1)}, r_2^{(n)})$ where $r_1^{(m-1)}$ is mapped to $r_2^{(n)}$ in the previous alignment, and $(r_1^{(m-1)}, r_1^{(m)})$ is in the set $alt_{RC}(R^{C_1(m-1)}, R^{C_1(m)})$. This set captures the mappings in the previous alignment that are affected by changes in relations.

3. It removes from the updated alignment $Align_R(O_1^{(m)}, O_2^{(n)})$ any mappings in the set alt that have a similarity score $\lambda_R(r_1^{(m)}, r_2^{(n)})$ below the threshold ϵ. This step ensures that only mappings with sufficient similarity are retained in the updated alignment.

4. It identifies the newly added relations new by looking for relations $r_1^{(m)}$ in $R^{C_1(m)}$ that are not already mapped in the previous alignment $Align_R(O_1^{(m-1)}, O_2^{(n)})$. These new relations are candidates for mapping to relations in $R^{C_2(n)}$.

Algorithm 15 Revalidating the existing mappings of relations

Input: $diff_R(O_1^{(m-1)}, O_1^{(m)}), Align_R(O_1^{(m-1)}, O_2^{(n)}), \epsilon$

Output: $Align_R(O_1^{(m)}, O_2^{(n)})$

1: $Align_R(O_1^{(m)}, O_2^{(n)}) := Align_R(O_1^{(m-1)}, O_2^{(n)});$

2: $alt = \{(r_1^{(m-1)}, r_2^{(n)}) \mid (r_1^{(m-1)}, r_2^{(n)}) \in Align_R(O_1^{(m-1)}, O_2^{(n)}) \land (r_1^{(m-1)}, r_1^{(m)}) \in alt_{R^C}(R^{C_1(m-1)}, R^{C_1(m)})\}$

3: $Align_R(O_1^{(m)}, O_2^{(n)}) := Align_R(O_1^{(m)}, O_2^{(n)}) \setminus \{(r_1^{(m-1)}, r_2^{(n)}) \mid (r_1^{(m-1)}, r_2^{(n)}) \in alt \land \lambda_R(r_1^{(m)}, r_2^{(n)}) < \epsilon\};$

4: $new := \{r_1^{(m)} \mid (r_1^{(m-1)}, r_1^{(m)}) \in alt_{R^C}(R^{C_1(m-1)}, R^{C_1(m)}) \land \neg \exists (r_1^{(m-1)}, r_2^{(n)}) \in Align_R(O_1^{(m-1)}, O_2^{(n)})\}$

5: **for all** $(r_1^{(m)}, r_2^{(n)}) \in new \times R^{C_2(n)}$ **do**

6:     **if** $\lambda_R(r_1^{(m)}, r_2^{(n)}) \geq \epsilon$ **then**

7:         $Align_R(O_1^{(m)}, O_2^{(n)}) := Align_R(O_1^{(m)}, O_2^{(n)}) \cup \{(r_1^{(m)}, r_2^{(n)})\}$

8:         **if** $\exists r_1'^{(m)} \in R^{C_1(m)} : (r_1'^{(m)} \leftarrow r_1^{(m)})$ **then**

9:             $Align_R(O_1^{(m)}, O_2^{(n)}) := Align_R(O_1^{(m)}, O_2^{(n)}) \cup \{(r_1'^{(m)}, r_2^{(n)})\}$

10:         **end if**

11:     **end if**

12: **end for**

13: **return** $Align_R(O_1^{(m)}, O_2^{(n)});$

---

5. For each pair of $(r_1^{(m)}, r_2^{(n)})$ where $r_1^{(m)}$ is a newly added relation and $r_2^{(n)}$ is a relation in $R^{C_2(n)}$, the algorithm checks if their similarity score $\lambda_R(r_1^{(m)}, r_2^{(n)})$ is above the threshold ϵ. If it is, the pair is added to the updated alignment $Align_R(O_1^{(m)}, O_2^{(n)})$. Additionally, if there is a relation $r_1'^{(m)}$ in $R^{C_1(m)}$ that is a child of $r_1^{(m)}$, the algorithm also includes the mapping $(r_1'^{(m)}, r_2^{(n)})$ in the updated alignment.

6. Finally, the algorithm returns the updated alignment $Align_R(O_1^{(m)}, O_2^{(n)})$.

The algorithm processes each relation added to or modified in the source ontology and compares it with every relation present in the target ontology. Since the changes made to the source ontology are typically limited in scope, the algorithm's overall complexity is primarily influenced by the number of relations in the target ontology. As a result, the algorithm's complexity remains within a quadratic bound, which means it does not exceed a quadratic growth rate.

This characteristic arises from the fact that the algorithm does not directly compare every pair of relations from both ontologies. Instead, it selectively analyzes the mappings between specific relations based on certain conditions. The algorithm first identifies a set of alternative mappings called 'alt,' which consists of relations in the existing alignment that satisfy specific criteria involving the changes made to the source ontology. The subsequent steps involve operations on this set and creating a new set called 'new' based on certain conditions.

Since the algorithm's execution time depends on the sizes of alt, $Align_R(O_1^{(m)}, O_2^{(n)})$, and new, it is primarily influenced by the number of relations in the target ontology. As long as the target ontology does not grow excessively, the algorithm's complexity will remain manageable, ensuring efficient execution.

In practical terms, as the size of the target ontology increases, the algorithm's execution time may grow proportionally or slightly faster due to the quadratic nature of the complexity. However, the algorithm remains scalable and suitable for scenarios where the number of relations in the target ontology is reasonably large, ensuring that the alignment and evolution process can be performed efficiently and effectively.

5.4.2.3   Removing mappings on the relation level

The final procedure presented in Algorithm 16 focuses on updating an existing alignment by removing stale mappings of deleted relations between two versions of ontologies. It takes as input the previous alignment, denoted as $Align_R(O_1^{(m-1)}, O_2^{(n)})$, and the differences in relations between the previous and current versions of ontology O_1, denoted as $diff_R(O_1^{(m-1)}, O_1^{(m)})$. The goal is to produce an updated alignment, denoted as $Align_R(O_1^{(m)}, O_2^{(n)})$, that reflects the removal of mappings involving deleted relations.

Algorithm 16 Removing stale mappings of deleted relations from the existing alignment

---

Input: $diff_R(O_1^{(m-1)}, O_1^{(m)}), Align_R(O_1^{(m-1)}, O_2^{(n)})$
Output: $Align_R(O_1^{(m)}, O_2^{(n)})$
1: $del := \{(r_1^{(m-1)}, r_2^{(n)}) \mid (r_1^{(m-1)}, r_2^{(n)}) \in Align_R(O_1^{(m-1)}, O_2^{(n)}) \wedge r_1^{(m-1)} \in del_R(R^{C_1(m-1)}, R^{C_1(m)})\}$;
2: $Align_R(O_1^{(m)}, O_2^{(n)}) := Align_R(O_1^{(m-1)}, O_2^{(n)}) \setminus del$;
3: **return** $Align_R(O_1^{(m)}, O_2^{(n)})$;

The algorithm follows the following steps:

1. It initializes an empty set del to store mappings involving deleted relations.

2. It iterates through each mapping $(r_1^{(m-1)}, r_2^{(n)})$ in the previous alignment $Align_R(O_1^{(m-1)}, O_2^{(n)})$. If the relation $r_1^{(m-1)}$ is found in the set of deleted relations $del_R(R^{C_1(m-1)}, R^{C_1(m)})$, the mapping is considered stale and added to the set del.

3. After examining all mappings, the algorithm updates the alignment by removing the mappings stored in the set del from the previous alignment. This is done by performing the set difference operation: $Align_R(O_1^{(m)}, O_2^{(n)}) := Align_R(O_1^{(m-1)}, O_2^{(n)}) \setminus del$.

4. Finally, the algorithm returns the updated alignment $Align_R(O_1^{(m)}, O_2^{(n)})$.

The algorithm ensures that the updated alignment consists only of valid mappings, considering the changes in relations between the two versions of the ontologies. The algorithm's computational complexity primarily depends on two steps: constructing the set del of stale mappings and updating the alignment by removing the mappings in del.

The construction of the set del involves iterating through the mappings in the previous alignment, which has a cardinality of $|Align_R(O_1^{(m-1)}, O_2^{(n)})|$. For each mapping, the algorithm checks if the relation is in the set of deleted relations. This step has a time complexity of $O(|Align_R(O_1^{(m-1)}, O_2^{(n)})|)$ since it requires iterating through all mappings once and checking membership in the set of deleted relations.

The set difference operation achieves updating the alignment by removing the mappings in the set del. The time complexity of this step depends on the size of the previous alignment, $|Align_R(O_1^{(m-1)}, O_2^{(n)})|$, and the size of the mappings to be removed, $|del|$. Since the size of set del is at most $|Align_R(O_1^{(m-1)}, O_2^{(n)})|$, the time complexity of this step is also $O(|Align_R(O_1^{(m-1)}, O_2^{(n)})|)$.

In summary, the computational complexity of the algorithm is mainly influenced by the size of the previous alignment, denoted as $|Align_R(O_1^{(m-1)}, O_2^{(n)})|$, since both constructing the set *del* and updating the alignment involve operations that scale linearly with this size. The algorithm efficiently ensures that only valid mappings are included in the updated alignment, considering the changes in relations between the ontologies.

5.4.3 Updating ontology alignment on the instance level

Maintaining ontology alignment at the instance level is a complex task entailed by several factors that may come into play when considering alignment at this level. For example, changes made at the concept level can ripple through the ontology, impacting concept alignments and mappings between instances. Consequently, a task decomposition into three substeps, such as checking for new mappings, validating and updating existing mappings, and removing potentially obsolete ones, is insufficient. Thus, an approach presented in this book section offers a more holistic, systematic perspective.

The solution has been divided into four procedures, each targeting a distinct scenario. Each scenario encompasses various modifications within ontologies, which can directly or indirectly impact instances. Therefore, each may influence instance alignment and must be considered separately.

5.4.3.1 Effects of instance and concept removal

The first procedure presented in Algorithm 17 addresses the effects of removing concepts and instances from maintained ontologies. The algorithm takes several inputs: the previous instance alignment $Align_I(O_1^{(m-1)}, O_2^{(n)})$, the current concept alignment $Align_C(O_1^{(m)}, O_2^{(n)})$ and the outcome of the difference function $diff_C(O_1^{(m-1)}, O_1^{(m)})$. The main goal is to produce the alignment on the instance level of ontologies O_1 and O_2 in their most recent states.

Algorithm 17 Applying effects of instance and concept removals in ontology alignment on the instance level alignment

---

Input: $Align_I(O_1^{(m-1)}, O_2^{(n)}), Align_C(O_1^{(m)}, O_2^{(n)}), diff_C(O_1^{(m-1)}, O_1^{(m)})$
Output: $Align_I(O_1^{(m)}, O_2^{(n)})$
1: $del := \{AL_{O_1,O_2}(c_1^{(m-1)}, c_2^{(n)}) \mid AL_{O_1,O_2}(c_1^{(m-1)}, c_2^{(n)}) \in Align_I(O_1^{(m-1)}, O_2^{(n)}) \wedge c_1^{(m-1)} \in del_C(O_1^{(m-1)}, O_1^{(m)})\}$
2: $Align_I(O_1^{(m)}, O_2^{(n)}) := Align_I(O_1^{(m-1)}, O_2^{(n)}) \setminus del$
3: **for all** $i_1^{(m-1)} \in del_I(I^{(m-1)}, I^{(m)})$ **do**
4:     **for all** $c_1^{(m-1)} \in Ins^{-1}(i_1^{(m-1)})$ **do**
5:        $AL_{O_1,O_2}(c_1^{(m)}, c_2^{(n)}) := AL_{O_1,O_2}(c_1^{(m)}, c_2^{(n)}) \setminus \{(i_1^{(m-1)}, i_2^{(n)}) \mid (i_1^{(m-1)}, i_2^{(n)}) \in AL_{O_1,O_2}(c_1^{(m-1)}, c_2^{(n)})\}$
6:     **end for**
7: **end for**
8: **return** $Align_I(O_1^{(m)}, O_2^{(n)})$;

The algorithm can be broken down into the following steps:

- The algorithm begins by identifying the mappings in the earlier instance alignment, $Align_I(O_1^{(m-1)}, O_2^{(n)})$, that involve instances whose corresponding concepts have been deleted (based on the output of $diff_C(O_1^{(m-1)}, O_1^{(m)})$). These mappings are collected in the set del.

- Next, the algorithm updates the instance alignment, $Align_I(O_1^{(m)}, O_2^{(n)})$, by removing the mappings in the set del from the previous instance alignment. This step eliminates the mappings associated with deleted concept instances, ensuring that the instance alignment remains consistent with the concept changes.

- The algorithm then iterates over the instances that have been deleted (based on $del_I(I^{(m-1)}, I^{(m)})$). For each deleted instance $i_1^{(m-1)}$, it further iterates over the concept instances, $c_1^{(m-1)}$, that correspond to the deleted instance. Within the nested loop, the algorithm removes the mappings between $c_1^{(m-1)}$ and $c_2^{(n)}$ in the concept alignment, $AL_{O_1,O_2}(c_1^{(m-1)}, c_2^{(n)})$, within the instance alignment. This step ensures that the instance alignment is updated to reflect the removal of deleted concept instances and their associated mappings.

- Finally, the updated instance alignment, $Align_I(O_1^{(m)}, O_2^{(n)})$, is returned as the output of the algorithm.

This algorithm updates the instance-level ontology alignment by considering concept alignment changes and concept differences between two ontology versions. It removes mappings involving deleted concepts and adjusts mappings for instances that have been removed or added.

Computing the set of mappings to be removed del involves iterating over the alignment $Align_I(O_1^{(m-1)}, O_2^{(n)})$ and identifying mappings that involve concepts marked for removal. The complexity of this step depends on the size of the alignment and the cost of checking for concept membership in the removal set. The complexity of this step can be approximated as $O(|AlignI(O^{(m-1)}, O^{(n)})| * |del_C(O_1^{(m-1)}, O_1^{(m)})|)$.

Updating the alignment $Align_I(O_1^{(m)}, O_2^{(n)})$ involves removing the mappings identified in the del set from the alignment $Align_I(O_1^{(m-1)}, O_2^{(n)})$. The complexity of this operation is proportional to the size of the del set. Therefore, the complexity can be approximated as $O(|del|)$.

The overall complexity of the algorithm can be expressed as approximately $O(|AlignI(O^{(m-1)}, O^{(n)})| * |del_C(O_1^{(m-1)}, O_1^{(m)})| + |del|)$, where $|AlignI(O^{(m-1)}, O^{(n)})|$ represents the number of mappings in the alignment $Align_I(O_1^{(m-1)}, O_2^{(n)})$, $|del_C(O_1^{(m-1)}, O_1^{(m)})|$ represents the size of the set of concepts marked for removal, and $|del|$ represents the size of the set of mappings to be removed. therefore, the complexity is influenced by the alignment size, the number of concepts marked for removal, and the number of mappings to be removed.

The above algorithm analysis indicates that it performs reasonably well, particularly for scenarios with many mappings and relatively few removals. If the number of removals is large, it still should not entail any additional problems since removing elements of instance alignment $Align_I(O_1^{(m-1)}, O_2^{(n)})$ to update it to $Align_I(O_1^{(m)}, O_2^{(n)})$ is a relatively straightforward operation.

5.4.3.2 Effects of concept addition

The second of the procedures (presented in Algorithm 18), which can be used to maintain ontology alignment on the instance level when mapped ontology evolves, addresses the situation in which new concepts and their instances are added to the ontology. It accepts four input parameters: the previous instance alignment $Align_I(O_1^{(m-1)}, O_2^{(n)})$, the current concept alignment $Align_C(O_1^{(m)}, O_2^{(n)})$, the concept differences $diff_C(O_1^{(m-1)}, O_1^{(m)})$, and a threshold value τ.

Algorithm 18 Applying effects of concept additions in ontology alignment on the instance level alignment

---

Input: $Align_I(O_1^{(m-1)}, O_2^{(n)}), Align_C(O_1^{(m)}, O_2^{(n)}), diff_C(O_1^{(m-1)}, O_1^{(m)}), \tau$
Output: $Align_I(O_1^{(m)}, O_2^{(n)})$
1: $new := \{(c_1^{(m)}, c_2^{(n)}) \mid c_1^{(m)} \in new_C(O_1^{(m-1)}, O_1^{(m)}) \wedge (c_1^{(m)}, c_2^{(n)}) \in Align_C(O_1^{(m)}, O_2^{(n)})\}$
2: **for all** $(c_1^{(m)}, c_2^{(n)}) \in new$ **do**
3:     $AL_{O_1,O_2}(c_1^{(m)}, c_2^{(n)}) := \{(i_1^{(m)}, i_2^{(n)}) \mid i_1^{(m)} \in c_1^{(m)} \wedge i_2^{(n)} \in c_2^{(n)} \wedge \lambda_I(v_{c_1}^{i_1(m)}, v_{c_2}^{i_2(n)})) \geq \tau\}$
4:     $Align_I(O_1^{(m)}, O_2^{(n)}) := Align_I(O_1^{(m)}, O_2^{(n)}) \cup \{AL_{O_1,O_2}(c_1^{(m)}, c_2^{(n)})\}$
5: **end for**
6: **return** $Align_I(O_1^{(m)}, O_2^{(n)})$;

The algorithm aims to designate the updated instance alignment $Align_I(O_1^{(m)}, O_2^{(n)})$ by taking the following steps:

- The algorithm initializes an empty set new.

- It iterates over the concept mappings in $Align_C(O_1^{(m)}, O_2^{(n)})$ and selects only those mappings where the concept $c_1^{(m)}$ from the current ontology $O_1^{(m)}$ is present in the set of new concepts $new_C(O_1^{(m-1)}, O_1^{(m)})$ (i.e., it is a newly added concept). The selected mappings are added to the new set.

- For each concept mapping $(c_1^{(m)}, c_2^{(n)})$ in the new set, the algorithm computes the instance alignment $AL_{O_1,O_2}(c_1^{(m)}, c_2^{(n)})$. It iterates over all instances $i_1^{(m)}$ in $c_1^{(m)}$ and all instances $i_2^{(n)}$ in $c_2^{(n)}$. It checks if the similarity measure $\lambda_I(v_{c_1}^{i_1(m)}, v_{c_2}^{i_2(n)})$ between the values of instance $i_1^{(m)}$ in concept $c_1^{(m)}$ and the values of instance $i_2^{(n)}$ in concept $c_2^{(n)}$ is greater than or equal to the threshold τ. If the condition is satisfied, the instance mapping $(i_1^{(m)}, i_2^{(n)})$ is added to $AL_{O_1,O_2}(c_1^{(m)}, c_2^{(n)})$.

- The computed instance alignment $AL_{O_1,O_2}(c_1^{(m)}, c_2^{(n)})$ for each concept mapping $(c_1^{(m)}, c_2^{(n)})$ in the new set is added to the current instance alignment $Align_I(O_1^{(m)}, O_2^{(n)})$.

- Finally, the updated instance alignment $Align_I(O_1^{(m)}, O_2^{(n)})$ is returned as the output of the algorithm.

The initial phase of the algorithm focuses on identifying new concept mappings by iterating through the set of newly introduced concepts in the updated ontology. Therefore, the computational complexity of this step is directly proportional to the size of the set $new_C(O_1^{(m-1)}, O_1^{(m)})$, as each concept mapping needs to be examined.

Once new concept mappings are identified, the algorithm determines the corresponding instance mappings. This step involves iterating through the instances of the mapped concepts and assessing a similarity function. The complexity of this step is influenced by two factors: the number of new concept mappings ($|new|$) and the sizes of the instance sets associated with each concept.

If the number of new concept mappings and the sizes of the respective instance sets are relatively small, the algorithm's computational complexity can be considered acceptable. In such cases, the runtime of the algorithm remains within reasonable limits. However, if these quantities grow significantly, the algorithm's complexity will increase accordingly, potentially leading to longer execution times.

5.4.3.3 Effects of concept and instance alterations

In this chapter of the book, the third procedure delves into the crucial matter of handling modifications that may arise within concepts and instances throughout the lifespan of an ontology. The procedure takes into account various inputs, namely $Align_I(O_1^{(m-1)}, O_2^{(n)})$, $Align_C(O_1^{(m)}, O_2^{(n)})$, $diff_C(O_1^{(m-1)}, O_1^{(m)})$, and ϵ. By utilizing these inputs, its primary objective is to calculate $Align_I(O_1^{(m)}, O_2^{(n)})$, which represents the updated alignment of the ontology.

Algorithm 19 Updating ontology alignment on the instance level

---

Input: $Align_I(O_1^{(m-1)}, O_2^{(n)}), Align_C(O_1^{(m)}, O_2^{(n)}), diff_C(O_1^{(m-1)}, O_1^{(m)}), \tau, \epsilon$

Output: $Align_I(O_1^{(m)}, O_2^{(n)})$

1: **for all** $(c_1^{(m-1)}, c_1^{(m)}) \in alt_C(O_1^{(m-1)}, O_1^{(m)})$ **do**

2:      **for all** $AL_{O_1,O_2}(c_1^{(m)}, c_2^{(n)}) \in Align_I(O_1^{(m)}, O_2^{(n)})\}$ **do**

3:          **if** $| A^{c_1(m-1)} | \neq | A^{c_1(m)} |$ **then**

4:              **for all** $(i_1^{(m)}, i_2^{(n)}) \in AL_{O_1,O_2}(c_1^{(m)}, c_2^{(n)})$ **do**

5:                  **if** $| \lambda_I(v_{c_1}^{i_1(m-1)}, v_{c_2}^{i_2(n)}) - \lambda_I(v_{c_1}^{i_1(m)}, v_{c_2}^{i_2(n)}) | \geq \epsilon$ **then**
$AL_{O_1,O_2}(c_1^{(m)}, c_2^{(n)}) := AL_{O_1,O_2}(c_1^{(m)}, c_2^{(n)}) \setminus \{(i_1^{(m-1)}, i_2^{(n)})\}$

6:              **end if**

7:          **end for**

8:          **else**

9:              $aux = \{i_2^{(n)} \mid i_2^{(n)} \in Ins(c_2^{(n)}) \wedge \neg \exists i_1'^{(m)} : (i_1'^{(m)}, i_2^{(n)})) \in AL_{O_1,O_2}(c_1^{(m)}, c_2^{(n)})\}$

10:             **for all** $(i_1^{(m)}, i_2^{(n)}) \in Ins(c_1^{(m)}) \times aux$ **do**

11:                 **if** $\lambda_I(v_{c_1}^{i_1(m)}, v_{c_2}^{i_2(n)})) \geq \tau$ **then**

12:                    $AL_{O_1,O_2}(c_1^{(m)}, c_2^{(n)}) := AL_{O_1,O_2}(c_1^{(m)}, c_2^{(n)}) \cup \{(i_1^{(m)}, i_2^{(n)}))\}$

13:               **end if**

14:             **end for**

15:          **end if**

16:      **end for**

17: **end for**

18: **return** $Align_I(O_1^{(m)}, O_2^{(n)})$;

The algorithm described in Algorithm 19 follows the steps outlined below:

- It iterates over each pair $(c_1^{(m-1)}, c_1^{(m)})$ in the set of modified classes $(alt_C(O_1^{(m-1)}, O_1^{(m)}))$.

- For each pair, the algorithm iterates through a set $AL_{O_1,O_2}(c_1^{(m)}, c_2^{(n)})$ representing the alignment of instances in $Align_I(O_1^{(m)}, O_2^{(n)})$. If the number of instances in $c_1^{(m-1)}$ is not equal to the number of instances in $c_1^{(m)}$, it proceeds to iterate over each pair $(i_1^{(m)}, i_2^{(n)})$ in $AL_{O_1,O_2}(c_1^{(m)}, c_2^{(n)})$.

- If the absolute difference between $\lambda_I(v_{c_1}^{i_1(m-1)}, v_{c_2}^{i_2(n)})$ and $\lambda_I(v_{c_1}^{i_1(m)}, v_{c_2}^{i_2(n)})$ is greater than or equal to the threshold value ϵ, the algorithm removes $(i_1^{(m-1)}, i_2^{(n)})$ from $AL_{O_1,O_2}(c_1^{(m)}, c_2^{(n)})$.

- When the number of instances in $c_1^{(m-1)}$ is not equal to the number of instances in $c_1^{(m)}$, the algorithm creates a set aux containing instances $i_2^{(n)}$ from $Ins(c_2^{(n)})$ that do not have a corresponding $i_1^{\prime(m)}$ such that $(i_1^{\prime(m)}, i_2^{(n)}) \in AL_{O_1,O_2}(c_1^{(m)}, c_2^{(n)})$.

- The algorithm adds all pairs $(i_1^{(m)}, i_2^{(n)})$ from the cartesian product $Ins(c_1^{(m)}) \times aux$ to $AL_{O_1,O_2}(c_1^{(m)}, c_2^{(n)})$.

- For each pair $(i_1^{(m)}, i_2^{(n)})$ in the cartesian product, if the alignment degree between the instances exceeds the threshold τ, formally represented as $\lambda_I(v_{c_1}^{i_1(m)}, v_{c_2}^{i_2(n)}) \geq \tau$, the algorithm considers them aligned and adds it to $AL_{O_1,O_2}(c_1^{(m)}, c_2^{(n)})$

- Finally, the algorithm returns the updated alignment $Align_I(O_1^{(m)}, O_2^{(n)})$.

The algorithm discussed in this section is characterized by its higher computational complexity compared to the other procedures presented in this chapter. It employs a nested loop structure, with an outer loop iterating over the set $alt_C(O_1^{(m-1)}, O_1^{(m)})$ of concepts modified in O_1, and an inner loop iterating over the instance alignments in $Align_I(O_1^{(m)}, O_2^{(n)})$. As a result, if these sets are large, the algorithm's runtime can become lengthy.

However, it is important to note that such modifications to classes and instance alignments are typically infrequent and tend to occur primarily during the early stages of ontology development. These modifications often take place before any substantial alignments have been established. As an ontology matures and reaches a certain level of stability, the occurrence of such changes becomes rare, typically involving only a small number of concepts.

Therefore, while the algorithm may have a higher computational cost due to its nested loops, in practice, its impact on runtime is mitigated by the infrequent and limited nature of the modifications it handles. As a result, the algorithm remains suitable for maintaining and updating ontology alignments, even in scenarios where the size of the modified classes and instance alignments is relatively large.

5.4.3.4 Refinement of instance level ontology alignment

The algorithm for ontology alignment refinement, as presented in Algorithm 20, is a final step in maintaining ontology alignment. Its purpose is to improve and refine the alignment at the instance level by considering ontological changes and incorporating new mappings that may have emerged due to ontology evolution. The algorithm takes several inputs: the previous instance alignment $Align_I(O_1^{(m-1)}, O_2^{(n)})$, the current class alignment $Align_C(O_1^{(m)}, O_2^{(n)})$, the differences in the class structure $diff_C(O_1^{(m-1)}, O_1^{(m)})$ appearing due to ontology evolution, and a threshold value τ.

The main objective of this algorithm is to enhance the instance-level alignment by considering potential new mappings that were not previously discovered and adjusting existing mappings. By doing so, the algorithm aims to achieve a more accurate and up-to-date alignment between the ontologies, eventually enriching it.

The procedure takes the following steps:

- The algorithm begins with a nested loop structure. The outer loop iterates over the modified classes in $O_1^{(m)}$, denoted as $c_1^{(m)}$. These are the classes that have changed from the previous version $O_1^{(m-1)}$ and have corresponding mappings in $O_2^{(n)}$ through $Align_C(O_1^{(m)}, O_2^{(n)})$. The loop ensures that only relevant classes are considered for alignment refinement.

Algorithm 20 Refining ontology alignment on the instance level

---

Input: $Align_I(O_1^{(m-1)}, O_2^{(n)}), Align_C(O_1^{(m)}, O_2^{(n)}), diff_C(O_1^{(m-1)}, O_1^{(m)}), \tau$

Output: $Align_I(O_1^{(m)}, O_2^{(n)})$

1: **for all** $c_1^{(m)} \in \{c_1^{(m)} \mid c_1^{(m)} \in C_1^{(m)} \wedge c_1^{(m-1)} \in C_1^{(m-1)} \wedge I^{c_1(m-1)} \neq I^{c_1(m)} \wedge \exists c_2^{(n)} \in$
$\quad C_2^{(n)} : (c_1^{(m)}, c_2^{(n)}) \in Align_C(O_1^{(m)}, O_2^{(n)})\}$ **do**

2:      **for all** $AL_{O_1,O_2}(c_1^{(m)}, c_2^{(n)}) \in Align_I(O_1^{(m)}, O_2^{(n)})$ **do**

3:          $dels = \{(i_1^{(m)}, i_2^{(n)}) \mid (i_1^{(m)}, i_2^{(n)}) \in AL_{O_1,O_2}(c_1^{(m)}, c_2^{(n)}) \wedge \lambda_I(v_{c_1}^{i_1(m)}, v_{c_2}^{i_2(n)}) < \tau\}$

4:          $new := \{i_1^{(m)} \mid i_1^{(m)} \in I_1^{(m)} \wedge \neg \exists (i_1^{(m)}, i_2^{(n)}) \in AL_{O_1,O_2}(c_1^{(m)}, c_2^{(n)})\}$

5:          $adds = \{(i_1^{(m)}, i_2^{(n)}) \mid (i_1^{(m)}, i_2^{(n)}) \in ((new_I(I_1^{(m-1)}, I_2^{(m)}) \cap Ins(c_1^{(m)}) \cup new) \times$
$\quad Ins(c_2^{(n)}) \wedge \lambda_I(v_{c_1}^{i_1(m)}, v_{c_2}^{i_2(n)}) \geq \tau\}$

6:          $AL_{O_1,O_2}(c_1^{(m)}, c_2^{(n)}) := AL_{O_1,O_2}(c_1^{(m)}, c_2^{(n)}) \setminus dels \cup adds$

7:      **end for**

8: **end for**

9: **return** $Align_I(O_1^{(m)}, O_2^{(n)})$;

- Within the outer loop, there is an inner loop that iterates over the instance alignments in $Align_I(O_1^{(m)}, O_2^{(n)})$. This loop enables examining and adjusting individual instance mappings for the given class pair $(c_1^{(m)}, c_2^{(n)})$.

- For each instance mapping $AL_{O_1,O_2}(c_1^{(m)}, c_2^{(n)})$, the algorithm identifies the instances to be deleted from the alignment. The set *dels* contains instances $(i_1^{(m)}, i_2^{(n)})$ that do not satisfy a similarity threshold τ, as determined by the similarity measure $\lambda_I(v_{c_1}^{i_1(m)}, v_{c_2}^{i_2(n)})$.

- Then, it generates the set *adds* of instance pairs $(i_1^{(m)}, i_2^{(n)})$, which belong to the Cartesian product of two sets: the first set is determined by the instances in the modified concept $c_1^{(m)}$ (either new instances or instances that were not previously aligned), and the second set consisting of instances belonging to the concept $c_2^{(n)}$.

- It checks if the similarity score, denoted as λ_I, between the attribute values of the instances $i_1^{(m)}$ and $i_2^{(n)}$ from the set *adds* exceeds the threshold τ. If the similarity score is above or equal to the threshold, the instance pair is considered for addition.

- It updates the instance alignment $AL_{O_1,O_2}(c_1^{(m)}, c_2^{(n)})$ by removing instances in *dels* and adding instances in *adds*.

- Finally, the refined alignment is returned as output $Align_I(O_1^{(m)}, O_2^{(n)})$

The algorithm's computational complexity depends on three main factors: the number of modified concepts in the ontology O_1, the number of concepts in the ontology O_2, and the number of existing instance alignments. Since the algorithm contains two nested loops, its complexity can be considered polynomial.

Despite the apparent challenges entailed by polynomial complexity, this characteristic is generally considered manageable within practical applications of ontology alignment. This manageability is contingent upon the ontologies remaining within reasonable size bounds. In such contexts, the polynomial growth in complexity does not preclude the algorithm from executing efficiently, thereby ensuring that refining ontology alignments remains feasible.

Furthermore, the manageability of the algorithm's complexity is also a consequence of its design. The algorithm minimizes unnecessary computations by focusing on only those concepts that have undergone modifications and leveraging precise criteria, for instance matching and alignment adjustments. This selective processing approach not only mitigates the potential impact of the polynomial complexity on performance but also enhances the algorithm's utility in dynamic environments where ontologies are subject to frequent updates.

5.5 Measuring the level of knowledge about ontology interoperability

In distributed systems, knowledge is distributed across multiple nodes within a complex infrastructure. Each node typically utilizes ontologies to formally represent its knowledge, which is crucial in modern semantic applications. To enable effective communication among these nodes, ontology alignment establishes a connection or bridge between two or more ontologies. This alignment facilitates the translation of content between ontologies, ensuring interoperability.

However, as business requirements evolve, ontologies need to be updated, which can disrupt communication between services within the system. In previous sections of this chapter, the author introduces a framework that addresses these challenges, allowing for the reestablishment of communication between knowledge-based systems that incorporate ontologies.

Nonetheless, an important question remains: How do modifications made to either ontology affect the combined knowledge potential when the two ontologies are aligned? Do these changes enhance or diminish the knowledge potential enabled by the alignment?

5.5.1 Formal definition of ontology interoperability measures

The main goal of this section of the book is to develop a measure that can be used to assess the extent to which updating the ontology alignment contributes to acquiring knowledge about the interoperability of the aligned ontologies.

Let us assume that two ontologies exist: O_1 and O_2, and the concept alignment $Align_C(O_1, O_2)$. The aforementioned task can be decomposed into two subtasks:

- To develop a function $\mu(O_1, O_2, Align_C(O_1, O_2))$ which for two ontologies O_1 and O_2 and the concept alignment $Align_C(O_1, O_2)$ between them, calculates their knowledge potential.

- To develop a function $\Delta(O_1^{(m)}, O_2^{(m)}, O_1^{(n)}, O_2^{(n)}, Align_C(O_1^{(m)}, O_2^{(m)}), Align_C(O_1^{(n)}, O_2^{(n)}))$ which returns values from range $[-100\%, \infty]$ and for ontologies O_1 and O_2 in their subsequent versions from moments in time $m, n \in TL$ (such that $O_1^{(m)} \prec O_1^{(n)}$ and $O_2^{(m)} \prec O_2^{(n)}$) calculates how the knowledge potential changed when considered ontologies and their alignment evolved.

In order to provide the above functions, several auxiliary elements must be defined. The knowledge potential of a given concept $c_r \in C_1$ within ontology O_1 in the context of the alignment $Align_C(O_1, O_2)$ can be calculated as follows:

$$\phi(O_1, c) = \sum_{c_s \in S_{NA}(Sub_C(c), Align_C(O_1, O_2))} Depth(S_{NA}(Sub_C(c), Align_C(O_1, O_2)), c_s) \quad (5.10)$$

where S_{NA} is an auxiliary function that for a subtree $S = Sub_C(c)$ (defined in Section 2.1), $c \in C_1$ removes from this subtree concepts (and their descendants) which have mappings within the alignment $Align(O_1, O_2)$. Formally, it can be defined as a function which returns a set adhering to the following criterion:

$$S_{NA}(S, Align_C(O_1, O_2)) = \{c \mid c \in S \wedge \neg \exists c_2 \in C_2 : (c_1, c_2) \in Align_C(O_1, O_2)\} \quad (5.11)$$

By analogy to Equation 5.10, the maximal knowledge potential of a concept can be calculated as follows:

$$\phi_{max}(O_1, c) = \sum_{c_s \in Sub_C(c)} Depth((Sub_C(c), c_s) \quad (5.12)$$

For given $c_1 \in C1$, $c_2 \in C2$, such that $(c_1, c_2) \in Align_C(O_1, O_2)$, Equation 5.10 allows calculating the knowledge potential of a selected mapping within the alignment $Align(O_1, O_2)$:

$$\sigma(c_1, O_1, c_2, O_2) = \begin{cases} \phi(O_1, c_1) + \phi(O_2, c_2) & \text{if } (c_1, c_2) \in Align_C(O_1, O_2) \\ 0 & \text{otherwise} \end{cases} \quad (5.13)$$

Equation 5.13 can be easily extended to estimate the overall knowledge potential of the whole alignment $Align(O_1, O_2)$:

$$\kappa(O_1, O_2, Align_C(O_1, O_2)) = \sum_{(c_1, c_2) \in Align_C(O_1, O_2)} \sigma(c_1, O_1, c_2, O_2) \quad (5.14)$$

Having the above elements, it is possible to formulate a set of postulates which must be met by the searched function $\mu(O_1, O_2)$:

- **P1.** $\mu(O_1, O_2, Align_C(O_1, O_2)) = 0 \iff Align_C(O_1, O_2) = \emptyset$ (in other words, the alignment of O_1 and O_2 is empty)

- **P2.** $\mu(O_1, O_2, Align_C(O_1, O_2)) = 1 \iff \forall_{(c_{r1}, c_{r2}) \in Align_C(O_1, O_2)}(c_{r1} \in Root(O_1) \wedge c_{r2} \in Root(O_2))$

P1 addresses the circumstance where the alignment, denoted as $Align_C(O_1, O_2)$, between ontologies O_1 and O_2 is nonexistent or empty. In such instances, knowledge potential is absent due to the lack of mappings between the concepts of the two ontologies. Accordingly, for this scenario, the value of $\mu(O_1, O_2)$ is set to its minimum, which is 0 – it reflects the intuition that without any form of alignment, the ontologies cannot contribute to mutual understanding or interoperability, hence offering no enhancement to knowledge.

P2 examines the situation where the existing mappings in the alignment $Align_C(O_1, O_2)$ exclusively link only the top-level concepts of both ontologies. Such mappings, while establishing a basic level of connectivity between O_1 and O_2, often fail to capture the nuanced and detailed relationships among the more specific concepts within the ontologies.

The final definition of the function μ is given below:

$$\mu(O_1, O_2, Align_C(O_1, O_2)) = \frac{\kappa(O_1, O_2, Align_C(O_1, O_2))}{\sum\limits_{c_1 \in Root(O_1)} \phi(O_1, c_1) + \sum\limits_{c_2 \in Root(O_2)} \phi(O_2, c_2)} \qquad (5.15)$$

When $Align_C(O_1, O_2)$ is empty, there are no mappings between concepts of O_1 and O_2. Consequently, the numerator $\kappa(O_1, O_2, Align_C(O_1, O_2))$ becomes 0 because no mappings exist to evaluate. With the numerator at 0, regardless of the values obtained through the denominator, the overall fraction evaluates to 0. It reflects the intuitive understanding that without any alignment, there is no contribution to mutual understanding or interoperability between the ontologies, thus fulfilling **P1**.

The function μ meets **P2** through its denominator, which sums ϕ of root concepts in both ontologies. The denominator effectively captures the broadest knowledge potential that could be harnessed through top-level concept alignments by focusing on root concepts. When the alignment exclusively consists of root concept mappings, the numerator, representing the actual knowledge potential harnessed, equals the maximum potential represented by the denominator, hence making μ evaluate to 1

Equation 5.15 measures the knowledge potential between two mapped ontologies, assuming they remain constant and unchanged over time. However, ontologies and their alignments are subject to various changes, ranging from minor to substantial. Therefore, it is essential to understand how changes applied to ontologies and the corresponding updates in the alignment between them impact their knowledge potential.

Assuming that $O_1^{(n)} \prec O_1^{(m)}$ and $O_2^{(n)} \prec O_2^{(m)}$ denote that ontology O_1 and O_2 have evolved between time n and time m, we are interested in comparing the knowledge potential of ontologies $O_1^{(n)}$ and $O_2^{(n)}$, along with their alignment, at time n, with the knowledge potential of the ontologies $O_1^{(m)}$ and $O_2^{(m)}$ after changes have been made, and the alignment has been updated. Therefore, the following calculation can be employed to assess the potential increase in knowledge after updating ontology mappings:

$$\Delta(O_1^{(m)}, O_2^{(m)}, O_1^{(n)}, O_2^{(n)}, Align_C(O_1^{(m)}, O_2^{(m)}), Align_C(O_1^{(n)}, O_2^{(n)})) =$$
$$(\frac{\mu(O_1^{(m)}, O_2^{(m)}, Align_C(O_1^{(m)}, O_2^{(m)}))}{\mu(O_1^{(n)}, O_2^{(n)}, Align_C(O_1^{(n)}, O_2^{(n)}))} - 1) * 100\% \qquad (5.16)$$

The above equation provides a means to quantify the change in knowledge regarding the interoperability of two ontologies resulting from updates in the ontologies and their alignment. It assumes that the initial knowledge potential between $O_1^{(n)}$ and $O_2^{(n)}$, denoted as $\mu(O_1^{(n)}, O_2^{(n)})$, is not equal to 0. This assumption is necessary because a knowledge increase of exactly 0 in the initial state of the ontology would leave us without a reference point for comparing subsequent changes.

The developed function returns values from the range $\Delta \in [-100\%, \infty)$. Positive values of Δ indicate a growth in knowledge compared to the earlier state, signifying an increase in the knowledge potential. Conversely, negative values of Δ indicate a decrease in the knowledge stored in the two ontologies, which reduces the knowledge potential.

TABLE 5.1
Pairs of ontologies used in the experiment

No	O_1	$|C_1|$	O_2	$|C_2|$
1	Cocus	55	Iasted	140
2	ConfTool	38	Sofsem	60
3	Ekaw	74	Sigkdd	49
4	CMT	36	Paperdyne	47
5	Edas	104	Iasted	140
6	Sofsem	60	Confious	57
7	OpenConf	62	Ekaw	74
8	Edas	104	Sofsem	60
9	OpenConf	62	Cocus	55
10	Edas	104	ConfTool	38

5.5.2   Experimental evaluation

5.5.2.1   Experimental procedure

The main aim of the experiment was to verify the applicability of the developed measure of Δ in the case of evolving ontology. Similar to the experiment described in Chapter 4 we used a set of selected ontologies from a dataset provided by the Ontology Alignment Evaluation Initiative[1] (*OAEI*), which are enlisted in Table 5.1. They all comply with the base ontology definition from Equation 2.1.

In order to study the process of ontology evolution, we have introduced some modifications to the first ontology (O_1) in each pair. These modifications involve the random addition or deletion of concepts within the ontology. By incorporating these changes, we aim to simulate ontologies' dynamic nature as they evolve. This approach allows us to observe and analyze the transformations that occur during the evolution of ontologies.

To ensure a comprehensive exploration of ontology evolution, we formulated nine scenarios, each representing a unique configuration of concept additions and deletions. These scenarios are detailed in Section 5.5.2.2, providing a diverse range of possibilities and potential pathways for the evolution of ontologies. Through these scenarios, we can gain valuable insights into the various trajectories that ontologies may follow as they evolve, shedding light on the factors and mechanisms that drive ontology changes.

We have generated two alignments for each pair of ontologies: one for the version before the evolution and another for the version after the evolution. These alignments serve as a means to compare and assess the changes that occur during the evolution process. To accomplish this, we utilized LogMap, a widely recognized tool for ontology matching ([99]). LogMap offers high scalability, incorporating reasoning and inconsistency repair capabilities. Its effectiveness has been demonstrated by its commendable performance in multiple OAEI campaigns [96, 97, 95].

Following the generation of alignments, we calculated the value of the Δ function for each two alignments for each ontology pair. The Δ function measures dissimilarity or difference between the alignments, enabling us to quantify and evaluate the changes that have occurred due to ontology evolution. The collected values are presented and analyzed in Section 5.5.2.3.

---

[1]https://oaei.ontologymatching.org/

5.5.2.2 Evolution scenarios

This chapter provides nine scenarios encompassing various modifications ontologies can take during their evolution. Understanding these diverse pathways is crucial for practical ontology engineering and maintenance; thus, by simulating these changes, we aim to capture the variability and complexity that can arise during evolution.

Scenario 1

Approximately 20% of random new concepts are added to the ontology. Newly added concepts must meet the following condition: for every new concept c_{new} incorporated into O_1, there must exist corresponding concepts c_{r1} in C_1 and c_{r2} in C_2, where the alignment between O_1 and O_2, denoted as $Align(O_1, O_2)$, includes the pair (c_{r1}, c_{r2}). Furthermore, the new concept c_{new} should be positioned within a subtree $S = Subtree(O, c_{r1})$, ensuring that the relationship (c_{r1}, c_{new}) is contained within O_1 and that the depth of c_{new} within S is equal to 1.

In this ontology evolution scenario, the process involves adding approximately 20% of random new concepts to the existing ontology, referred to as O_1. However, adding new concepts follows specific conditions to maintain alignment and coherence with another ontology, denoted as O_2, through their corresponding concepts in C_1 and C_2. Alignment between O_1 and O_2 is represented by the set $Align(O_1, O_2)$, which includes pairs of corresponding concepts (c_{r1}, c_{r2}).

For a new concept c_{new} to be incorporated into O_1, it must satisfy two criteria. First, there should exist corresponding concepts c_{r1} in C_1 and c_{r2} in C_2, meaning that the alignment between the two ontologies includes the pair (c_{r1}, c_{r2}). This condition ensures that the new concept aligns with the existing knowledge in O_1 and maintains consistency with O_2.

Second, the new concept c_{new} should be positioned within a subtree S, a subset of O_1 and representing a specific branch of knowledge associated with c_{r1}. This constraint ensures that the relationship (c_{r1}, c_{new}) is contained within O_1, preserving the hierarchical structure and semantic coherence of the ontology. Additionally, the depth of c_{new} within S should equal 1, implying that it is directly connected to c_{r1} and maintains a close relationship within the subtree.

By incorporating new concepts that satisfy these conditions, the ontology evolution aims to expand the knowledge representation while preserving alignment with another ontology and maintaining the ontology's structural integrity and semantic consistency.

Scenario 2

Approximately 20% of new random concepts are incorporated into the ontology, with each concept satisfying the following condition: for every new concept c_{new} added to ontology O_1, there exists a corresponding concept c_{r1} in C_1 and c_{r2} in C_2 where (c_{r1}, c_{r2}) is part of the alignment $Align(O_1, O_2)$. Additionally, the new concept c_{new} is located within a specific subtree $S = Subtree(O, c_{r1})$ such that the relationship (c_{r1}, c_{new}) exists and the depth of c_{new} within S is either 1 or 2.

In this ontology evolution scenario, the objective is to introduce approximately 20% of new random concepts into the existing ontology, denoted as O_1. Each newly added concept, denoted as c_{new}, needs to meet specific criteria to ensure alignment with another ontology, referred to as O_2, through corresponding concepts c_{r1} in C_1 and c_{r2} in C_2.

To be incorporated into O_1, a new concept c_{new} must satisfy two conditions. Firstly, there must be corresponding concepts c_{r1} in C_1 and c_{r2} in C_2 such that the alignment $Align(O_1, O_2)$ includes the pair (c_{r1}, c_{r2}). This condition ensures that the new concept maintains consistency and correspondence between the two ontologies. Secondly, c_{new} should be positioned within a specific subtree, denoted as S, a subset of O_1. This subtree represents a cohesive ontology section associated with the concept c_{r1}. The requirement is that the relationship (c_{r1}, c_{new}) exists within O_1, indicating a connection between the new concept and c_{r1}. Additionally, the depth of c_{new} within S can be either 1 or 2, meaning it can either directly relate to c_{r1} or be connected to a concept one level below c_{r1} within the subtree.

The ontology expands its knowledge representation by incorporating new concepts that fulfil these conditions while maintaining alignment with O_2. This approach ensures that the newly added concepts integrate smoothly into the existing ontology, aligning with the existing knowledge and establishing relationships within specific ontology sections.

Scenario 3

Adding approximately 20% of new concepts to the ontolo O_1 while ensuring the following condition: for each new concept c_{new} added to O_1, there exist corresponding concepts $c_{r1} \in C_1$ and $c_{r2} \in C_2$ in the reference alignment $Align(O_1, O_2)$. Additionally, the new concept c_{new} is located within the subtree $Subtree(O_1, c_{r1})$.

In this ontology evolution scenario, the goal is to introduce approximately 20% of new concepts into the existing ontology O_1. Incorporating these new concepts follows a specific condition to ensure alignment with another ontology O_2 through corresponding concepts c_{r1} in C_1 and c_{r2} in C_2.

Adding a new concept c_{new} to O_1 must meet two important criteria. First, there must be corresponding concepts c_{r1} in C_1 and c_{r2} in C_2 that form part of the reference alignment $Align(O_1, O_2)$. This condition ensures the new concept maintains a coherent connection between the two ontologies. Secondly, the new concept c_{new} should be placed within the subtree $Subtree(O_1, c_{r1})$, which represents a specific section of O_1 associated with the concept c_{r1}.

Following these guidelines, the ontology expands by incorporating new concepts that satisfy the alignment condition and are positioned within the relevant subtree. This approach ensures that the new concepts align with the existing knowledge represented by O_2 and are placed in appropriate sections of O_1 to maintain coherence and consistency within the ontology.

Scenario 4

Adding approximately 20% of randomly selected new concepts to the ontology, subject to the following condition: for every new concept c_{new} added to ontology O_1, there are no corresponding concepts c_{r1} in C_1 and c_{r2} in C_2 such that $(c_{r1}, c_{r2}) \in Align(O_1, O_2)$ and $(c_{new}, c_{r1}) \in Subtree(O_1, c_{r1})$.

In this ontology evolution scenario, precisely the same as in previous scenarios, the objective is to introduce approximately 20% of new concepts into the existing ontology O_1. All new concepts must meet a condition which states that for each new concept c_{new} added to O_1, there should be no corresponding concepts c_{r1} in C_1 and c_{r2} in C_2 such that (c_{r1}, c_{r2}) belongs to the alignment $Align(O_1, O_2)$ and (c_{new}, c_{r1}) exists in the subtree $Subtree(O_1, c_{r1})$.

This condition ensures that the newly added concepts do not have corresponding concepts in the alignment between O_1 and O_2 and do not form part of the existing subtree structure. By imposing this constraint, the intention is to introduce fresh and independent concepts into the ontology that do not duplicate or overlap with the current knowledge represented in the alignment or the subtree. By adhering to this condition, the ontology undergoes expansion with new concepts that bring unique and distinct information. This allows for the enrichment of the ontology with unrelated concepts, thus broadening its scope.

Scenario 5

Including approximately 10% of random new concepts that meet the following requirement: for every new concept c_{new} added to ontology O_1, there exists a corresponding concept c' in the original set of concepts C_1, such that c_{new} is equal to c'.

In this ontology evolution scenario, the goal is to incorporate approximately 10% of randomly selected new concepts into the existing ontology O_1. However, a specific requirement must be met when adding these new concepts.

The requirement states that for each new concept c_{new} added to O_1, there must exist a corresponding concept c' in the original set of concepts C_1 such that c_{new} is equal to c'. In other words, the new concepts introduced are identical to concepts already present in the ontology. By satisfying this requirement, the ontology is expanded with duplicate concepts, effectively increasing the representation of existing knowledge within O_1.

Including such duplicates can serve various purposes, such as providing alternative labels or synonyms for existing concepts, enabling cross-referencing between different parts of the ontology, or accommodating different perspectives or naming conventions within the domain.

Scenario 6

Adding approximately 10% of random new concepts, all of which meet the following condition: for each new concept c_{new} introduced to ontology O_1, there exist corresponding concepts c_{r1} in C_1 and c_{r2} in C_2 such that the pair (c_{r1}, c_{r2}) is aligned in $Align(O_1, O_2)$. Additionally, the new concept c_{new} is located within the subtree $Subtree(O_1, c_{r1})$, and there exists a concept c' in C_2 where c_{new} is equivalent to c'.

In this ontology evolution scenario, the objective is to add approximately 10% new concepts to the existing ontology O_1. For each new concept c_{new} introduced to O_1, there must exist corresponding concepts c_{r1} in the original set of concepts C_1 and c_{r2} in the reference alignment $Align(O_1, O_2)$. This requirement ensures that the pair (c_{r1}, c_{r2}) is aligned in the ontology alignment, indicating a semantic relationship between them.

Additionally, every new concept c_{new} must be positioned within the subtree $Subtree(O_1, c_{r1})$, implying that it is a part of the existing knowledge structure and inherits the hierarchical relationships of c_{r1}. Furthermore, a concept c' must exist in the second ontology O_2 where c_{new} is equivalent to c'. This equivalence between c_{new} and c' suggests that they represent the same underlying concept but may have different labels or terms in the respective ontologies, ensuring that c_{new} is integrated into the ontology coherently.

Scenario 7

Approximately 5% of concepts are removed randomly from ontology O_1 in a way that ensures each removed concept c_{rem} satisfies the following condition: there exist corresponding concepts c_{r1} in C_1 and c_{r2} in C_2 such that they are aligned in $Align(O_1, O_2)$, and c_{rem} is located within the subtree $Subtree(O_1, c_{r1})$ of c_{r1}.

In this scenario of ontology evolution, we randomly remove approximately 5% of concepts from ontology O_1. The selection for removal adheres to a precise criterion: for each concept c_{rem} to be removed, corresponding concepts c_{r1} in C_1 and c_{r2} in C_2 must exist. These corresponding concepts should be aligned within $Align(O_1, O_2)$, ensuring that c_{rem} resides within the subtree $Subtree(O_1, c_{r1})$ rooted at c_{r1}.

This criterion guarantees that the removed concept c_{rem} belongs to the hierarchical organization under c_{r1}, thereby preserving the semantic relationships and structural coherence within that ontology section. This approach maintains the integrity and cohesiveness of the ontology's knowledge framework by carefully selecting c_{rem} for removal from O_1.

Scenario 8

Approximately 5% of concepts are removed randomly from the ontology, ensuring that each removed concept c_{rem} from ontology O_1 meets the following condition: there exist corresponding concepts c_{r1} in C_1 and c_{r2} in C_2 such that the pair (c_{r1}, c_{r2}) is aligned in $Align(O_1, O_2)$, and $\phi(O_1, c_{r1})$ attains its maximum value.

In the given scenario, the ontology O_1 is subjected to the removal of approximately 5% of its concepts. However, the removal process is not arbitrary but follows a specific criterion to preserve the ontology structure's most valuable and well-connected concepts.

Certain conditions must be satisfied for each concept c_{rem} that is removed from ontology O_1. First, there must exist corresponding concepts c_{r1} in C_1 and c_{r2} in C_2 such that the pair (c_{r1}, c_{r2}) is aligned in the alignment $Align(O_1, O_2)$, which ensures that there is a semantic correspondence between the concepts being removed and concepts in the reference ontology. Additionally, the concept c_{r1} is selected based on its knowledge potential $\phi(O_1, c_{r1})$ – the objective is to identify the concept with the maximum knowledge potential value within the ontology O_1.

Scenario 9

Two concepts and their subtrees are removed from the ontology, where each removed concept c_{rem} has corresponding concepts $c_{r1} \in C_1$ and $c_{r2} \in C_2$ in the reference alignment $Align(O_1, O_2)$. The chosen concepts for removal are those with the maximal local similarity $\phi(O_1, c_{r1})$.

The knowledge potential, denoted by $\phi(O_1, c_{r1})$, refers to the measure of the potential knowledge or significance associated with a given concept c_{r1} within the ontology O_1. By ensuring that the removed concepts meet these conditions, we guarantee they have direct counterparts in O_2 and are aligned with them in the reference alignment.

The condition of selecting concepts with the maximum knowledge potential, as measured by $\phi(O_1, c_{r1})$, implies that the removed concepts possess the highest potential knowledge or significance within the ontology O_1. These concepts are highly informative and crucial for knowledge representation and integration. Thus, their removal may significantly impact the overall alignment quality and knowledge coherence between the ontologies.

5.5.2.3   Result analysis

This part of the book analyses the experiment outcomes detailed in Section 5.5.2.1. Table 5.2 provides raw data collected during the procedure.

The experimental results have been statistically analyzed, with a significance level of $\alpha = 0.05$ chosen for hypothesis testing. The objective was to investigate the correlation between the Δ values and the percentages of changes introduced in the ontologies. The changes were quantified by calculating the ratio of added/removed concepts to the total number of concepts in the initial state of each ontology. For additions, the score was multiplied by 100%, and for removals, it was multiplied by -100%.

Initially, we checked the samples for a normal distribution but rejected the appropriate hypothesis, which allows us to claim that the data did not follow a normal distribution. Consequently, we calculated Spearman's rank correlation coefficient, obtaining a value of 0.603969, with an associated p-value extremely low ($1.13e^{-15}$). These results demonstrate a moderate positive correlation between the Δ value and the percentage of changes applied to the ontologies. This correlation affirms the initial assumption's validity and confirms that modifications in the ontologies and their mappings significantly influence the assessment of knowledge increase.

The results presented in Table 5.2 (initially published in [118]) provide valuable insights into the effectiveness of the Δ measure in capturing knowledge changes resulting from the applied evolution scenarios. The intuitive nature of the Δ values demonstrates its ability to reflect the expected outcomes of each scenario.

The results presented in Table 5.2, initially published in [118], offer valuable insights into the efficacy of the Δ measure for detecting changes in knowledge about ontology interoperability arising from various evolution scenarios. The Δ measure's intuitiveness is evident in its capacity to accurately mirror the anticipated results of each scenario, thereby demonstrating its practical utility.

In scenarios where knowledge growth was expected (Scenarios 1, 2, 3, and 5), the Δ values indicate increased knowledge, which suggests that the addition of new concepts, aligned with corresponding concepts in the reference ontology, contributes to the enrichment of knowledge within the ontologies. Conversely, in scenarios involving the removal of concepts (Scenarios 7, 8, and 9), the negative Δ values accurately capture the decrease in knowledge resulting from eliminating relevant concepts.

Scenarios 4 and 6 were particularly interesting as they presented more complex dynamics. In Scenario 4, the added concepts did not lead to a noticeable increase in knowledge, as they were incorporated in a way that did not significantly affect the overall structure and interconnectedness of the ontology. Similarly, in Scenario 6, although concepts were copied between ontologies, the resulting similarity did not translate into a significant knowledge increase, emphasizing the importance of expressive conceptual additions rather than mere duplication.

TABLE 5.2

The results of the experiment

No	Scenario								
	1	2	3	4	5	6	7	8	9
1	12.88	21.24	29.79	-8.87	-2.06	4.05	-0.14	-3.72	-65.12
2	1.23	56.55	7.92	-10.98	17.33	-9.52	-9.32	8.06	-8.90
3	-0.20	47.95	11.04	-13.08	6.36	9.43	21.15	-6.55	-5.13
4	-1.74	28.57	20.81	-12.70	2.65	-23.79	-35.60	-28.15	-32.22
5	20.99	36.45	50.44	-16.07	65.10	39.28	-22.57	-13.45	-36.15
6	64.00	29.41	120.68	-21.53	24.00	-3.53	-100.00	-36.10	-81.65
7	13.66	32.80	33.37	-20.44	105.03	87.40	-13.73	-4.05	-46.90
8	-3.44	60.52	4.01	-12.18	34.02	23.75	-9.23	-4.45	-16.79
9	17.68	33.62	47.12	-28.88	28.65	0.35	-49.24	-4.91	-88.02
10	6.97	50.00	21.44	-21.84	10.35	-3.06	-13.23	-5.63	-50.68

While most of the calculated Δ values align with our expectations, it is essential to note the limitations of the measure. Single or insignificant changes may not substantially impact the Δ values, making it difficult to determine the direction of change solely based on these values. Therefore, it is crucial to consider the context and significance of modifications when interpreting Δ results, enabling a comprehensive understanding of knowledge evolution in ontologies.

The findings highlight the effectiveness of the Δ measure in capturing the overall knowledge change in the ontologies. They also emphasize the need for considering the magnitude and significance of modifications to accurately interpret Δ values and conclude the direction of knowledge change. In summary, most of the Δ values align with our expectations, reflecting the anticipated knowledge increase or decrease in ontology alignments.

5.6 Conclusions

This chapter explores various aspects of managing ontology evolution and versioning in maintaining ontology alignment. It provides insights into handling changes in ontologies, measuring their significance, updating ontology alignments, and methods for measuring the increase of knowledge about ontology interoperability.

While some of the elements discussed in this chapter may have already been presented in the author's previous works, there are also new and original elements that have been introduced here:

- Section 5.2 focuses on managing the change history of ontologies. It discusses the importance of recording and tracking ontological changes over time. The research fundamentals have been previously published in [114], and the formal definitions have been extensively reviewed and consolidated with more recent advances.

- The subsequent Section 5.3 focuses on the subject of measuring the significance of change in evolving ontologies. It provides methodologies for evaluating the importance of modifications at different levels of ontologies, such as concepts, relations, and instances. These methods serve as criteria for triggering the utilization of algorithms that validate and potentially update ontology alignments to ensure their coherence with the evolved ontologies. The initial work has been outlined in [115], but this book provides a more cohesive approach to this task.

- In Section 5.4, the book explores updating ontology alignments in the light of ontology evolution. It discusses strategies and techniques (partially published in [116], [117], [119]) for realigning ontologies after their evolution. It includes updating alignments at the concept, relation, and instance levels, ensuring that the mappings between ontologies remain consistent, accurate, and up-to-date.

- Section 5.5 delves into methods for quantifying the increase in knowledge regarding ontology interoperability, which have been presented in their initial form in [118]. This part of the chapter introduces a measure that calculates the degree to which knowledge about the interoperability between two ontologies has changed due to the evolution of ontologies and their alignment. This measure is a valuable tool for assessing the impact of ontology updates on the overall understanding of compatibility between ontologies. Therefore, it provides invaluable insights into the effectiveness of alignment maintenance efforts.

The methods discussed in this chapter provide a systematic approach to dealing with ontology evolution in the context of ontology alignment. These methods ensure that the alignment remains accurate and up-to-date by addressing different scenarios and considering the ontological changes.

The complexity of the provided algorithms is influenced by several factors, including the size of the ontologies, the number of changes that occur, and the specific matching and evaluation techniques employed. In situations where the number of changes is significant, ontology alignment maintenance algorithms may become impractical or too time-consuming to run.

It is important to note that these algorithms are not intended to create new alignments from scratch. The main strength of these algorithms lies in their ability to maintain alignments when the changes made to the ontologies are relatively small compared to the overall size of the involved ontologies.

6

Advanced methods of assessing ontology alignment

As shown in Chapters 3, 4, and 5 designating new alignments between ontologies or maintaining existing ones are both complex tasks. The former is computationally expensive, and different solutions may yield multiple competitive ontology alignments. Latter involves modifying existing mappings, which may lead to breaking already established correspondences.

In this context, developing a robust evaluation mechanism for ontology alignment is essential. The well-known approach (used earlier in this book) to this task uses the methodology proposed by the Ontology Alignment Evaluation Initiative (OAEI), which is a non-profit organization that, since 2004, has hosted annual campaigns evaluating ontology matching technologies. These campaigns utilize a structured dataset comprising various ontologies categorized into thematic groups—or "tracks"—accompanied by predetermined reference alignments, deemed the standard for correctness. The evaluation process involves comparing participant-generated alignments against these reference standards to derive traditional metrics such as Precision, Recall, and F1-measure, facilitating a quantitative assessment of alignment quality.

However, the reliance on predefined reference alignments is a significant constraint of the OAEI methodology, particularly when considering the application of ontologies in real-world scenarios where such alignments are typically unavailable. This limitation complicates objective evaluation and selection of the most appropriate alignment among several candidates, as the absence of a reference standard prevents the assessment. Moreover, if a reference alignment exists, new ones would not be needed.

The above considerations underscore the need for innovative evaluation strategies, which should be capable of assessing ontology alignment quality autonomously. In this chapter, such a framework is proposed. It does not require pre-existing reference alignments and relies solely on the knowledge within the aligned ontologies.

6.1 Content-based methods of assessing ontology alignment quality

In practical scenarios where one needs to align two ontologies, numerous methods are available, each yielding varying results. The apparent absence of a reference alignment poses a significant challenge, as it leaves a fundamental question unanswered: how does a system architect or researcher determine the best alignment when no reference alignment allows for calculating metrics like Precision and Recall? These metrics are relatively straightforward to compute and interpret, but can only be computed in situations with a reference alignment available. In the opposite situation, the mappings must be evaluated based solely on the content of the ontologies.

DOI: 10.1201/9781003437888-6

As defined by Equation 2.1, the concepts' taxonomy characterizes concepts and, in consequence, their instances. Let us consider an ontology, with some general concepts on top of the hierarchy tree. These top-level concepts represent high levels of abstraction, providing a general framework for understanding various elements within the ontology. As one navigates deeper into the ontology, more specific subclasses and concepts are encountered, each offering a finer level of detail and granularity. They represent a more intricate understanding of a particular domain, which implies that the knowledge associated with these concepts is more detailed and contextually rich.

This observation forms the basis for our approach to assessing ontology mappings. We claim that mappings of concepts located lower in the hierarchy carry greater significance - they represent connections between highly specialized and detailed concepts in the ontologies. In contrast, mappings involving high-level, more general concepts capture more general, less informative connections, which may be less valuable in practical applications.

Based on the above remarks, we introduce two functions (further described and formally defined in Section 6.1.1) that can serve as criteria for assessing ontology alignments, both based on the depth of the mapped concepts:

1. **A function $\Lambda_C : \tilde{O} \times \tilde{O} \times \widetilde{AL_C} \rightarrow \mathbb{R}^+$ for assessing ontology mappings at the concept level based on depth of mapped concepts.** It calculates a real value that reflects the degree to which the aligned concepts are deep within the ontologies. Higher values of Λ_C indicate that the mappings connect concepts placed deeper in the hierarchy, signifying a more detailed and specialized alignment. Conversely, lower values suggest that the mappings involve more general and less specific concepts.

2. **A function $\Lambda_I : \tilde{O} \times \tilde{O} \times \widetilde{AL_I} \rightarrow \mathbb{R}^+$ for assessing ontology mappings at the instance level based on the depth of their classes.** Similar to Λ_C, Λ_I considers the classes' depth but does so on the instance level. It calculates a real value, which indicates whether the mapped instances are associated with concepts deep within the ontology hierarchy. Higher values of Λ_I signify that the mapped instances are connected to more specialized and detailed concepts. In comparison, lower values suggest mappings involving instances associated with broader and less specific concepts.

The second factor influencing concepts and instances is their relationships with other concepts and instances. This is especially visible when analyzing the concept's hierarchy. A significant observation is that when ontology alignments include mappings of concepts located within the same subtree of their taxonomy (in other words – with a high level of continuity between them), they are more accurate and provide more meaningful interpretation. From the user's perspective, having a smaller, focused alignment is usually more valuable than a set of mappings involving unrelated classes across entire ontologies. Such alignment provides a clear view of the connections between concepts and instances and, consequently, is easier to understand, manage, and utilize.

Based on these considerations, we introduce two additional functions (described and defined in Section 6.1.2) for assessing ontology alignments that leverage the continuity of mapped classes:

1. **A function $\Gamma_C : \tilde{O} \times \tilde{O} \times \widetilde{AL_C} \rightarrow \mathbb{R}^+$ for assessing ontology mappings on the concept level based on continuity of mapped concepts.** When applied, Γ_C calculates a numerical value that quantifies the level of continuity among the mapped concepts. Higher values of Γ_C indicate that the mapped concepts are logically connected, forming a cohesive area within the ontology hierarchy. On the other hand, lower values of Γ_C imply that the evaluated alignment contains mappings of concepts dispersed throughout whole ontologies.

2. **A function $\Gamma_I : \tilde{O} \times \tilde{O} \times \widetilde{AL_I} \to \mathbb{R}^+$ for assessing ontology mappings on the instance level based on instance continuity.** Similar to Γ_C, Γ_I calculates a numerical value, reflecting the level of continuity of mapped instances. Higher values of Γ_I indicate that the mappings connect more instances belonging to the same concepts, while lower values indicate that the assessed alignment is a set of random, scattered mappings.

The four functions Λ_C, Λ_I, Γ_C, and Γ_I that will be described in this chapter form a novel approach to evaluating the quality of ontology alignments based only on the content of the aligned ontologies. What sets them apart is their independence from any pre-existing reference alignments. They provide a holistic evaluation of alignment quality, surpassing the limitations of traditional metrics such as Precision and Recall, which becomes particularly invaluable in real-world applications.

6.1.1 Assessing Ontology Mappings via Concept Depth

This section of the book focuses on two approaches to evaluating ontology alignments by examining the depth of mapped concepts: Λ_C assesses the quality of concept-level mappings, while Λ_I evaluates instance mappings. Notably, Λ_I takes into account that an instance can be associated with multiple concepts and, therefore, represents multiple objects from the ontology domain. By doing so it is able to incorporate the information about concept depths.

All of the methods proposed in this section utilize a function γ_D, which assigns a scoring to a given mapping $\langle c_1, c_2 \rangle$ based on the depths of c_1 and c_2. For two (A, V)-based ontologies $O_1 = (C_1, H_1, R^{C_1}, I_1, R^{I_1})$ and $O_2 = (C_2, H_2, R^{C_2}, I_2, R^{I_2})$ and the alignment $Align_C(O_1, O_2)$ (defined according to Definition 2.13) it has the following signature:

$$\gamma_D : \tilde{O} \times \tilde{O} \times \widetilde{AL_C} \times Align_C(O_1, O_2) \to \mathbb{R}^+ \tag{6.1}$$

The function must meet the following postulate:

- **P1.** $\gamma_D(O_1, O_2, Align_C(O_1, O_2), \langle c_1, c_2 \rangle) \geq \gamma_D(O_1, O_2, Align_C(O_1, O_2), \langle c_1', c_2' \rangle) \iff Depth(c_1, O_1) \geq Depth(c_1', O_1) \vee Depth(c_2, O_2) \geq Depth(c_2', O_2) \iff$

The given postulate states that for two different alignments of concepts taken from two independent ontologies, the value of γ_D should be higher for mapping concepts placed deeper within the hierarchy. Utilizing Definition 2.19 of inconsistent mappings (denoted with a symbol $\not\sim$), the function γ_D takes a concept pair $\langle c_1', c_2' \rangle \in C_1 \times C_2$ and yields a positive real number. It is defined below:

$$\gamma_D(O_1, O_2, Align_C(O_1, O_2), \langle c_1, c_2 \rangle) =$$
$$\begin{cases} 0 & \text{if } \langle c_1, c_2 \rangle \not\sim Align_C(O_1, O_2) \\ \frac{1}{Depth(O_1) - Depth(H_1, c_1) + 1} + \frac{1}{Depth(O_2) - Depth(H_2, c_2) + 1} & \text{otherwise} \end{cases}$$
$$\tag{6.2}$$

The function γ_D, as defined above, assigns a score to a pair of mapped concepts $\langle c_1, c_2 \rangle$ between two ontologies O_1 and O_2 based on their depth within their respective hierarchies. The function operates under two conditions:

- If the concept pair $\langle c_1, c_2 \rangle$ is deemed inconsistent with the alignment $Align_C(O_1, O_2)$, γ_D returns a value of 0, indicating no contribution to the alignment score from this pair due to inconsistency.

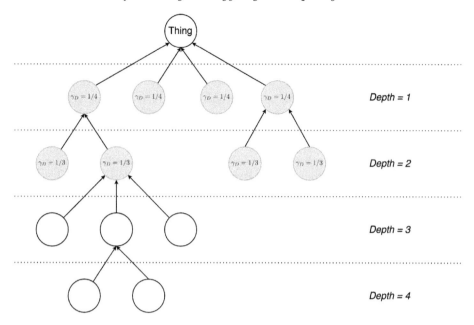

FIGURE 6.1
Example values of γ_D for concepts from single ontology

- Otherwise, it calculates the score as the sum of the inverses of the adjusted depth differences for each concept in its ontology. The adjusted depth difference is given by the total depth of the ontology minus the depth of the concept in question plus one. This adjustment ensures that deeper concepts contribute a higher score to the alignment evaluation, reflecting the intuition that deeper concepts are more specific and their correct alignment indicates a more semantically meaningful correspondence.

The postulate **P1** states that the value of γ_D for a pair of concepts is greater or equal to that for another pair if at least one of the concepts in the first pair is deeper (or at the same depth) in its respective ontology hierarchy than its counterpart in the second pair. It is caused by the fact that the γ_D formula assigns higher scores to concepts located deeper in the ontology due to the inverse relationship between the score and the adjusted depth difference. Deeper concepts reduce the denominator in the formula, resulting in a larger overall score. Therefore, the function γ_D satisfies postulate **P1**.

Figure 6.1 shows the exemplary values of γ_D through a visual representation of a part of a source ontology included in an alignment. Grey circles represent the concepts that have been successfully mapped to the corresponding concepts in a target ontology. The specific details of the target ontology are not crucial for illustrating the main idea of γ_D; the figure mainly demonstrates how the depth-based scoring function applies in the context of evaluating ontology alignment.

With a method for evaluating a single mapping using the function γ_D, extending this evaluation to encompass every mapping within a specific alignment $Align_C(O_1, O_2)$ becomes a simple procedure. The proposed approach entails applying γ_D to each mapping contained within the alignment.

Definition 6.1 *A method for evaluating ontology alignment on the concept level based on depth of mapped concepts is a function with a signature* $\Lambda_C : \widetilde{O} \times \widetilde{O} \times \widetilde{AL_C} \to \mathbb{R}^+$ *defined* as:

$$\Lambda_C(O_1, O_2, Align_C(O_1, O_2)) = \sum_{\langle c_1, c_2 \rangle \in Align_C(O_1, O_2)} \gamma_D(O_1, O_2, Align_C(O_1, O_2), \langle c_1, c_2 \rangle)$$

(6.3)

The presented method allows for a comprehensive and consistent assessment of the concept alignment by iterating through all the mappings. In Figure 6.1, the overall value of Λ_C scored by the presented alignment and calculated based on partial values of γ_D, equals 2.34.

Adapting Λ_C to operate at the instance level is relatively uncomplicated. This adaptation can be accomplished using the Ins^{-1} function defined in Equation 2.14. This function inputs a specific instance identifier, represented by the symbol i. In response, it returns a set of concepts retrieved from a specified ontology in which this particular instance identifier, i, has been applied.

Definition 6.2 *A method for evaluating ontology alignment on the instance level based on depth of their concepts is a function with a signature* $\Lambda_I : \widetilde{O} \times \widetilde{O} \times \widetilde{AL}_I \times \widetilde{AL}_C \to \mathbb{R}^+$ *defined as:*

$$\Lambda_I(O_1, O_2, Align_I(O_1, O_2), Align_C(O_1, O_2)) =$$

$$\sum_{\langle i_1, i_2 \rangle \in Align_I(O_1, O_2)}$$

(6.4)

$$\max_{\langle c_1, c_2 \rangle \in (Ins^{-1}(c_1, O_1) \times Ins^{-1}(c_2, O_2)) \cap Align_C(O_1, O_2)}$$

$$\gamma_D(O_1, O_2, Align_C(O_1, O_2), \langle c_1, c_2 \rangle)$$

The function Λ_I Λ_I takes four main inputs: two ontologies, O_1 and O_2, and two alignments, $Align_I(O_1, O_2)$ and $Align_C(O_1, O_2)$. Its goal is to compute a real-valued score that reflects the alignment quality of instances $Align_I(O_1, O_2)$ by considering the depth of their concepts.

Λ_I begins by iterating over pairs of instances, denoted as $\langle i_1, i_2 \rangle$, within the instance alignment $Align_I(O_1, O_2)$. For each instance pair $\langle i_1, i_2 \rangle$, the function iterates over pairs of concepts, denoted as $\langle c_1, c_2 \rangle$. These concepts are drawn from the sets of concepts to which instances i_1 and i_2 belong (using the function Ins^{-1} from Equation 2.14). This forms a Cartesian product of concept sets restricted to those pairs $\langle c_1, c_2 \rangle$ that are also present in the alignment $Align_C(O_1, O_2)$. Within the set of $\langle c_1, c_2 \rangle$ pairs, the function identifies the pair with the highest value of γ_D, which measures the depth-based relevance and quality of the concept mapping between O_1 and O_2. The function Λ_I calculates and accumulates the γ_D scores for the selected $\langle c_1, c_2 \rangle$ pairs. The sum of all these individual scores is the final result returned by Λ_I.

Figure 6.2 shows example scores assigned to instances of concepts within a specific ontology. Small grey circles illustrate instances successfully mapped to corresponding instances in another ontology, with their encompassing concepts represented as white circles around the grey ones. The figure also shows the accumulated values of γ_D, indicating depth-based scores for each group of instances.

In this section, we introduced two methods, Λ_C and Λ_I, which assess the quality of ontology alignments. These methods analyze alignments by evaluating the depth of corresponding concepts, enabling a detailed examination at both the concept and instance levels. By focusing on the depth within the ontology, both measures ensure that the

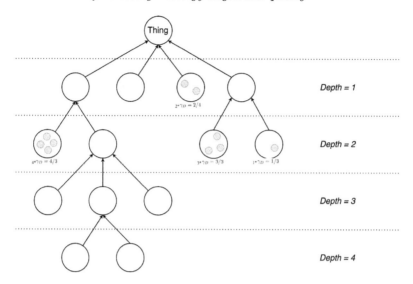

FIGURE 6.2
Example calculation of partial γ_D for instances' concepts

evaluation is not only about whether concepts and instances align but also how these alignments reflect the conceptual hierarchy and interconnectedness of the domains.

6.1.2   Continuity Based Methods For Assessing Ontology Mappings

This section of the book is devoted to assessing ontology alignment based on the continuity of concepts. When some ontology alignment contains mappings of concepts that have no apparent connection, the alignment may appear disorganized and chaotic, suggesting that its content has been created accidentally.

An example of this situation occurs when two distinct entities share the same names, creating homonyms. In such cases, if the shared name is the sole common attribute between these entities, it becomes unlikely that their parent and child concepts would be logically mapped together. Consequently, the mapping between them appears coincidental at best. On the contrary, one can reasonably expect higher accuracy and precision in ontology alignments, where mappings involve concepts that are part of the same taxonomic subtrees or hierarchies.

These observations have inspired the development of two functions, namely Γ_C and Γ_I, designed to evaluate the mappings of concepts and instances by assigning scores to groups of concepts that form coherent subtrees within ontologies.

Initially, we must define a method to generate a collection of subtrees within a given ontology, denoted as $O = (C, R^C, I, R^I, H)$. In this context, subtrees are sets of concepts sharing a common ancestor within the concept hierarchy represented by H. To achieve this, we have defined a function called $subtrees_O(O)$ as follows:

$$subtrees_O(O) = \{subtree \in 2^C \mid \exists c' \in C, \forall c \in subtree : (c, c') \in H\} \qquad (6.5)$$

Essentially, the above function returns a collection of subsets from the set of concepts C. A subset qualifies as a subtree of H if, for every concept within that subset, denoted as c, there exists a common ancestor, represented as r, within the concept hierarchy H. In other words, all concepts in a specific subset share a common ancestor in the ontology's hierarchy.

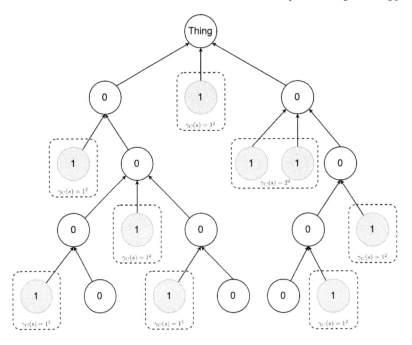

FIGURE 6.3
Example values of γ_C for concepts from single ontology

An individual item s from the set provided by the function $subtrees_O(O)$ can be assigned a rating using the following approach:

$$\gamma_C(s) = |s|^2 \tag{6.6}$$

The function computes the rating by squaring the number of elements in the given subtree. Consequently, the larger the subset s, the higher the rating it receives, emphasizing the continuity of specific subtrees within the ontology's hierarchy.

For an illustration of the function γ_C's applicability, please see Figures 6.3 and 6.4. Assume that the grey-highlighted concepts on both figures are parts of two distinct, competing alignments – these concepts form different subtrees, delineated by dotted lines around some selected concepts. With the scoring function γ_C in mind, it becomes relatively straightforward to devise a method, Γ_C, which calculates the overall alignment scores by summing the values of γ_C for subtrees formed by concepts from the two compared alignments.

Building upon this concept, we see that the alignment in Figure 6.3 scores lower, achieving an overall score of 11, whereas the alignment in Figure 6.4 secures a significantly higher score of 49. This difference highlights the critical role of evaluating alignments not by the number of mappings but by analyzing coherence, depth, and semantic relatedness among mapped concepts, as measured by γ_C. Thus, although the alignment in Figure 6.3 may contain a higher number of mappings, it is considered less effective than the one in Figure 6.4, which demonstrates a more prominent continuity among the concepts involved.

Definition 6.3 *A method for evaluating ontology alignment on the concept level based on continuity of mapped concepts can be defined as a function* Γ_C *with a signature* $\Gamma_C : \tilde{O} \times \tilde{O} \times \tilde{A} \to \mathbb{N}$. *It calculates the value of the scoring function* γ_C *for every subtree formed by*

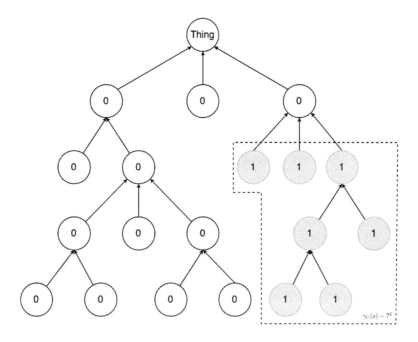

FIGURE 6.4
Example calculation of Γ_C for concepts from single ontology

concepts participating in the evaluated alignment in both ontologies:

$$\Gamma_C(O_1, O_2, Align_C(O_1, O_2)) =$$
$$\sum_{s \in subtrees_O^A(O_1, Align_C(O_1, O_2))} \gamma_C(s) + \sum_{s \in subtrees_O^A(O_2, Align_C(O_1, O_2))} \gamma_C(s) \quad (6.7)$$

The helper function $subtrees_O^A$, used in Equation 6.7, modifies the $subtrees_O(O)$ function from Equation 6.5 to select subtrees from the ontology O that are part of the alignment $Align_C(O_1, O_2)$. This function aims to ensure that it does not return subtrees that overlap; in other words, it avoids returning smaller subtrees that are subsets of larger subtrees also included in the set. An auxiliary function $subtrees_O^{A+}$ is introduced, generating a set of potentially overlapping, redundant subtrees without considering the exclusion criteria.

$$subtrees_O^{A+}(O_1, Align_C(O_1, O_2)) =$$
$$\{subtree \in subtrees_O(O_1) \mid \forall c_1 \in subtree \, \exists c_2 \in C_2 : (c_1, c_2) \in Align_C(O_1, O_2)\} \quad (6.8)$$

Based on the above function, it is possible to define the expected function $subtrees_O^A$ which refines the output of $subtrees_O^{A+}$:

$$subtrees_O^A(O_1, Align_C(O_1, O_2)) =$$
$$\{s \in subtrees_O^{A+}(O_1) \mid \neg \exists s' \in subtrees_O^{A+}(O_1) : s \subset s'\} \quad (6.9)$$

After generating the initial set of subtrees with $subtrees_O^{A+}(O_1)$, the function $subtrees_O^A$ actively filters this collection to exclude any subtrees that overlap or are redundant. It examines each subtree s from the collection produced by $subtrees_O^A + (O_1)$ to determine if another subtree s' in the collection encompasses s. If it finds such a superset s', indicating that s forms part of a larger subtree s', the function discards s. This filtering process ensures that $subtrees_O^A$'s final output includes no overlapping or redundant subtrees.

The most difficult step in the presented method is finding the largest subtrees formed by concepts in the given alignment. In other words – how to determine the output of the function $subtrees_O^A$, further used to compute the expected value of Γ_C. To overcome this issue, we have developed the imperative procedure described in Algorithm 21. The algorithm takes as input two ontologies: $O_1 = (C_1, H_1, R^{C_1}, I_1, R^{I_1})$ and $O_2 = (C_2, H_2, R^{C_2}, I_2, R^{I_2})$, together with their alignment at concept level, $Align_C(O_1, O_2)$. The algorithm proceeds in the following steps:

- It starts by calculating the continuity scores for both O_1 and O_2, referred to as CS_1 and CS_2, respectively. These scores are computed using an auxiliary subprocedure called GETCONTINUITYSCORE.

- The subprocedure GETCONTINUITYSCORE, used in the computation, takes as input the alignment $Align_C(O_1, O_2)$, one of the processed ontologies O, a set of concepts from that ontology, and a boolean flag $isRoot$ indicating whether the yielded concepts are direct descendants of the ontology's root.

- The subprocedure initializes an empty set t to keep track of concepts with consistent mappings within $Align_C(O_1, O_2)$ and forming a subtree with other elements of t. It also initializes a variable CS set to 0, accumulating partial continuity scores.

Algorithm 21 Procedure for calculating values of Γ_C

Input: O_1, O_2, $Align_C(O_1, O_2)$
Output: Γ_C
1:   $CS_1 :=$ GETCONTINUITYSCORE $(Align_C(O_1, O_2), O_1, Root(O_1), true)$
2:   $CS_2 :=$ GETCONTINUITYSCORE $(Align_C(O_1, O_2), O_2, Root(O_2), true)$
3:   $\Gamma_C := CS_1 + CS_2$
4:   **return** Γ_C
5:   **procedure** GETCONTINUITYSCORE($Align_C(O_1, O_2), O, conceptList, isRoot$)
6:     $t := \emptyset$
7:     $CS := 0$
8:     **for all** $concept \in conceptList$ **do**
9:       $cs :=$ GETCONTINUITYSCORE($Align_C(O_1, O_2), O, Sub_D(O, concept), false$)
10:      **if** $\exists \langle c, c' \rangle \in Align_C(O_1, O_2) : (concept \in \{c, c'\}) \wedge \langle c, c' \rangle \sim Align_C(O_1, O_2)$ **then**
11:        $t := t \cup \{concept\} \cup cs[0]$
12:        $CS := CS + cs[1]$
13:      **else**
14:        $CS := CS + cs[1] + \gamma_C(cs[0])$
15:      **end if**
16:     **end for**
17:     **if** $isRoot$ **then**
18:       **return** $CS + \gamma_C(t)$
19:     **else**
20:       **return** (t, CS)
21:     **end if**
22: **end procedure**

- For each *concept* from the provided set of concepts and its descendants, the subprocedure recursively calls itself and stores the partial output in the variable *cs*.

- If a consistent mapping $\langle c, c' \rangle$ exists in $Align_C(O_1, O_2)$ where *concept* = *c* or *concept* = *c'*, the subprocedure incorporates *concept* and the result of its recursive call into the set *t*. It also increments the partial continuity score CS by the points accrued from the previously completed subtrees of *concept*'s ancestors. If no such mapping exists, the procedure marks the subtree as fully traversed and scored, increasing the partial CS value by the sum of collected scores and those computed for its ancestors.

- The GETCONTINUITYSCORE subprocedure either returns a single continuity score when called with a truthy value of the *isRoot* flag or outputs a pair that includes a set of concepts from O forming a subtree with the given one and a partial continuity score.

- The algorithm calculates the final continuity score value, Γ_C, by adding CS_1 and CS_2 together and then returns this sum as the output of the entire procedure.

Having discussed the evaluation of ontology alignment at the concept level, we now focus on assessing the alignment at the instance level. As defined in Equation 2.10, concepts are instantiated as instances. Thus, while concepts serve as organizational elements that categorize instances based on shared characteristics at different specificity levels, instances lack inherent meaning and gain semantic value only within the context of specific concepts.

Therefore, evaluating ontology alignments at the instance level must navigate the described duality. The measure proposed next, Γ_I, aims to address this complex interplay by offering a comprehensive evaluation of alignment quality. Section 2.3 defines, through Equations 2.32 and 2.33, the instance level alignment of ontologies O_1 and O_2 (denoted as $Align_I(O_1, O_2)$) as a collection of instance alignments corresponding to already aligned concepts. Each element of $Align_I(O_1, O_2)$, a set $AL_{O_1,O_2}(c_1, c_2)$, encompasses mappings of instances between concepts c_1 and c_2. The method assigns a rating to each $AL_{O_1,O_2}(c_1, c_2)$ within the context of a specific concept c as follows:

$$\gamma_I(AL_{O_1,O_2}(c_1, c_2), c) = \left| \{i \in c \mid \exists (i_1, i_2) \in AL_{O_1,O_2}(c_1, c_2) : i = i_1 \vee i = i_2 \} \right|^2 \quad (6.10)$$

The function γ_I calculates its value from the count of unique instances i in concept c included in the instance-level alignment $AL_{O_1,O_2}(c_1, c_2)$. By squaring this number to accentuate differences, the function ensures that alignments with more matching instances receive a higher rating.

For a visual representation of this concept, refer to Figures 6.5 and 6.6. Each figure depicts the same ontology involved in two distinct alignments. Here, instances and their corresponding concepts appear as small circles within larger ones, with grey circles indicating instances included in an alignment. Beneath each concept with mapped instances, the corresponding value of γ_I appears, illustrating the function's application.

Figure 6.5 shows that, at most, two instances from the same class map to each other, revealing a somewhat scattered alignment. Summing all individual values of γ_I, we obtain an overall ranking of 26. On the other hand, Figure 6.6 displays an alignment where all instances of several concepts are comprehensively mapped, with the sum of γ_I values reaching 53.

The preference for the alignment in Figure 6.6 originates from its enhanced usability from a user's perspective. Although this alignment might be smaller in size, it offers greater value. Since aligning different ontologies aims to augment specialist knowledge, the focused alignment in Figure 6.6 serves as a more effective tool for knowledge integration, capturing the intricacies of the ontology domain more accurately. In other words, the quality of an ontology alignment should be evaluated not merely by the number of mappings but by the meaningfulness and specificity of those mappings. This perspective is the base rationale for defining γ_I.

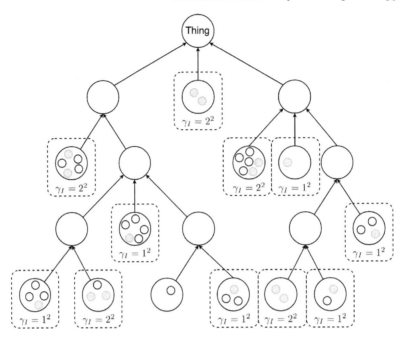

FIGURE 6.5
Example calculation of Γ_I for instances from single ontology

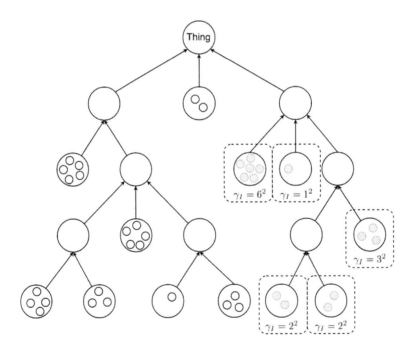

FIGURE 6.6
Example calculation of Γ_I for instances from single ontology

Definition 6.4 *A method for assessing ontology mappings on the instance level based on instance continuity* is a function Γ_I with a signature $\Gamma_I : \tilde{O} \times \tilde{O} \times \widetilde{AL}_I \to \mathbb{N}$ defined as a sum of each concept pair's instance-level alignment rating:

$$\Gamma_I(O_1, O_2, Align_I(O_1, O_2)) =$$
$$\sum_{(c_1, c_2) \in C_1 \times C_2} \left(\gamma_I(AL_{O_1, O_2}(c_1, c_2), c_1) + \gamma_I(AL_{O_1, O_2}(c_1, c_2), c_2) \right) \qquad (6.11)$$

Algorithm 22 Procedure for calculating values of Γ_I

Input: $O_1, O_2, Align_I(O_1, O_2)$
Output: Γ_I
1: $\Gamma_I := 0$
2: **for all** $c_1, c_2 \in C_1 \times C_2$ **do**
3:      **if** $AL_{O_1, O_2}(c_1, c_2) \in Align_I(O_1, O_2)$ **then**
4:          $\gamma_1 := \gamma_I(AL_{O_1, O_2}(c_1, c_2), c_1)$
5:          $\gamma^2 := \gamma_I(AL_{O_1, O_2}(c_1, c_2), c_2)$
6:          $\Gamma^2 := \Gamma_I + \gamma_1 + \gamma_2$
7:      **end if**
8: **end for**
9: **return** Γ_I

We have developed the procedural approach to calculating a value of Γ_I described in Algorithm 22. The algorithm takes as input two ontologies: $O_1 = (C_1, H_1, R^{C_1}, I_1, R^{I_1})$ and $O_2 = (C_2, H_2, R^{C_2}, I_2, R^{I_2})$, along with their alignment on the instance level, $Align_I(O_1, O_2)$. It takes the following steps:

- To accumulate the overall quality score as the algorithm progresses, it starts with initializing a variable Γ_I to zero.

- It uses a nested loop to iterate over all possible pairs of concepts, c_1 from ontology O_1 and c_2 from ontology O_2, as indicated by $C_1 \times C_2$.

- For every pair of concepts (c_1, c_2), the algorithm verifies whether an instance-level alignment exists for these concepts in $Align_I(O_1, O_2)$ before proceeding with the evaluation.

- The algorithm calculates two quality ratings, γ_1 and γ_2, using the function γ_I and the instance alignments $AL_{O_1, O_2}(c_1, c_2)$, which represent the quality of the instance-level alignment for c_1 and c_2 with respect to this concept pair.

- The values of γ_1 and γ_2 are added to the Γ_I variable to accumulate the alignment quality as the algorithm proceeds to the next concept pair.

- After iterating through all concept pairs and evaluating their instance-level alignments, the algorithm returns the final value of Γ_I as the output.

In this section, we introduce two methods, Γ_C and Γ_I, that evaluate the quality of ontology alignments at both the concept and instance levels. These methods highlight the critical role of continuity. Both functions complement the depth-based methods, Λ_C and Λ_I, discussed in the preceding section.

In conclusion, the four developed functions Λ_C, Λ_I, Γ_C, and Γ_I establish a novel framework for comparing ontology alignments based solely on the content of the aligned ontologies. Their distinct feature is their independence from any pre-existing reference alignments. Therefore, they surpass the limitations of traditional metrics such as Precision and Recall, offering a broader, practical perspective on evaluating alignment quality. It is especially valuable in real-world applications as it offers a robust methodology applicable to a variety of knowledge integration and interoperability tasks. The book's next section will demonstrate the applicability of the proposed methods.

6.2 Applicability analysis

This section demonstrates the practical value of the metrics Λ_C, Λ_I, Γ_C, and Γ_I. It is crucial to underscore that our objective is not to directly compare these metrics against conventional measures like Precision or Recall, which offer valuable insights into the correctness and completeness of ontology alignments. However, they rely on the availability of reference alignments for comparison, limiting their applicability in real-world scenarios.

The methods introduced in the preceding sections of this book take a distinct approach by concentrating on the depth and continuity of the assessed alignments. Therefore, they fundamentally differ in nature from traditional metrics – they possess different properties and serve different purposes, rendering direct comparisons inappropriate.

The core objective of this chapter is to demonstrate that our metrics are not intended to replace existing measures. Instead, they are designed to complement and enhance the existing toolkit for evaluating ontology alignments. By showcasing their practical utility, we aim to provide evidence of how these metrics can coexist with traditional measures, offering a more comprehensive and insightful approach to assessing alignment quality and utility in various real-world applications.

This section is divided into two subsections. The first will describe the applicability analysis in the context of a widely regarded dataset prepared by the Ontology Alignment Evaluation Initiative (OAEI). In the second part, we will use the algorithms discussed in Chapter 5 to illustrate the practical significance of Λ_C, Λ_I, Γ_C, and Γ_I in the context of ontology evolution.

6.2.1 In the context of OAEI datasets

This section of the book demonstrates the practical application of ontology alignment evaluation measures introduced in previous sections. We utilize data from the Ontology Alignment Evaluation Initiative (OAEI), which offers a comprehensive benchmark dataset. This dataset comprises a collection of ontologies and reference mappings curated by OAEI organizers, along with mappings contributed by participants, generated through their respective solutions. Due to the fact, that it includes only alignments of concepts and instances to facilitate our analysis, we will divide it into two stages. The first stage will concentrate on the concept level, which constitutes the majority of OAEI's data. Subsequently, the second stage will focus on the applicability of the developed framework on the instance level.

For the first stage of the analysis, we chose data from 2018 OAEI contest[1], during which, participants had the opportunity to test their systems in twelve different categories. From

---

[1]https://oaei.ontologymatching.org/2018/

TABLE 6.1
Ontology statistics from selected OAEI ontology matching tracks

Ontology	Number of Concepts	Maximal Depth
Anatomy track		
Adult Mouse Anatomy	2744	9
NCI Thesaurus	3304	14
Biodiversity and Ecology track		
Flora Phenotype Ontology	28932	13
Plant Trait Ontology	1504	14
Large Biomedical Ontologies track (1)		
Foundational Model of Anatomy	10157	20
SNOMED CT	13412	34
Large Biomedical Ontologies track (2)		
Foundational Model of Anatomy	3696	20
NCI Thesaurus	6488	14

this extensive dataset, we have selected seven ontologies: "Adult Mouse Anatomy", "NCI Thesaurus", "Flora Phenotype Ontology", "Plant Trait Ontology", "SNOMED CT", and two variants of the "Foundational Model of Anatomy" ontology. We wanted to use fairly large ontologies, therefore we selected ontologies that contained a minimum of 1500 concepts. This resulted in four pairs of ontologies, each accompanied by their respective reference alignments. These pairs fall under three primary categories: "Anatomy", "Biodiversity and Ecology", and "Large Biomedical Ontologies".

The detailed information about the selected ontologies can be found in Table 6.1. It is worth noting that, in some cases, the competition organizers made adjustments to the ontologies to include only elements relevant to the specific task, which is why the number of concepts within the Foundational Model of Anatomy ontology varies.

Submission done by contest participants for ontology pairs from Table 6.1 allows us to collect forty competing alignments. As aforementioned, for each alignment OAEI provided the values of Precision, Recall, and F1-measure, and for the purpose of this chapter, also for each alignment we computed Λ_C and Γ_C.

Since both Λ_C and Γ_C do not yield normalized values within the range of $[0,1]$, we have taken the additional step of calculating normalized values for Λ_C and Γ_C with respect to reference alignments prepared by OAEI for each pair of considered ontologies. In this context, let's assume that some alignment is denoted as $Align(O_1, O_2)$, and the reference alignment is denoted as $Align_{ref}(O_1, O_2)$. The normalized values of Λ_C and Γ_C, which we will refer to as $\widehat{\Lambda_C}$ and $\widehat{\Gamma_C}$, can be calculated as follows:

$$\widehat{\Lambda_C}(O_1, O_2, Align(O_1, O_2)) = \frac{\Lambda_C(O_1, O_2, Align(O_1, O_2)}{\Lambda_C(O_1, O_2, Align_{ref}(O_1, O_2))} \qquad (6.12)$$

$$\widehat{\Gamma_C}(O_1, O_2, Align(O_1, O_2)) = \frac{\Gamma_C(O_1, O_2, Align(O_1, O_2)}{\Gamma_C(O_1, O_2, Align_{ref}(O_1, O_2))} \qquad (6.13)$$

TABLE 6.2
Scores obtained by individual matchers in **Anatomy** track for ontologies **Adult Mouse Anatomy** and **NCI Thesaurus**

Matcher	Precision	Recall	F1	$\widehat{\Lambda_C}$	$\widehat{\Gamma_C}$
ALIN	0.998	0.611	0.758	0.630	0.430
ALOD2Vec	0.996	0.648	0.785	0.667	0.477
AML	0.950	0.936	0.943	0.984	1.076
DOME	0.997	0.615	0.761	0.632	0.433
FCAMapX	0.941	0.791	0.859	0.843	0.712
Holontology	0.976	0.294	0.451	0.282	0.131
KEPLER	0.958	0.741	0.836	0.783	0.605
LogMap	0.918	0.880	0.846	0.918	0.746
LogMapBio	0.888	0.908	0.898	1.026	0.994
LogMapLite	0.962	0.728	0.828	0.770	0.566
POMAP++	0.919	0.877	0.897	0.957	0.945
SANOM	0.888	0.844	0.865	0.957	0.948
XMap	0.929	0.865	0.896	0.924	0.883

Since all of the ontologies from the OAEI dataset are expressed in OWL format ([7]), and their corresponding alignments are stored in RDF format ([32]). Thus, to implement the measures defined in the preceding sections of this book, we chose to use the Java programming language, specifically version 8, in combination with the Apache Jena framework ([2]).

Apache Jena is an open-source software framework designed to support the development of applications related to creating and processing semantic web and linked data. This framework offers a robust interface for loading and working with data stored in RDF or OWL file formats. Moreover, Apache Jena incorporates an efficient implementation of the SPARQL query engine ([166]), which enables SQL-like navigation through OWL and RDF files, facilitating the manipulation of ontology data.

Table 6.2 presents an overview of results from the Anatomy track, which encompass the names of the systems that participated in generating the alignments, along with their corresponding scores for Precision, Recall, and F1-Measure, obtained during the OAEI campaign, and values of $\widehat{\Lambda_C}$ and $\widehat{\Gamma_C}$. Table 6.3 follows the same structure and provides results for the Biodiversity and Ecology track. Likewise, Tables 6.4 and 6.5 contain results from the Large Biomedical Ontologies tracks.

The values collected from Tables 6.2, 6.3, 6.4, and 6.4 together make up five samples of Precision, Recall, F1-measure, $\widehat{\Lambda_C}$ and $\widehat{\Gamma_C}$. However, before proceeding with any further analysis, it is crucial to determine whether these data sets adhere to a normal distribution. To accomplish this, we conducted a nonparametric Kolmogorov-Smirnov test, the results of which are outlined in Table 6.6. The p-values calculated for each sample are all greater than the assumed significance level of $\alpha = 0.01$. Therefore, we have no grounds to reject the null hypotheses which state that the samples of Precision, Recall, F1-measure, $\widehat{\Lambda_C}$ and $\widehat{\Gamma_C}$ come from a normal distribution.

The primary objective of the analysis is to determine whether a correlation exists between conventional metrics, namely Precision, Recall, F1-measure, and newly introduced measures such as $\widehat{\Lambda_C}$ and $\widehat{\Gamma_C}$. Since the data samples are all from a normal distribution,

---

[2]https://jena.apache.org/

TABLE 6.3
Scores obtained by individual matchers in **Biodiversity and Ecology** track for ontologies **Flora Phenotype Ontology** and **Plant Trait Ontology**

Matcher	Precision	Recall	F1	$\widehat{\Lambda_C}$	$\widehat{\Gamma_C}$
AML	0.880	0.840	0.860	0.942	0.895
Lily	0.813	0.586	0.681	0.729	0.547
LogMap	0.817	0.787	0.802	0.935	0.982
LogMapBio	0.803	0.787	0.795	0.947	1.007
LogMapLite	0.987	0.661	0.755	0.637	0.392
POMap	0.663	0.709	0.685	1.165	0.908
XMap	0.987	0.619	0.761	0.638	0.415

TABLE 6.4
Scores obtained by individual matchers in OAEI **Large Biomedical Ontologies** track for ontologies **Foundational Model of Anatomy** and **SNOMED CT**

Matcher	Precision	Recall	F1	$\widehat{\Lambda_C}$	$\widehat{\Gamma_C}$
ALOD2Vec	0.941	0.213	0.347	0.182	0.061
AML	0.923	0.762	0.835	0.803	0.662
DOME	0.988	0.198	0.330	0.160	0.052
FCAMapX	0.955	0.815	0.879	0.853	0.657
KEPLER	0.822	0.424	0.559	0.450	0.251
LogMap	0.947	0.690	0.798	0.718	0.321
LogMapBio	0.947	0.693	0.800	0.722	0.332
LogMapLite	0.968	0.208	0.342	0.173	0.058
POMAP++	0.906	0.260	0.404	0.227	0.081
XMap	0.962	0.647	0.774	0.669	0.402

TABLE 6.5
Scores obtained by individual matchers in OAEI **Large Biomedical Ontologies** track for ontologies **Foundational Model of Anatomy** and **NCI Thesaurus**

Matcher	Precision	Recall	F1	$\widehat{\Lambda_C}$	$\widehat{\Gamma_C}$
ALOD2Vec	0.972	0.839	0.901	0.845	0.748
AML	0.958	0.910	0.933	0.912	0.763
DOME	0.985	0.764	0.861	0.756	0.503
FCAMapX	0.948	0.911	0.929	0.940	0.865
KEPLER	0.960	0.831	0.891	0.841	0.881
LogMap	0.944	0.897	0.920	0.920	0.747
LogMapBio	0.941	0.902	0.921	0.929	0.914
LogMapLite	0.967	0.819	0.887	0.829	0.676
POMAP++	0.979	0.814	0.889	0.808	0.637
XMap	0.977	0.783	0.869	0.778	0.514

TABLE 6.6

Verification of normal distribution of ontology alignment
evaluation measures

Sample name	Test statistic D	p-value
Precision	0.231	0.023
Recall	0.163	0.214
F1-measure	0.250	0.011
$\widehat{\Lambda}_C$	0.168	0.186
$\widehat{\Gamma}_C$	0.110	0.680

we can use the Intraclass Correlation Coefficient (abbreviated as ICC) ([11]). This method
is usually applied when a finite group of judges evaluates a finite set of objects to measure
the agreement degree in their assessments. Depending on the scenario, there are three main
models of using ICC:

- **Model 1**. For each of the randomly chosen objects, a set of judges is also randomly
  selected from the entire population of judges.

- **Model 2**. A group of judges is randomly selected from a population of judges, and each
  judge evaluates all possible objects.

- **Model 3**. All judges provide ratings for all objects.

Calculating the ICC returns a value from a range $[-1, 1]$, which can be interpreted according
to the following rules:

- When ICC is approximately 1, it indicates a robust concordance among the evaluations
  made by different "judges". This reflects a high variance between evaluated objects and
  a low variance between the judges' assessments.

- An ICC value close to 0 suggests a lack of concordance among judges' evaluations of
  individual objects. This shows a low variance between objects and a high variance among
  judges' assessments.

- In the case of ICC approximately equal to -1, a negative intraclass coefficient is treated
  similarly to when ICC is around 0.

In our scenario, we treat each ontology alignment evaluation measure as a "judge" and
the alignments created by different OAEI participants as the assessed objects. Such an
approach allows us to choose the third model of ICC.

We evaluated all alignments using Precision, Recall, F1-measure, $\widehat{\Lambda}_C$, and $\widehat{\Gamma}_C$.
Subsequently, we calculated the value of ICC for six pairs of measures ($\widehat{\Lambda}_C - Precision$,
$\widehat{\Lambda}_C - Recall$, $\widehat{\Lambda}_C$-F1-measure, $\widehat{\Gamma}_C - Precision$, $\widehat{\Gamma}_C - Recall$, $\widehat{\Gamma}_C$-F1-measure). The collected
outcomes can be found in Table 6.7. Additionally, Figures 6.7, 6.8, and 6.9, show individual
values of the compared metrics.

We observe notable ICC values for the Recall measure, 0.934 for $\widehat{\Lambda}_C$ and 0.837 for $\widehat{\Gamma}_C$.
These high ICC values signify strong correlations between Recall and the newly proposed
measures. To further illustrate this relationship, please refer to Figure 6.7, which visually
represents the observed correlations. The acquired values of ICC show that as the values of
Recall increase, there is an increase in the values of $\widehat{\Lambda}_C$ and $\widehat{\Gamma}_C$.

TABLE 6.7

Results of the intraclass correlation coefficient analysis

	$\widehat{\Lambda_C}$	$\widehat{\Gamma_C}$
Recall	0.934	0.837
Precision	-0.179	-0.159
F1-measure	0.838	0.697

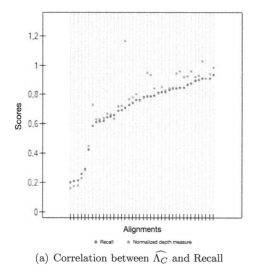

(a) Correlation between $\widehat{\Lambda_C}$ and Recall   (b) Correlation between $\widehat{\Gamma_C}$ and Recall

FIGURE 6.7

Correlation of Recall

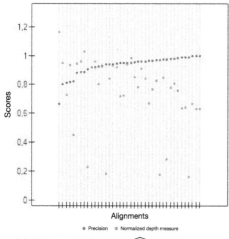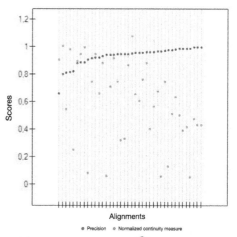

(a) Correlation between $\widehat{\Lambda_C}$ and Precision   (b) Correlation between $\widehat{\Gamma_C}$ and Precision

FIGURE 6.8

Correlation of Precision

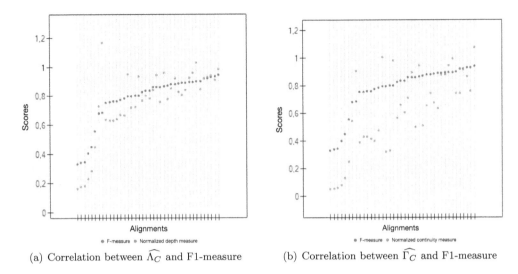

(a) Correlation between $\widehat{\Lambda_C}$ and F1-measure   (b) Correlation between $\widehat{\Gamma_C}$ and F1-measure

FIGURE 6.9
Correlation of F1-measure

Conversely, when analyzing the Precision measure, we notice low ICC values, -0.179 for $\widehat{\Lambda_C}$ and -0.159 for $\widehat{\Gamma_C}$. These low ICC values suggest a lack of correlation between Precision and the newly introduced measures, as depicted in Figure 6.8.

Eventually, we find that for the F1-measure and $\widehat{\Lambda_C}$, the ICC value is 0.838, and for $\widehat{\Gamma_C}$, it equals 0.697, which suggests moderate correlations between evaluated methods, as shown in Figure 6.8. However, remember that the F1-measure is a composition of both Precision and Recall. Consequently, the nature of the F1-measure affects the observed moderate correlations. More specifically, Recall positively impacts the ICC value, enhancing it, while Precision decreases the final value.

We used the F-test to verify the intraclass correlation coefficient's significance. The analyzed values are derived from an interval scale from a normal distribution and are related, so they meet all the conditions for using this test. The null hypothesis is that there is no correspondence between the test sets, and the assumed significance level is $\alpha = 0.05$. The results can be found in Table 6.8.

The results of the conducted F-tests confirm the previous observations. Both proposed methods for assessing the mapping of ontologies are not consistent with precision, but are consistent with completeness and F1-measure at a high level.

The second part of the analysis focused on the level of instances. Similar to the experiment described in Section 4.4, we selected the IIMB (ISLab Instance Matching Benchmark) dataset ([3]) as our dataset. This dataset comprises 80 pairs (further referred to as alignment test cases) of ontologies, each accompanied by a reference alignment. For more comprehensive information about this dataset, please refer to Section 4.4.2, which describes our fuzzy logic-based framework for ontology alignment experimentally verified using the same dataset.

This stage of the analysis required some additional preprocessing. As per Definitions 6.2 and 6.4, both measures, Λ_I and Γ_I, require that instances within an ontology are assigned to at least one concept, as defined in Equation 2.3. Such an approach follows the standard ontology development practices, which recommend associating instances with specific concepts ([147]).

TABLE 6.8

Results of the significance verification of intraclass correlation coefficient analysis using F-test

Sample 1	Sample 2	F-test value	p-value
$\widehat{\Lambda_C}$	*Precision*	0.696	0.869
$\widehat{\Lambda_C}$	*Recall*	29.362	< 0.00001
$\widehat{\Lambda_C}$	*F1 − measure*	11.318	< 0.00001
$\widehat{\Gamma_C}$	*Precision*	0.725	0.84
$\widehat{\Gamma_C}$	*Recall*	11.327	< 0.00001
$\widehat{\Gamma_C}$	*F1 − measure*	5.606	< 0.00001

After examining the IIMB dataset, we discovered that, in many cases, the instances in the ontologies were not assigned to any concept. To address this issue (rendered our proposed measures inapplicable), we selected only those test cases from the initial set of 80 ontology pairs where instances had assigned concepts. This selection process resulted in a dataset containing 45 ontology pairs. We generated alignments for each of these pairs using the external system LogMap ([99]), a widely recognized and highly regarded ontology alignment solution. Subsequently, we assessed each produced alignment against a reference alignment to compute Precision, Recall, and F1-measures. Additionally, we calculated the values of Λ_I and Γ_I. The collected results after normalization can be found in Table 6.9.

Similar to the analysis of Λ_C and Γ_C, initially, we started with checking whether the collected data followed the normal distribution. Unfortunately, the results of this test indicated that none of the data samples come from the normal distribution. Consequently, we opted to employ Spearman's rank-order correlation coefficient, and a summary of gathered results can be found in Table 6.10.

For Recall, there is a moderate positive correlation with $\widehat{\Lambda_I}$ (0.511) and a strong positive correlation with $\widehat{\Gamma_I}$ (0.899). Precision shows a very weak positive correlation with $\widehat{\Lambda_I}$ (0.039) and a moderate positive correlation with $\widehat{\Gamma_I}$ (0.555). F1-measure shows a moderate positive correlation with $\widehat{\Lambda_I}$ (0.492) and a strong positive correlation with $\widehat{\Gamma_I}$ (0.893).

In this section, we have provided the applicability analysis of ontology alignment evaluation measures in the context of the most broadly used benchmark dataset provided by the Ontology Alignment Evaluation Initiative (OAEI). By assessing the correlation between classic metrics like Recall, Precision, and F1-measure and the proposed Λ_C, Λ_I, Γ_C and Γ_I, we have showcased their utility. The findings underline that, rather than replacing the traditional methods, the developed framework can serve as valuable enhancement, offering a different perspective on the quality of ontology alignments, both at the concept and instance levels.

6.2.2 In the context of ontology evolution

Let us assume that two ontologies exist – the source ontology O_1 and the target ontology O_2. Moreover, let us assume an established, verified alignment $Align(O_1, O_2)$ exists between them. Obviously, when some significant changes are introduced over time to one of those ontologies, it may render the initial alignment obsolete.

TABLE 6.9
LogMap scores of $\widehat{\Lambda_I}$, $\widehat{\Gamma_I}$, Precision, Recall, and F1-measure for in IIMB benchmark

Test Case	$\widehat{\Lambda_I}$	$\widehat{\Gamma_I}$	Precision	Recall	F1
001	0.965	0.998	0.937	0.984	0.960
002	0.971	0.845	0.803	0.871	0.836
003	0.978	0.902	0.838	0.907	0.871
004	0.966	0.994	0.929	0.973	0.950
005	0.569	0.421	0.944	0.600	0.734
006	0.902	0.879	0.942	0.926	0.934
007	0.970	1.000	0.938	0.997	0.967
008	0.971	1.000	0.938	0.997	0.967
009	0.957	0.878	0.849	0.893	0.870
010	0.921	0.872	0.888	0.893	0.891
011	1.000	0.881	0.804	0.888	0.844
012	0.975	0.996	0.931	0.992	0.960
013	0.970	1.000	0.941	0.997	0.968
014	0.999	0.878	0.804	0.890	0.845
015	0.660	0.530	0.913	0.658	0.764
016	0.960	0.905	0.893	0.937	0.914
017	0.963	0.998	0.937	0.978	0.957
018	0.613	0.480	0.934	0.622	0.747
019	0.975	0.846	0.804	0.874	0.837
020	0.961	0.998	0.939	0.978	0.958
021	0.963	0.998	0.937	0.978	0.957
022	0.960	0.997	0.932	0.975	0.953
023	0.960	0.997	0.932	0.975	0.953
024	0.969	0.999	0.938	0.992	0.964
025	0.969	0.999	0.933	0.995	0.963
026	0.964	0.998	0.932	0.984	0.957
027	0.971	1.000	0.938	0.997	0.967
028	0.963	0.998	0.937	0.978	0.957
029	0.965	0.998	0.935	0.986	0.960
030	0.960	0.997	0.932	0.975	0.953
031	0.965	0.998	0.933	0.986	0.959
032	0.964	0.998	0.932	0.978	0.955
033	0.969	0.999	0.933	0.995	0.963
034	0.968	0.998	0.933	0.986	0.959
035	0.968	0.999	0.936	0.995	0.964
036	0.973	1.000	0.936	0.997	0.966
037	0.960	0.997	0.934	0.975	0.954
038	0.969	0.999	0.938	0.992	0.964
039	0.969	0.999	0.933	0.995	0.963
040	0.960	0.997	0.932	0.975	0.953
049	0.004	0.000	0.250	0.500	0.333
050	0.007	0.001	0.143	0.500	0.222
063	0.493	0.262	0.943	0.963	0.953
070	0.460	0.247	0.935	0.989	0.961
077	0.003	0.000	0.500	0.500	0.500

TABLE 6.10
Results of Spearman's rank-order correlation coefficient analysis

Measure pair	Correlation value
Recall - $\widehat{\Lambda_I}$	0.511
Recall - $\widehat{\Gamma_I}$	0.899
Precision - $\widehat{\Lambda_I}$	0.039
Precision - $\widehat{\Gamma_I}$	0.555
F1-measure - $\widehat{\Lambda_I}$	0.492
F1-measure - $\widehat{\Gamma_I}$	0.893

The conventional approach in such a situation would involve reapplying ontology alignment methods from scratch for the new versions of the considered ontologies. However, given the computational complexity and resource-intensive nature of ontology alignment, this may not be the most efficient solution. Therefore, it would be beneficial if a set of algorithms existed that, based on a description of changes applied to ontologies, could revalidate and update existing ontology alignments.

In Chapter 5, the author proposes a novel framework to address the issue considered above. The current section of the book will focus on leveraging these algorithms to illustrate the practical significance of assessing the quality of ontology alignments defined in this chapter.

The main idea is straightforward – collect two alignments of ontologies in their initial state and their state after evolution, created from scratch by some prominent ontology alignment system (like previously incorporated LogMap tool [95]). Then, apply algorithms from Chapter 5 on alignments in their initial state, considering how ontologies changed over time, resulting in their updated version. Eventually, assed the quality of all collected alignments using methods provided in this chapter. If calculated values do not significantly differ, we can claim that algorithms from Chapter 5 produce alignments with at least similar quality to the ones designated by processing whole ontologies from scratch using some ontology alignment systems.

The first step to achieving this goal is choosing a benchmark dataset. Our initial plan was to rely on OAEI's benchmarks, which have been mentioned and utilized multiple times in this book. The rationale behind this choice was rooted in the fact that the Ontology Alignment Evaluation Initiative has been organizing annual campaigns since 2004 dedicated to evaluating ontology matching technologies. These campaigns are built upon benchmark datasets, comprising numerous ontologies grouped into thematic sets and pre-prepared reference alignments. As such, we anticipated that the benchmark data would undergo modifications and evolve annually to mimic real-world applications of ontologies and reflect the ever-changing landscape of business requirements. However, we observed that the dataset provided by OAEI did not undergo such changes, and in the subsequent campaigns, only new benchmark ontologies were added to the pool.

To address this situation, we opted to handpick ontologies from the OAEI dataset and subject them to predefined modification scenarios. These scenarios simulated various real-world alterations that actively maintained ontologies may undergo. We created twelve distinct scenarios, each representing a specific type of change or update that could occur in a maintained ontology.

Since most of OAEI's benchmarks are focused solely on the concept level of ontologies, we decided to limit the experiment only to this level. Eventually, we decided to use ontologies from the Conference Track from the OAEI datasets used during the 2021 campaign. It includes 16 ontologies related to the conference organization domain, along with their pairwise alignments. From this extensive collection, we randomly selected the *confOf* ontology as a source ontology, denoted as O_1, and the *CMT* ontology as a target ontology, denoted as O_2.

As the external ontology alignment system, the LogMap tool ([95]) was chosen, which generated a base alignment, referred to as $Align_{LogMap}(O_1^{(m)}, O_2^{(n)})$, between the source ontology $O_1^{(m)}$ and the target ontology $O_2^{(n)}$ using them in their initial states m and n respectively.

The final procedure can be outlined as follows:

1. For each of the twelve modification scenarios, apply it to the source ontology $O_1^{(m)}$, transitioning it to a modified state denoted as $O_1^{(m+1)}$.

2. Generate an ontology change log, denoted as $Log(O_1)$, which documents the specific modifications made to transition from $O_1^{(m)}$ to $O_1^{(m+1)}$ using a function called $diff_C(C_1^{(m)}, C_1^{(m+1)})$ from Equation 5.4.

3. Generate a new alignment, $Align_{LogMap}(O_1^{(m+1)}, O_2^{(n)})$, between the modified source ontology $O_1^{(m+1)}$ and the target ontology $O_2^{(n)}$ using LogMap.

4. Update the original alignment, $Align(O_1^{(m)}, O_2^{(n)})$, to follow the changes introduced in the source ontology $O_1^{(m+1)}$ using appropriate algorithms from Section 5.4, resulting in the updated alignment $Align(O_1^{(m+1)}, O_2^{(n)})$.

5. Since we restricted the experiment only to the level of concepts, calculate alignment quality metrics Λ_C and Γ_C for all of the collected alignments. This step includes:

    (a) Calculating $\Lambda_C(O_1^{(m+1)}, O_2^{(n)}, Align_{LogMap}(O_1^{(m+1)}, O_2^{(n)}))$. The sample of collected values will be further abbreviated as $\Lambda_C(Align_{LogMap})$.

    (b) Calculating $\Lambda_C(O_1^{(m+1)}, O_2^{(n)}, Align(O_1^{(m+1)}, O_2^{(n)}))$. The sample of collected values will be further abbreviated as $\Lambda_C(Align)$.

    (c) Calculating $\Gamma_C(O_1^{(m+1)}, O_2^{(n)}, Align_{LogMap}(O_1^{(m+1)}, O_2^{(n)}))$. The sample of collected values will be further abbreviated as $\Gamma_C(Align_{LogMap})$

    (d) Calculating $\Gamma_C(O_1^{(m+1)}, O_2^{(n)}, Align(O_1^{(m+1)}, O_2^{(n)}))$. The sample of collected values will be further abbreviated as $\Gamma_C(Align)$

The collected results are presented in Table 6.12.

TABLE 6.11
Results of the significance verification of intraclass correlation coefficient analysis using F-test

Sample 1	Sample 2	F-test value	p-value
$\Lambda_C(Align_{LogMap})$	$\Lambda_C(Align)$	1.079	0.89
$\Gamma_C(Align_{LogMap})$	$\Gamma_C(Align)$	1.575	0.43

TABLE 6.12

Λ_C and Γ_C scores of alignments generated by LogMap and maintenance algorithms

Scenario	LogMap		Updated alignment	
	Λ_C	Γ_C	Λ_C	Γ_C
No changes	2.949	16	2.949	16
Removing 5 concepts	1.699	8	1.699	8
Adding 5 related concepts	4.250	29	3.550	23
Modifying 5 concepts	2.366	14	1.699	10
Adding and removing 5 concept	3.466	22	2.099	13
Adding and modifying 5 concept	3.333	22	2.633	17
Modifying and removing 5 concept	1.116	6	0.450	4
Adding, removing, and modifying 5 concept	2.183	16	0.850	9
Removing 20 concepts	1.283	4	1.283	4
Adding 20 related 5 concepts	3.199	17	3.449	18
Modifying 20 concepts	1.700	8	0.450	6
Removing 40 concepts	0.000	0	0.000	0
Adding 40 related 5 concepts	3.883	20	2.783	15

TABLE 6.13
Results of t-test verification of samples $\Lambda_C(Align_{LogMap})$-$\Lambda_C(Align)$ and $\Gamma_C(Align_{LogMap})$-$\Gamma_C(Align)$

Sample 1	Sample 2	t-test value	p-value
$\Lambda_C(Align_{LogMap})$	$\Lambda_C(Align)$	1.22	0.234
$\Gamma_C(Align_{LogMap})$	$\Gamma_C(Align)$	1.01	0.32

As previously, any further analysis must be preceded by checking whether or not the collected samples come from the normal distribution. For this purpose, we used the Shapiro-Wilk test. For all samples ($\Lambda_C(Align_{LogMap})$, $\Lambda_C(Align)$, $\Gamma_C(Align_{LogMap})$ and $\Gamma_C(Align)$), we received p-value higher than the accepted significance level $\alpha = 0.05$. The statistical test values were equal to 0.971, 0.971, 0.974, and 0.978, respectively. Such results allow us to claim that all the samples follow the normal distribution.

The next step involves verification of variance equality. For this purpose, we used the F-test. The collected results can be found in Table 6.11. It can be easily noticed that for the accepted significance level $\alpha = 0.05$, the obtained values confirm the equality of variances of pairs of samples $\Lambda_C(Align_{LogMap})$-$\Lambda_C(Align)$ and $\Gamma_C(Align_{LogMap})$-$\Gamma_C(Align)$.

Ultimately, we opted to use the t-test to assess whether two approaches for generating ontology alignments produced results of comparable quality. These approaches involve creating ontology alignments from scratch using LogMap and updating initial alignments using algorithms from Chapter 5, represented by two sample pairs: $\Lambda_C(Align_{LogMap})$-$\Lambda_C(Align)$ and $\Gamma_C(Align_{LogMap})$-$\Gamma_C(Align)$. The accepted significance level α was equal to 0.05.

The statistical analysis results can be found in Table 6.13. Since all the p-values are greater than the assumed α level and the statistic values for samples $\Lambda_C(Align_{LogMap})$-$\Lambda_C(Align)$ and $\Gamma_C(Align_{LogMap})$-$\Gamma_C(Align)$. equal 1.22 and 1.01, respectively, the analysis confirms that the quality of the alignments produced by compared methods is indeed similar.

In summary, the experimental procedure detailed in this section serves a dual purpose. First, it offers a comprehensive assessment of how well ontology alignment maintenance methods, as discussed in Chapter 5, can effectively handle changes within ontologies. This investigation demonstrates the feasibility of updating ontology alignments solely based on the evolution of ontologies, eliminating the need to restart ontology alignment processes from scratch and reprocess entire ontologies, which carries practical implications, particularly concerning the complexity of these methods.

This fact leads to a second achievement in this section – the practical applicability of ontology alignment evaluation methods. These evaluation methods become very useful when conventional measures such as Precision or Recall are either inapplicable or do not serve the intended purpose. This finding highlights the versatility and real-world utility of the evaluation techniques proposed in the current chapter.

6.3   Conclusions

As discussed throughout this book, ontology alignment tackles the seemingly straightforward task of identifying which elements of two ontologies describe the same aspects of the real world. Numerous diverse approaches have been proposed in the literature, emphasizing the importance of establishing a reliable method for evaluating their results.

Traditionally, the primary approach for assessing the quality of mappings between two ontologies involves a comparison against reference alignments, which entails the computation of Precision and Recall values. These reference alignments are typically accessible in benchmark datasets, notably by the Ontology Alignment Evaluation Initiative (OAEI). However, in real-world scenarios, the availability of ground truth reference alignments is often impractical. Thus, evaluating alignment quality must rely on alternative criteria.

The main contribution of this chapter is the introduction of a novel framework for comparing ontology alignments, rendering the need for reference mappings obsolete in real-world applications of ontologies and ontology alignments.

While some concepts discussed in this chapter have been previously addressed in the author's earlier works ([156], [86], [155]), it is essential to highlight that this chapter presents new content, as outlined below:

- The description of the proposed approaches for evaluating ontology alignments based on concepts' depths in Section 6.1.1 offers deeper insights into these methods. It not only refines them to follow consistent formal foundations but also extends their applicability to scenarios where certain instances can be assigned to multiple different concepts, which enriches the versatility and robustness of the proposed approaches.

- Methods based on concepts' continuity discussed in Section 6.1.2 were entirely rewritten to compensate for the new formal foundations provided in Chapter 2, which provides a more robust and comprehensive overview of the advantages and disadvantages of the proposed solution.

- The discussion on the applicability of developed methods given in Section 6.2 has not been previously published in such a level of detail. It provides a careful analysis of the properties of presented functions and a much broader scope of scenarios where the given functions can be applied.

In conclusion, the chapter's contribution mainly consists of the introduction of four functions: Λ_C, Λ_I, Γ_C, and Γ_I, which form a novel framework for evaluating the quality of ontology alignments based only on the content of the aligned ontologies. It is worth noting that these methods operate independently of any pre-existing reference alignments. Their primary objective is not to validate the correctness of specific mappings but rather to evaluate their quality within the context of the hierarchical structure of ontologies. In other words, they offer a more comprehensive perspective on alignment quality that extends beyond conventional metrics such as Precision and Recall, thus providing a more holistic understanding and broader perspective on alignment quality.

Part IV

Final Remarks

7

Conclusions

This book's main subject is finding matching elements extracted from independent ontologies, which in the literature is frequently referred to as ontology alignment. The book presents an extended, more complete, unified version of the author's latest research. It discusses aspects spanning from providing a foundational formal model for both ontologies and their alignments through aspects related to designating them using a multistrategy approach made possible by incorporating fuzzy logic, ending on aspects of evaluating the quality of ontology alignments.

Overall, the book can be treated as a description of a complete formal framework for ontology alignment and a summary of the author's previous achievements, which have been presented in over twenty scientific papers. They have been published in prestigious scientific journals and proceedings of international conferences, published by, among others, IEEE, Springer and Elsevier [82], [83], [84], [85], [86], [87], [114], [115], [116], [117], [118], [119], [120], [121], [149], [155], [156], [157], [158], [159].

All of the formal tools have been consolidated under a consistent mathematical notation. In addition to presenting a cohesive synthesis of past research, the book also introduces several new methods and extended experimental results. Thereby, it forms a valuable resource for both academic and practical applications in the field of ontology alignment.

As described in Chapter 1, the contribution of this book includes the following elements:

- A formal model of ontology, its internal elements (concepts, relations, and instances), and their structures, including a novel notion of attributes' and relations' semantics based on propositional calculus.

- Method of providing attributes' semantics.

- Method of providing relations semantics.

- A formal model of ontology alignment.

- A set of formal criteria for detecting inconsistencies in ontology mappings.

- Fuzzy logic framework for ontology alignment, which includes:
    - Fuzzy logic-based methods for aligning ontologies on the concept level.
    - Fuzzy logic-based methods for aligning ontologies on the relation level.
    - Fuzzy logic-based methods for aligning ontologies on the instance level.

- Results of experimental verification of fuzzy logic framework for ontology alignment and its comparison with competitive solutions in the light of the state-of-the-art benchmark datasets provided by the Ontology Alignment Evaluation Initiative.

- A formal model of time, ontology repository, and ontology log used to track changes in evolving ontologies.

DOI: 10.1201/9781003437888-7

- A set of difference functions providing methods to describe changes applied to ontologies throughout their maintenance and evolution.

- A set of functions for assessing the significance of ontology modifications for the concept, relation, and instance levels.

- A framework for revalidating and updating ontology alignments based on information about ontology evolution, which includes

  - A set of methods for updating ontology alignment on the concept level.
  - A set of methods for updating ontology alignment on the relation level.
  - A set of methods for updating ontology alignment on the instance level.

- A method for measuring the level of ontologies interoperability and the results of its experimental evaluation.

- A content-based framework for assessing ontology alignment quality, which includes:

  - Methods for assessing ontology mappings based on concept depth.
  - The continuity-based methods for assessing ontology mappings.

- Experimental evaluation of a content-based framework for assessing ontology alignment quality, which includes:

  - Comparison with traditional metrics in the context of datasets provided by the Ontology Alignment Evaluation Initiative
  - Applicability analysis in ontology evolution utilizing the developed framework for updating ontology alignment.

In conclusion, this book significantly contributes to the field of ontology alignment, thoroughly addressing the complexities and challenges of the field. Obviously, it does not cover all the related topics, and numerous unresolved issues and unexplored problems still await further investigation ([150]). Some of the future research directions may include:

- The application of advanced machine learning techniques, including deep learning and large language models, to enhance the ontology alignment process. Future work could explore the integration of these models for generating new mappings or refining existing ones, leveraging the latest advancements in artificial intelligence ([77], [181], [209]).

- Global expansion of the Internet caused rapid expansion of multilanguage data, making aligning ontologies expressed in different languages increasingly important. Addressing issues entailed by differences in languages has recently gained some research attention ([91], [102]).

- The growing size and complexity of ontologies necessitate scalable and efficient alignment algorithms. Future research could focus on optimizing the computational resources required for alignment tasks, potentially employing distributed computing and cloud technologies to accommodate large-scale ontologies ([141], [174]).

Bibliography

[1] Ismail Akbari and Mohammad Fathian. A novel algorithm for ontology matching. *Journal of Information Science*, 36(3):324–334, 2010.

[2] Ismail Akbari, Mohammad Fathian, and Kambiz Badie. An improved mlma+ and its application in ontology matching. In *2009 Innovative Technologies in Intelligent Systems and Industrial Applications*, pages 56–60. IEEE, 2009.

[3] Alsayed Algergawy, Michelle Cheatham, Daniel Faria, Alfio Ferrara, Irini Fundulaki, Ian Harrow, Sven Hertling, Ernesto Jiménez-Ruiz, Naouel Karam, Abderrahmane Khiat, et al. Results of the ontology alignment evaluation initiative 2018. In *13th International Workshop on Ontology Matching col-located with the 17th International Semantic Web Conference, Monterey, CA, USA*, October 8–12, 2018, volume 2288, pages 76–116, 2018.

[4] Sarah M. Alghamdi, Fernando Zhapa-Camacho, and Robert Hoehndorf. A-lion - alignment learning through inconsistency negatives of the aligned ontologies. In Pavel Shvaiko, Jérôme Euzenat, Ernesto Jiménez-Ruiz, Oktie Hassanzadeh, and Cássia Trojahn, editors, *Proceedings of the 17th International Workshop on Ontology Matching (OM 2022) co-located with the 21st International Semantic Web Conference (ISWC 2022)*, Hangzhou, China, held as a virtual conference, October 23, 2022, volume 3324 of *CEUR Workshop Proceedings*, pages 137–144. CEUR-WS.org, 2022.

[5] Alex Alves, Kate Revoredo, and Fernanda Araújo Baião. Ontology alignment based on instances using hybrid genetic algorithm. In *Organizational Memories*, 2012.

[6] Yuan An, Alexander Kalinowski, and Jane Greenberg. Otmaponto: optimal transport-based ontology matching. In Pavel Shvaiko, Jérôme Euzenat, Ernesto Jiménez-Ruiz, Oktie Hassanzadeh, and Cássia Trojahn, editors, *Proceedings of the 16th International Workshop on Ontology Matching co-located with the 20th International Semantic Web Conference (ISWC 2021), Virtual conference, October 25, 2021*, volume 3063 of *CEUR Workshop Proceedings*, pages 185–192. CEUR-WS.org, 2021.

[7] Antoniou, Grigoris, and Frank Van Harmelen. "Web Ontology Language: OWL." *Handbook on Ontologies in Information Systems*, 67–92, Springer-Verlag, 2003.

[8] Robert Arp, Barry Smith, and Andrew D Spear. *Building ontologies with basic formal ontology*. MIT Press, 2015.

[9] Manuel Atencia and Marco Schorlemmer. An interaction-based approach to semantic alignment. *Journal of Web Semantics*, 12:131–147, 2012.

[10] Ben Athiwaratkun, Andrew Wilson, and Anima Anandkumar. Probabilistic FastText for multi-sense word embeddings. In Iryna Gurevych and Yusuke Miyao, editors, *Proceedings of the 56th Annual Meeting of the Association for Computational Linguistics (Volume 1: Long Papers)*, pages 1–11, Melbourne, Australia, July 2018. Association for Computational Linguistics.

[11] John J Bartko. The intraclass correlation coefficient as a measure of reliability. *Psychological Reports*, 19(1):3–11, 1966.

[12] Christian Borgelt. An implementation of the fp-growth algorithm. In *Proceedings of the 1st international workshop on open source data mining: frequent pattern mining implementations*, KDD05: The Eleventh ACM SIGKDD International Conference on Knowledge Discovery and Data Mining Chicago Illinois 21 August 2005 pages 1–5, 2005.

[13] Enrico G. Caldarola and Antonio M. Rinaldi. A multi-strategy approach for ontology reuse through matching and integration techniques. In Stuart H. Rubin and Thouraya Bouabana-Tebibel, editors, *Quality Software Through Reuse and Integration*, pages 63–90, Cham, 2018. Springer International Publishing.

[14] Silvio Domingos Cardoso, Marcos Da Silveira, and Cédric Pruski. Construction and exploitation of an historical knowledge graph to deal with the evolution of ontologies. *Knowledge-Based Systems*, 194:105508, 2020.

[15] Michelle Cheatham and Pascal Hitzler. String similarity metrics for ontology alignment. In *The Semantic Web – ISWC 2013*, pages 294–309, Berlin, Heidelberg, 2013. Springer Berlin Heidelberg.

[16] Michelle Cheatham, Catia Pesquita, Daniela Oliveira, and Helena B McCurdy. The properties of property alignment on the semantic web. *International Journal of Metadata, Semantics and Ontologies*, 13(1):42–56, 2018.

[17] Guanrong Chen, Trung Tat Pham, and NM Boustany. Introduction to fuzzy sets, fuzzy logic, and fuzzy control systems. *Applied Mechanics Reviews*, 54(6):B102–B103, 2001.

[18] Guowei Chen and Songmao Zhang. Fcamapx results for oaei 2018. In *OM@ ISWC*, pages 160–166, 2018.

[19] Jiaoyan Chen, Pan Hu, Ernesto Jimenez-Ruiz, Ole Magnus Holter, Denvar Antonyrajah, and Ian Horrocks. Owl2vec*: Embedding of owl ontologies. *Machine Learning*, 110(7):1813–1845, 2021.

[20] Jiaoyan Chen, Ernesto Jiménez-Ruiz, Ian Horrocks, Denvar Antonyrajah, Ali Hadian, and Jaehun Lee. Augmenting ontology alignment by semantic embedding and distant supervision. In Ruben Verborgh, Katja Hose, Heiko Paulheim, Pierre-Antoine Champin, Maria Maleshkova, Oscar Corcho, Petar Ristoski, and Mehwish Alam, editors, *The Semantic Web*, pages 392–408, Cham, 2021. Springer International Publishing.

[21] Kenneth Ward Church. Word2vec. *Natural Language Engineering*, 23(1):155–162, 2017.

[22] Rudi L Cilibrasi and Paul MB Vitanyi. The google similarity distance. *IEEE Transactions on Knowledge and Data Engineering*, 19(3):370–383, 2007.

[23] Pablo Cingolani and Jesus Alcala-Fdez. jfuzzylogic: a robust and flexible fuzzy-logic inference system language implementation. In *2012 IEEE International Conference on Fuzzy Systems*, pages 1–8. IEEE, 2012.

[24] William W Cohen, Pradeep Ravikumar, Stephen E Fienberg, et al. A comparison of string distance metrics for name-matching tasks. In *IIWeb*, volume 3, pages 73–78, 2003.

[25] Gene Ontology Consortium. The gene ontology (go) database and informatics resource. *Nucleic Acids Research*, 32(suppl_1):D258–D261, 2004.

[26] Gene Ontology Consortium. The gene ontology resource: 20 years and still going strong. *Nucleic Acids Research*, 47(D1):D330–D338, 2019.

[27] Isabel F Cruz, Flavio Palandri Antonelli, and Cosmin Stroe. Agreementmaker: efficient matching for large real-world schemas and ontologies. *Proceedings of the VLDB Endowment*, 2(2):1586–1589, 2009.

[28] Jomar Da Silva, Kate Revoredo, Fernanda Baião, and Jérôme Euzenat. Alin: improving interactive ontology matching by interactively revising mapping suggestions. *The Knowledge Engineering Review*, 35:e1, 2020.

[29] Jomar da Silva, Kate Revoredo, Fernanda Baiao, and Cabral Lima. ALIN results for OAEI 2022. In Pavel Shvaiko, Jérôme Euzenat, Ernesto Jiménez-Ruiz, Oktie Hassanzadeh, and Cássia Trojahn, editors, *Proceedings of the 17th International Workshop on Ontology Matching (OM 2022) co-located with the 21th International Semantic Web Conference (ISWC 2022), Hangzhou, China, held as a virtual conference, October 23, 2022*, volume 3324 of *CEUR Workshop Proceedings*, pages 129–136. CEUR-WS.org, 2022.

[30] Jomar da Silva, Kate Revoredo, Fernanda Araujo Baião, and Cabral Lima. ALIN results for OAEI 2021. In Pavel Shvaiko, Jérôme Euzenat, Ernesto Jiménez-Ruiz, Oktie Hassanzadeh, and Cássia Trojahn, editors, *Proceedings of the 16th International Workshop on Ontology Matching co-located with the 20th International Semantic Web Conference (ISWC 2021), Virtual conference, October 25, 2021*, volume 3063 of *CEUR Workshop Proceedings*, pages 109–116. CEUR-WS.org, 2021.

[31] Viviane Torres Da Silva, Jéssica Soares Dos Santos, Raphael Thiago, Elton Soares, and Leonardo Guerreiro Azevedo. Owl ontology evolution: understanding and unifying the complex changes. *The Knowledge Engineering Review*, 37:e10, 2022.

[32] Brickley Dan. Rdf vocabulary description language 1.0: Rdf schema. *http://www. w3. org/TR/rdf-schema/*, 2004.

[33] Evangelia Daskalaki, Giorgos Flouris, Irini Fundulaki, and Tzanina Saveta. Instance matching benchmarks in the era of linked data. *Journal of Web Semantics*, 39:1–14, 2016.

[34] Jérôme David and Jérôme Euzenat. On fixing semantic alignment evaluation measures. In *Proc. 3rd ISWC workshop on ontology matching (OM)*, pages 25–36. No commercial editor., 2008.

[35] Jérôme David, Jérôme Euzenat, François Scharffe, and Cássia Trojahn dos Santos. The alignment api 4.0. *Semantic web*, 2(1):3–10, 2011.

[36] Kalyanmoy Deb, Amrit Pratap, Sameer Agarwal, and TAMT Meyarivan. A fast and elitist multiobjective genetic algorithm: Nsga-ii. *IEEE transactions on evolutionary computation*, 6(2):182–197, 2002.

[37] Gerard Deepak, Naresh Kumar, and A Santhanavijayan. A semantic approach for entity linking by diverse knowledge integration incorporating role-based chunking. *Procedia Computer Science*, 167:737–746, 2020.

[38] Juliana Medeiros Destro, Júlio Cesar dos Reis, Ricardo da Silva Torres, and Ivan L. M. Ricarte. Ontology changes-driven semantic refinement of cross-language biomedical ontology alignments. In Ali Hasnain, Vít Nováček, Michel Dumontier, and Dietrich Rebholz-Schuhmann, editors, *Proceedings of the Workshop on Semantic Web Solutions for Large-Scale Biomedical Data Analytics co-located with 18th International Semantic Web Conference (ISWC 2019)*, Auckland, New Zealand, October 27th, 2019, volume 2477 of *CEUR Workshop Proceedings*, pages 1–15. CEUR-WS.org, 2019.

[39] Kevin Donnelly et al. Snomed-ct: The advanced terminology and coding system for ehealth. *Studies in Health Technology and Informatics*, 121:279, 2006.

[40] Miriam Oliveira dos Santos, Carlos Eduardo Ribeiro de Mello, and Tadeu Moreira de Classe. A useful tool to support the ontology alignment repair. In Ricardo Cerri and Ronaldo C. Prati, editors, *Intelligent Systems*, pages 201–215, Cham, 2020. Springer International Publishing.

[41] William F Dowling and Jean H Gallier. Linear-time algorithms for testing the satisfiability of propositional horn formulae. *The Journal of Logic Programming*, 1(3):267–284, 1984.

[42] Sefika Efeoglu. Graphmatcher: a graph representation learning approach for ontology matching. In Pavel Shvaiko, Jérôme Euzenat, Ernesto Jiménez-Ruiz, Oktie Hassanzadeh, and Cássia Trojahn, editors, *Proceedings of the 17th International Workshop on Ontology Matching (OM 2022) co-located with the 21th International Semantic Web Conference (ISWC 2022)*, Hangzhou, China, held as a virtual conference, October 23, 2022, volume 3324 of *CEUR Workshop Proceedings*, pages 174–180. CEUR-WS.org, 2022.

[43] Sefika Efeoglu. Graphmatcher system presentation. In Pavel Shvaiko, Jérôme Euzenat, Ernesto Jiménez-Ruiz, Oktie Hassanzadeh, and Cássia Trojahn, editors, *Proceedings of the 18th International Workshop on Ontology Matching co-located with the 22nd International Semantic Web Conference (ISWC 2023)*, Athens, Greece, November 7, 2023, volume 3591 of *CEUR Workshop Proceedings*, pages 154–156. CEUR-WS.org, 2023.

[44] Marc Ehrig and Jérôme Euzenat. Relaxed precision and recall for ontology matching. In Benjamin Ashpole, Marc Ehrig, Jérôme Euzenat, and Heiner Stuckenschmidt, editors, *Integrating Ontologies '05, Proceedings of the K-CAP 2005 Workshop on Integrating Ontologies*, Banff, Canada, October 2, 2005, volume 156 of *CEUR Workshop Proceedings*. CEUR-WS.org, 2005.

[45] Jérôme Euzenat. Semantic precision and recall for ontology alignment evaluation. In Manuela M. Veloso, editor, *IJCAI 2007, Proceedings of the 20th International Joint Conference on Artificial Intelligence*, Hyderabad, India, January 6-12, 2007, pages 348–353, 2007.

[46] Jérôme Euzenat. Interaction-based ontology alignment repair with expansion and relaxation. In *IJCAI 2017-26th International Joint Conference on Artificial Intelligence*, pages 185–191. AAAI Press, 2017.

[47] Jérôme Euzenat, Pavel Shvaiko, et al. *Ontology matching*, volume 18. Springer, 2007.

[48] Jérôme Euzenat and Pavel Shvaiko. *Ontology matching: Second edition.* Springer, 10 2013.

[49] Omaima Fallatah, Ziqi Zhang, and Frank Hopfgartner. A hybrid approach for large knowledge graphs matching. In Pavel Shvaiko, Jérôme Euzenat, Ernesto Jiménez-Ruiz, Oktie Hassanzadeh, and Cássia Trojahn, editors, *Proceedings of the 16th International Workshop on Ontology Matching co-located with the 20th International Semantic Web Conference (ISWC 2021), Virtual conference*, October 25, 2021, volume 3063 of *CEUR Workshop Proceedings*, pages 37–48. CEUR-WS.org, 2021.

[50] Omaima Fallatah, Ziqi Zhang, and Frank Hopfgartner. Kgmatcher+ results for OAEI 2022. In Pavel Shvaiko, Jérôme Euzenat, Ernesto Jiménez-Ruiz, Oktie Hassanzadeh, and Cássia Trojahn, editors, *Proceedings of the 17th International Workshop on Ontology Matching (OM 2022) co-located with the 21th International Semantic Web Conference (ISWC 2022)*, Hangzhou, China, held as a virtual conference, October 23, 2022, volume 3324 of *CEUR Workshop Proceedings*, pages 181–187. CEUR-WS.org, 2022.

[51] Daniel Faria, Catia Pesquita, Emanuel Santos, Isabel F Cruz, and Francisco M Couto. Agreementmakerlight: A scalable automated ontology matching system. In *Proceedings of the 10th International Conference on Data Integration in the Life Sciences (DILS 2014)*, pages 29–32. Citeseer, 2014.

[52] Daniel Faria, Catia Pesquita, Emanuel Santos, Matteo Palmonari, Isabel F Cruz, and Francisco M Couto. The agreementmakerlight ontology matching system. In *On the Move to Meaningful Internet Systems: OTM 2013 Conferences: Confederated International Conferences: CoopIS, DOA-Trusted Cloud, and ODBASE 2013, Graz, Austria*, September 9–13, 2013. *Proceedings*, pages 527–541. Springer, 2013.

[53] Daniel Faria, Catia Pesquita, Teemu Tervo, Francisco M Couto, and Isabel F Cruz. Aml and amlc results for oaei 2019. In *Proceedings of the 14th International Workshop on Ontology Matching co-located with the 18th International Semantic Web Conference (ISWC)*, volume 2536, 2019.

[54] Daniel Faria, Marta Silva, Pedro Cotovio, Lucas Ferraz, Laura Balbi, and Catia Pesquita. Results for matcha and matcha-dl in oaei 2023. 2023.

[55] Daniel Faria, Marta Contreiras Silva, Pedro Cotovio, Patrícia Eugénio, and Catia Pesquita. Matcha and matcha-dl results for OAEI 2022. In Pavel Shvaiko, Jérôme Euzenat, Ernesto Jiménez-Ruiz, Oktie Hassanzadeh, and Cássia Trojahn, editors, *Proceedings of the 17th International Workshop on Ontology Matching (OM 2022) co-located with the 21th International Semantic Web Conference (ISWC 2022)*, Hangzhou, China, held as a virtual conference, October 23, 2022, volume 3324 of *CEUR Workshop Proceedings*, pages 197–201. CEUR-WS.org, 2022.

[56] Alfio Ferrara, Stefano Montanelli, Jan Noessner, and Heiner Stuckenschmidt. Benchmarking matching applications on the semantic web. In *The Semantic Web: Research and Applications: 8th Extended Semantic Web Conference, ESWC 2011*, Heraklion, Crete, Greece, May 29–June 2, 2011, *Proceedings, Part II 8*, pages 108–122. Springer, 2011.

[57] Daniel Fleischhacker and Heiner Stuckenschmidt. Implementing semantic precision and recall. In Pavel Shvaiko, Jérôme Euzenat, Fausto Giunchiglia, Heiner

Stuckenschmidt, Natalya Fridman Noy, and Arnon Rosenthal, editors, *Proceedings of the 4th International Workshop on Ontology Matching (OM-2009) collocated with the 8th International Semantic Web Conference (ISWC-2009)*, Chantilly, USA, October 25, 2009, volume 551 of *CEUR Workshop Proceedings*. CEUR-WS.org, 2009.

[58] Giorgos Flouris, Dimitris Manakanatas, Haridimos Kondylakis, Dimitris Plexousakis, and Grigoris Antoniou. Ontology change: classification and survey. *The Knowledge Engineering Review*, 23(2):117–152, 2008.

[59] Fausto Giunchiglia, Fiona McNeill, Mikalai Yatskevich, Juan Pane, Paolo Besana, and Pavel Shvaiko. Approximate structure-preserving semantic matching. In *On the Move to Meaningful Internet Systems: OTM 2008: OTM 2008 Confederated International Conferences, CoopIS, DOA, GADA, IS, and ODBASE 2008, Monterrey, Mexico, November 9–14, 2008, Proceedings, Part II*, pages 1217–1234. Springer, 2008.

[60] Fausto Giunchiglia, Mikalai Yatskevich, F Mcneill, et al. Structure preserving semantic matching. In Proceedings of the 2nd International Workshop on Ontology Matching: OM-2007, volume 304, pages 13–24. CEUR, 2007.

[61] Birte Glimm, Ian Horrocks, Boris Motik, Giorgos Stoilos, and Zhe Wang. Hermit: an owl 2 reasoner. *Journal of Automated Reasoning*, 53:245–269, 2014.

[62] Fumiko Kano Glückstad. Terminological ontology and cognitive processes in translation. In *Proceedings of the 24th Pacific Asia Conference on Language, Information and Computation*, Institute of Digital Enhancement of Cognitive Processing, Waseda University, Tohoku University, Sendai, Japan, pages 629–636, 2010.

[63] Christine Golbreich, Evan K Wallace, and Peter F Patel-Schneider. Owl 2 web ontology language new features and rationale. *W3C working draft, W3C (June 2009) http://www. w3. org/TR/2009/WD-owl2-new-features-20090611*, 2009.

[64] Wael H Gomaa, Aly A Fahmy, et al. A survey of text similarity approaches. *International Journal of Computer Applications*, 68(13):13–18, 2013.

[65] Francis Gosselin and Amal Zouaq. SORBET: A siamese network for ontology embeddings using a distance-based regression loss and BERT. In Terry R. Payne, Valentina Presutti, Guilin Qi, María Poveda-Villalón, Giorgos Stoilos, Laura Hollink, Zoi Kaoudi, Gong Cheng, and Juanzi Li, editors, *The Semantic Web – ISWC 2023 – 22nd International Semantic Web Conference*, Athens, Greece, November 6-10, 2023, *Proceedings, Part I*, volume 14265 of *Lecture Notes in Computer Science*, pages 561–578. Springer, 2023.

[66] Francis Gosselin and Amal Zouaq. Sorbetmatcher results for oaei 2023. 2023.

[67] Bernardo Cuenca Grau, Ian Horrocks, Boris Motik, Bijan Parsia, Peter Patel-Schneider, and Ulrike Sattler. Owl 2: The next step for owl. *Journal of Web Semantics*, 6(4):309–322, 2008. Semantic Web Challenge 2006/2007.

[68] Anika Groß, Michael Hartung, Andreas Thor, and Erhard Rahm. How do computed ontology mappings evolve? – A case study for life science ontologies. In Tudor Groza, Dimitris Plexousakis, and Vít Novácek, editors, *Proceedings of the 2nd Joint Workshop on Knowledge Evolution and Ontology Dynamics*, Boston, MA, USA, November 12, 2012, volume 890 of *CEUR Workshop Proceedings*. CEUR-WS.org, 2012.

[69] Thomas R Gruber. A translation approach to portable ontology specifications. *Knowledge acquisition*, 5(2):199–220, 1993.

[70] Bill Gates Happi Happi, Géraud Fokou Pelap, Danai Symeonidou, and Pierre Larmande. Dlinker results for OAEI 2022. In Pavel Shvaiko, Jérôme Euzenat, Ernesto Jiménez-Ruiz, Oktie Hassanzadeh, and Cássia Trojahn, editors, *Proceedings of the 17th International Workshop on Ontology Matching (OM 2022) co-located with the 21th International Semantic Web Conference (ISWC 2022)*, Hangzhou, China, held as a virtual conference, October 23, 2022, volume 3324 of *CEUR Workshop Proceedings*, pages 166–173. CEUR-WS.org, 2022.

[71] Michael Hartung, Anika Groß, and Erhard Rahm. Conto–diff: generation of complex evolution mappings for life science ontologies. *Journal of Biomedical Informatics*, 46(1):15–32, 2013.

[72] Michael Hartung, Toralf Kirsten, and Erhard Rahm. Analyzing the evolution of life science ontologies and mappings. In *Data Integration in the Life Sciences: 5th International Workshop, DILS 2008*, Evry, France, June 25–27, 2008. *Proceedings 5*, pages 11–27. Springer, 2008.

[73] Terry F Hayamizu, Mary Mangan, John P Corradi, James A Kadin, and Martin Ringwald. The adult mouse anatomical dictionary: a tool for annotating and integrating data. *Genome biology*, 6(3):1–8, 2005.

[74] Wei He, Xiaoping Yang, and Dupei Huang. A hybrid approach for measuring semantic similarity between ontologies based on wordnet. In Hui Xiong and W. B. Lee, editors, *Knowledge Science, Engineering and Management*, pages 68–78, Berlin, Heidelberg, 2011. Springer Berlin Heidelberg.

[75] Wei He, Xiaoping Yang, and Dupei Huang. A hybrid approach for measuring semantic similarity between ontologies based on wordnet. In *International Conference on Knowledge Science, Engineering and Management*, pages 68–78. Springer, 2011.

[76] Yuan He, Jiaoyan Chen, Denvar Antonyrajah, and Ian Horrocks. Biomedical ontology alignment with bert. In *OM@ISWC*, 2021.

[77] Yuan He, Jiaoyan Chen, Denvar Antonyrajah, and Ian Horrocks. BERTMap: a BERT-based ontology alignment system. In *Proceedings of the AAAI Conference on Artificial Intelligence* (Vol. 36, No. 5, pp. 5684–5691). February 20–27, 2024, Vancouver, Canada.

[78] Sven Hertling and Heiko Paulheim. Webisalod: providing hypernymy relations extracted from the web as linked open data. In *The Semantic Web–ISWC 2017: 16th International Semantic Web Conference*, Vienna, Austria, October 21–25, 2017, *Proceedings, Part II 16*, pages 111–119. Springer, 2017.

[79] Sven Hertling and Heiko Paulheim. Atbox results for oaei 2021. In *CEUR Workshop Proceedings*, volume 3063, pages 137–143. RWTH Aachen, 2021.

[80] Sven Hertling and Heiko Paulheim. Olala: Ontology matching with large language models. In *Proceedings of the 12th Knowledge Capture Conference 2023*, K-CAP '23: Knowledge Capture Conference, Pensacola FL, USA, pages 131–139, 2023.

[81] Sven Hertling and Heiko Paulheim. Olala results for oaei 2023. 2023.

[82] Bogumila Hnatkowska, Adrianna Kozierkiewicz, and Marcin Pietranik. OWL RL to framework for ontological knowledge integration preliminary transformation. In Ngoc Thanh Nguyen, Kietikul Jearanaitanakij, Ali Selamat, Bogdan Trawinski, and Suphamit Chittayasothorn, editors, *Intelligent Information and Database Systems – 12th Asian Conference, ACIIDS 2020*, Phuket, Thailand, March 23–26, 2020, *Proceedings, Part I*, volume 12033 of *Lecture Notes in Computer Science*, pages 37–48. Springer, 2020.

[83] Bogumiła Hnatkowska, Adrianna Kozierkiewicz, and Marcin Pietranik. Semi-automatic definition of attribute semantics for the purpose of ontology integration. *IEEE Access*, 8:107272–107284, 2020.

[84] Bogumiła Hnatkowska, Adrianna Kozierkiewicz, and Marcin Pietranik. Fuzzy based approach to ontology relations alignment. In *2021 IEEE International Conference on Fuzzy Systems (FUZZ-IEEE)*, pages 1–7. IEEE, 2021.

[85] Bogumiła Hnatkowska, Adrianna Kozierkiewicz, and Marcin Pietranik. Fuzzy logic framework for ontology instance alignment. In *Computational Science–ICCS 2022: 22nd International Conference*, London, UK, June 21–23, 2022, *Proceedings, Part II*, pages 653–666. Springer International Publishing Cham, 2022.

[86] Bogumila Hnatkowska, Adrianna Kozierkiewicz, Marcin Pietranik, and Hai Bang Truong. Assessing ontology alignments on the level of instances. In Ngoc Thanh Nguyen, Lazaros Iliadis, Ilias Maglogiannis, and Bogdan Trawinski, editors, *Computational Collective Intelligence – 13th International Conference, ICCCI 2021, Rhodes*, Greece, September 29 – October 1, 2021, *Proceedings*, volume 12876 of *Lecture Notes in Computer Science*, pages 42–52. Springer, 2021.

[87] Bogumiła Hnatkowska, Adrianna Kozierkiewicz, Marcin Pietranik, and Hai Bang Truong. Hybrid approach to designating ontology attribute semantics. In *Computational Collective Intelligence: 14th International Conference, ICCCI 2022*, Hammamet, Tunisia, September 28–30, 2022, *Proceedings*, pages 351–363. Springer International Publishing Cham, 2022.

[88] Aidan Hogan, Eva Blomqvist, Michael Cochez, Claudia dÁmato, Gerard De Melo, Claudio Gutierrez, Sabrina Kirrane, José Emilio Labra Gayo, Roberto Navigli, Sebastian Neumaier, et al. Knowledge graphs. *ACM Computing Surveys (Csur)*, 54(4):1–37, 2021.

[89] Laura Hollink, Mark Van Assem, Shenghui Wang, Antoine Isaac, and Guus Schreiber. Two variations on ontology alignment evaluation: Methodological issues. In *The Semantic Web: Research and Applications: 5th European Semantic Web Conference, ESWC 2008, Tenerife, Canary Islands*, Spain, June 1–5, 2008 *Proceedings 5*, pages 388–401. Springer, 2008.

[90] Rachael P Huntley, Tony Sawford, Maria J Martin, and Claire O'Donovan. Understanding how and why the gene ontology and its annotations evolve: the go within uniprot. *GigaScience*, 3(1):2047–217X, 2014.

[91] Shimaa Ibrahim, Said Fathalla, Jens Lehmann, and Hajira Jabeen. Toward the multilingual semantic web: Multilingual ontology matching and assessment. *IEEE Access*, 11:8581–8599, 2023.

[92] Valentina Ivanova, Benjamin Bach, Emmanuel Pietriga, and Patrick Lambrix. Alignment cubes: Towards interactive visual exploration and evaluation of multiple ontology alignments. In Claudia d'Amato, Miriam Fernandez, Valentina Tamma, Freddy Lecue, Philippe Cudré-Mauroux, Juan Sequeda, Christoph Lange, and Jeff Heflin, editors, *The Semantic Web – ISWC 2017*, pages 400–417, Cham, 2017. Springer International Publishing.

[93] Shaoxiong Ji, Shirui Pan, Erik Cambria, Pekka Marttinen, and S Yu Philip. A survey on knowledge graphs: Representation, acquisition, and applications. *IEEE Transactions on Neural Networks and Learning Systems*, 33(2):494–514, 2021.

[94] Yong Jiang, Xinmin Wang, and Hai-Tao Zheng. A semantic similarity measure based on information distance for ontology alignment. *Information Sciences*, 278:76–87, 2014.

[95] E. Jimenez-Ruiz. Logmap family participation in the oaei 2021. In *16th International Workshop on Ontology Matching (OM 2021)*, volume 3063, pages 175–177, January 2021. Copyright © 2021 for the individual papers by the papers' authors.

[96] Ernesto Jiménez-Ruiz. Logmap family participation in the oaei 2019. In *CEUR Workshop Proceedings*. CEUR-WS. org, 2019.

[97] Ernesto Jiménez-Ruiz. Logmap family participation in the OAEI 2020. In *Proceedings of the 15th International Workshop on Ontology Matching co-located with the 19th International Semantic Web Conference (ISWC 2020) Virtual conference (originally planned to be in Athens, Greece), November 2, 2020.*, volume 2788, pages 201–203. CEUR-WS, 2020.

[98] Ernesto Jiménez-Ruiz. Logmap family participation in the OAEI 2022. In Pavel Shvaiko, Jérôme Euzenat, Ernesto Jiménez-Ruiz, Oktie Hassanzadeh, and Cássia Trojahn, editors, *Proceedings of the 17th International Workshop on Ontology Matching (OM 2022) co-located with the 21th International Semantic Web Conference (ISWC 2022)*, Hangzhou, China, held as a virtual conference, October 23, 2022, volume 3324 of *CEUR Workshop Proceedings*, pages 188–190. CEUR-WS.org, 2022.

[99] Ernesto Jiménez-Ruiz and Bernardo Cuenca Grau. Logmap: Logic-based and scalable ontology matching. In *The Semantic Web–ISWC 2011: 10th International Semantic Web Conference*, Bonn, Germany, October 23–27, 2011, *Proceedings, Part I 10*, pages 273–288. Springer, 2011.

[100] Ernesto Jiménez-Ruiz, Antón Morant, and Bernardo Cuenca Grau. Logmap results for OAEI 2011. In Pavel Shvaiko, Jérôme Euzenat, Tom Heath, Christoph Quix, Ming Mao, and Isabel F. Cruz, editors, *Proceedings of the 6th International Workshop on Ontology Matching*, Bonn, Germany, October 24, 2011, volume 814 of *CEUR Workshop Proceedings*. CEUR-WS.org, 2011.

[101] Cliff A Joslyn, Patrick Paulson, and Amanda White. Measuring the structural preservation of semantic hierarchy alignments. In *Proceedings of the 4th International Conference on Ontology Matching*, volume 551, pages 61–72. Citeseer, 2009.

[102] Marouen Kachroudi. Revisiting indirect ontology alignment: New challenging issues in cross-lingual context. *arXiv preprint arXiv:2104.01628*, 2021.

[103] Marouen Kachroudi, Gayo Diallo, and Sadok Ben Yahia. Kepler at oaei 2018. *OM@ ISWC*, 2018:173–178, 2018.

[104] Peter Kardos, Zsolt Szanto, and Richard Farkas. Wombocombo results for oaei 2022. 2022.

[105] Yevgeny Kazakov, Markus Krötzsch, and František Simančík. The incredible elk: From polynomial procedures to efficient reasoning with el ontologies. *Journal of Automated Reasoning*, 53(1):1–61, 2014.

[106] Jan Martin Keil. Efficient bounded jaro-winkler similarity based search. *BTW 2019*, 2019.

[107] Jacob Devlin Ming-Wei Chang Kenton and Lee Kristina Toutanova. Bert: Pre-training of deep bidirectional transformers for language understanding. In *Proceedings of naacL-HLT*, volume 1, page 2, 2019.

[108] Muhammad Humayun Khan, Sadaqat Jan, Imran Khan, and Ibrar Ali Shah. Evaluation of linguistic similarity measurement techniques for ontology alignment. In *2015 International Conference on Emerging Technologies (ICET)*, pages 19-20 December 2015, Peshawar, Pakistan.

[109] Asad Masood Khattak, Khalid Latif, and Sungyoung Lee. Change management in evolving web ontologies. *Knowledge-Based Systems*, 37:1–18, 2013.

[110] Asad Masood Khattak, Zeeshan Pervez, Wajahat Ali Khan, Adil Mehmood Khan, Khalid Latif, and SY Lee. Mapping evolution of dynamic web ontologies. *Information Sciences*, 303:101–119, 2015.

[111] Abderrahmane Khiat and Moussa Benaissa. A new instance-based approach for ontology alignment. *International Journal on Semantic Web and Information Systems (IJSWIS)*, 11(3):25–43, 2015.

[112] Haridimos Kondylakis and Dimitris Plexousakis. Ontology evolution without tears. *Journal of Web Semantics*, 19:42–58, 2013.

[113] Daniel Kossack, Niklas Borg, Leon Knorr, and Jan Portisch. TOM matcher results for OAEI 2021. In Pavel Shvaiko, Jérôme Euzenat, Ernesto Jiménez-Ruiz, Oktie Hassanzadeh, and Cássia Trojahn, editors, *Proceedings of the 16th International Workshop on Ontology Matching co-located with the 20th International Semantic Web Conference (ISWC 2021)*, Virtual conference, October 25, 2021, volume 3063 of *CEUR Workshop Proceedings*, pages 193–198. CEUR-WS.org, 2021.

[114] Adrianna Kozierkiewicz and Marcin Pietranik. A formal framework for the ontology evolution. In *Intelligent Information and Database Systems: 11th Asian Conference, ACIIDS 2019*, Yogyakarta, Indonesia, April 8–11, 2019, *Proceedings, Part I 11*, pages 16–27. Springer International Publishing, 2019.

[115] Adrianna Kozierkiewicz and Marcin Pietranik. Triggering ontology alignment revalidation based on the degree of change significance on the ontology concept level. In *Business Information Systems: 22nd International Conference, BIS 2019*, Seville, Spain, June 26–28, 2019, *Proceedings, Part I 22*, pages 137–148. Springer International Publishing, 2019.

[116] Adrianna Kozierkiewicz and Marcin Pietranik. Updating ontology alignment on the concept level based on ontology evolution. In *Advances in Databases and Information Systems: 23rd European Conference, ADBIS 2019*, Bled, Slovenia, September 8–11, 2019, *Proceedings 23*, pages 201–214. Springer International Publishing, 2019.

[117] Adrianna Kozierkiewicz. and Marcin Pietranik. Updating ontology alignment on the relation level based on ontology evolution. In *Proceedings of the 15th International Conference on Evaluation of Novel Approaches to Software Engineering – ENASE*, pages 241–248. INSTICC, SciTePress, 2020.

[118] Adrianna Kozierkiewicz., Marcin Pietranik., and Karolina Kania. A method for estimating potential knowledge increase after updating ontology mapping. In *Proceedings of the 16th International Conference on Evaluation of Novel Approaches to Software Engineering – ENASE*, pages 173–180. INSTICC, SciTePress, 2021.

[119] Adrianna Kozierkiewicz, Marcin Pietranik, and Loan TT Nguyen. Updating ontology alignment on the instance level based on ontology evolution. In *Database and Expert Systems Applications: 31st International Conference, DEXA 2020, Bratislava, Slovakia*, September 14–17, 2020, *Proceedings, Part II 31*, pages 301–311. Springer International Publishing, 2020.

[120] Adrianna Kozierkiewicz, Marcin Pietranik, Mateusz Olsztynski, and Loan T. T. Nguyen. Updating the result ontology integration at the concept level in the event of the evolution of their components. In Ngoc Thanh Nguyen, Yannis Manolopoulos, Richard Chbeir, Adrianna Kozierkiewicz, and Bogdan Trawinski, editors, *Computational Collective Intelligence – 14th International Conference, ICCCI 2022*, Hammamet, Tunisia, September 28-30, 2022, *Proceedings*, volume 13501 of *Lecture Notes in Computer Science*, pages 51–64. Springer, 2022.

[121] Adrianna Kozierkiewicz, Marcin Pietranik, and Jankowiak Wojciech. Fuzzy logic framework for ontology concepts alignment. In *Intelligent Information and Database Systems: 15th Asian Conference, ACIIDS 2023*, Phuket, Thailand, July 24–26, 2023, *Proceedings, Part I 11*, pages 16–27. Springer International Publishing, 2023.

[122] Huanyu Li, Zlatan Dragisic, Daniel Faria, Valentina Ivanova, Ernesto Jiménez-Ruiz, Patrick Lambrix, and Catia Pesquita. User validation in ontology alignment: functional assessment and impact. *The Knowledge Engineering Review*, 34:e15, 11, 2019.

[123] Weizhuo Li. Combining sum-product network and noisy-or model for ontology matching. In Pavel Shvaiko, Jérôme Euzenat, Ernesto Jiménez-Ruiz, Michelle Cheatham, and Oktie Hassanzadeh, editors, *Proceedings of the 10th International Workshop on Ontology Matching Collocated with the 14th International Semantic Web Conference (ISWC 2015)*, Bethlehem, PA, USA, October 12, 2015, volume 1545 of *CEUR Workshop Proceedings*, pages 35–39. CEUR-WS.org, 2015.

[124] Weizhuo Li, Shiqi Zhou, Qiu Ji, and Bingjie Lu. Gmap results for OAEI 2021. In Pavel Shvaiko, Jérôme Euzenat, Ernesto Jiménez-Ruiz, Oktie Hassanzadeh, and Cássia Trojahn, editors, *Proceedings of the 16th International Workshop on Ontology Matching co-located with the 20th International Semantic Web Conference (ISWC 2021)*, *Virtual conference*, October 25, 2021, volume 3063 of *CEUR Workshop Proceedings*, pages 152–159. CEUR-WS.org, 2021.

[125] Yankai Lin, Zhiyuan Liu, Maosong Sun, Yang Liu, and Xuan Zhu. Learning entity and relation embeddings for knowledge graph completion. In *Proceedings of the AAAI Conference on Artificial Intelligence*, volume 29, 2015.

[126] Xiulei Liu, Qiang Tong, Xuhong Liu, and Zhihui Qin. Ontology matching: State of the art, future challenges, and thinking based on utilized information. *IEEE Access*, 9:91235–91243, 2021.

[127] Yanbin Liu, Linchao Zhu, Makoto Yamada, and Yi Yang. Semantic correspondence as an optimal transport problem. In *Proceedings of the IEEE/CVF Conference on Computer Vision and Pattern Recognition*, pages 4463–4472, 2020.

[128] Vincenzo Loia, Giuseppe Fenza, Carmen De Maio, and Saverio Salerno. Hybrid methodologies to foster ontology-based knowledge management platform. In *2013 IEEE Symposium on Intelligent Agents (IA)*, pages 36–43. IEEE, 2013.

[129] Alexander Maedche and Steffen Staab. Measuring similarity between ontologies. In *International Conference on Knowledge Engineering and Knowledge Management*, pages 251–263. Springer, 2002.

[130] Christopher D. Manning, Prabhakar Raghavan, and Hinrich Schütze. *Introduction to Information Retrieval*. Cambridge University Press, 2008.

[131] Viviana Mascardi, Angela Locoro, and Paolo Rosso. Automatic ontology matching via upper ontologies: A systematic evaluation. *IEEE Transactions on Knowledge and Data Engineering*, 22(5):609–623, 2009.

[132] Deborah L McGuinness, Richard Fikes, James Rice, and Steve Wilder. An environment for merging and testing large ontologies. In *KR*, pages 483–493, 2000.

[133] F Martin McNeill and Ellen Thro. *Fuzzy logic: a practical approach*. Academic Press, 2014.

[134] Fiona McNeill, Paolo Besana, Juan Pane, and Fausto Giunchiglia. Service integration through structure-preserving semantic matching. In *Cases on Semantic Interoperability for Information Systems Integration: Practices and Applications*, pages 64–82. IGI Global, 2010.

[135] Christian Meilicke. *Alignment incoherence in ontology matching*. PhD thesis, University of Mannheim, 2011.

[136] Lingling Meng, Runqing Huang, and Junzhong Gu. A review of semantic similarity measures in wordnet. *International Journal of Hybrid Information Technology*, 6(1):1–12, 2013.

[137] David Miller. An ontology for future airspace system architectures. In *2017 IEEE/AIAA 36th Digital Avionics Systems Conference (DASC)*, pages 1–8. IEEE, 2017.

[138] George A Miller. Wordnet: a lexical database for english. *Communications of the ACM*, 38(11):39–41, 1995.

[139] Majid Mohammadi. Bayesian evaluation and comparison of ontology alignment systems. *IEEE Access*, 7:55035–55049, 2019.

[140] Majid Mohammadi and Jafar Rezaei. Evaluating and comparing ontology alignment systems: an mcdm approach. *Journal of Web Semantics*, 64:100592, 2020.

[141] Imadeddine Mountasser, Brahim Ouhbi, Ferdaous Hdioud, and Bouchra Frikh. Semantic-based big data integration framework using scalable distributed ontology matching strategy. *Distributed and Parallel Databases*, 39:891–937, 2021.

[142] Christopher J Mungall, Carlo Torniai, Georgios V Gkoutos, Suzanna E Lewis, and Melissa A Haendel. Uberon, an integrative multi-species anatomy ontology. *Genome Biology*, 13(1):1–20, 2012.

[143] Sophie Neutel and Maaike HT de Boer. Towards automatic ontology alignment using bert. In *AAAI Spring Symposium: Combining Machine Learning with Knowledge Engineering*, 2021.

[144] Thi Thuy Anh Nguyen and Stefan Conrad. Combination of lexical and structure-based similarity measures to match ontologies automatically. In Ana Fred, Jan L. G. Dietz, Kecheng Liu, and Joaquim Filipe, editors, *Knowledge Discovery, Knowledge Engineering and Knowledge Management*, pages 101–112, Berlin, Heidelberg, 2013. Springer Berlin Heidelberg.

[145] Thi Thuy Anh Nguyen and Stefan Conrad. Ontology matching using multiple similarity measures. In *2015 7th International Joint Conference on Knowledge Discovery, Knowledge Engineering and Knowledge Management (IC3K)*, volume 1, pages 603–611. IEEE, 2015.

[146] Ikechukwu Nkisi-Orji, Nirmalie Wiratunga, Stewart Massie, Kit-Ying Hui, and Rachel Heaven. Ontology alignment based on word embedding and random forest classification. In Michele Berlingerio, Francesco Bonchi, Thomas Gärtner, Neil Hurley, and Georgiana Ifrim, editors, *Machine Learning and Knowledge Discovery in Databases*, pages 557–572, Cham, 2019. Springer International Publishing.

[147] N. Noy and Deborah Mcguinness. Ontology development 101: A guide to creating your first ontology. *Knowledge Systems Laboratory*, 32, 01 2001.

[148] Natalya Fridman Noy, Mark A Musen, et al. Algorithm and tool for automated ontology merging and alignment. In *Proceedings of the 17th National Conference on Artificial Intelligence (AAAI-00)*. Available as SMI technical report SMI-2000-0831, volume 115. sn, 2000.

[149] Cezary Orlowski, Pawel Kaplanski, Ngoc Thanh Nguyen, and Marcin Pietranik. The use of an ontotrigger for designing the ontology of a model maturity capsule. *Int. J. Softw. Eng. Knowl. Eng.*, 26(5):715–732, 2016.

[150] Inès Osman, Sadok Ben Yahia, and Gayo Diallo. Ontology integration: Approaches and challenging issues. *Information Fusion*, 71:38–63, 2021.

[151] Lorena Otero-Cerdeira, Francisco J Rodríguez-Martínez, and Alma Gómez-Rodríguez. Ontology matching: A literature review. *Expert Systems with Applications*, 42(2):949–971, 2015.

[152] Pierre-Henri Paris, Fayçal Hamdi, and Samira Si-said Cherfi. A study about the use of owl 2 semantics in rdf-based knowledge graphs. In *The Semantic Web: ESWC 2020 Satellite Events: ESWC 2020 Satellite Events*, Heraklion, Crete, Greece, May 31–June 4, 2020, Revised Selected Papers 17, pages 181–185. Springer, 2020.

[153] Romana Pernischová. The butterfly effect in knowledge graphs: Predicting the impact of changes in the evolving web of data. ISWC, 2019.

[154] Catia Pesquita, Daniel Faria, Emanuel Santos, and Francisco M. Couto. 2013. To repair or not to repair: reconciling correctness and coherence in ontology reference alignments. In *Proceedings of the 8th International Conference on Ontology Matching – Volume 1111 (OM'13)*. CEUR-WS.org, Aachen, DEU, 13–24.

[155] Marcin Pietranik and Adrianna Kozierkiewicz. Methods of managing the evolution of ontologies and their alignments. *Applied Intelligence*, 2023.

[156] Marcin Pietranik, Adrianna Kozierkiewicz, and Mateusz Wesołowski. Assessing ontology mappings on a level of concepts and instances. *IEEE Access*, 8:174845–174859, 2020.

[157] Marcin Pietranik and Ngoc Thanh Nguyen. A multi-attribute based framework for ontology aligning. *Neurocomputing*, 146:276–290, 2014.

[158] Marcin Pietranik and Ngoc Thanh Nguyen. Framework for ontology evolution based on a multi-attribute alignment method. In *2nd IEEE International Conference on Cybernetics, CYBCONF 2015*, Gdynia, Poland, June 24–26, 2015, pages 108–112. IEEE, 2015.

[159] Marcin Pietranik, Ngoc Thanh Nguyen, and Cezary Orlowski. Increasing the efficiency of ontology alignment by tracking changes in ontology evolution. In Dosam Hwang, Jason J. Jung, and Ngoc Thanh Nguyen, editors, *Computational Collective Intelligence. Technologies and Applications – 6th International Conference, ICCCI 2014*, Seoul, Korea, September 24–26, 2014. *Proceedings*, volume 8733 of *Lecture Notes in Computer Science*, pages 394–403. Springer, 2014.

[160] Jan Portisch, Michael Hladik, and Heiko Paulheim. Wiktionary matcher. In *CEUR Workshop Proceedings*, volume 2536, pages 181–188. RWTH Aachen, 2020.

[161] Jan Portisch and Heiko Paulheim. Alod2vec matcher. In Pavel Shvaiko, Jérôme Euzenat, Ernesto Jiménez-Ruiz, Michelle Cheatham, and Oktie Hassanzadeh, editors, *Proceedings of the 13th International Workshop on Ontology Matching co-located with the 17th International Semantic Web Conference, OM@ISWC 2018*, Monterey, CA, USA, October 8, 2018, volume 2288 of *CEUR Workshop Proceedings*, pages 132–137. CEUR-WS.org, 2018.

[162] M Pour, A. Algergawy, Florence Amardeilh, Reihaneh Amini, Omaima Fallatah, Daniel Faria, Irini Fundulaki, Ian Harrow, Sven Hertling, Pascal Hitzler, et al. Results of the ontology alignment evaluation initiative 2021. In *Proceedings of the 16th International Workshop on Ontology Matching (OM 2021)*, volume 3063, pages 62–108. CEUR, 2021.

[163] M Pour, A. Algergawy, Reihaneh Amini, Daniel Faria, Irini Fundulaki, Ian Harrow, Sven Hertling, Ernesto Jiménez-Ruiz, Clement Jonquet, Naouel Karam, et al. Results of the ontology alignment evaluation initiative 2020. In *Proceedings of the 15th International Workshop on Ontology Matching (OM 2020)*, volume 2788, pages 92–138. CEUR, 2020.

[164] M Pour, A Algergawy, P Buche, LJ Castro, J Chen, H Dong, O Fallatah, D Faria, I Fundulaki, S Hertling, et al. Results of the ontology alignment evaluation initiative 2022. In *Proceedings of the 17th International Workshop on Ontology Matching (OM 2022)* co-located with the 21th International Semantic Web Conference (ISWC 2022) Hangzhou, China, held as a virtual conference, October 23, 2022.

[165] Mina Abd Nikooie Pour, Alsayed Algergawy, Patrice Buche, Leyla Jael Castro, Jiaoyan Chen, Adrien Coulet, Julien Cufi, Hang Dong, Omaima Fallatah, Daniel Faria, et al. Results of the ontology alignment evaluation initiative 2023. In *18th International Workshop on Ontology Matching collocated with the 22nd International Semantic Web Conference ISWC-2023*, November 7th, 2023, Athens, Greece.

[166] Bastian Quilitz and Ulf Leser. Querying distributed rdf data sources with sparql. In *The Semantic Web: Research and Applications: 5th European Semantic Web Conference, ESWC 2008*, Tenerife, Canary Islands, Spain, June 1-5, 2008 *Proceedings 5*, pages 524–538. Springer, 2008.

[167] Erhard Rahm and Philip A Bernstein. A survey of approaches to automatic schema matching. *the VLDB Journal*, 10:334–350, 2001.

[168] Dominique Ritze, Christian Meilicke, Ondrej Šváb-Zamazal, and Heiner Stuckenschmidt. A pattern-based ontology matching approach for detecting complex correspondences. In *ISWC Workshop on Ontology Matching*, chantilly (VA US), pages 25–36, 2009.

[169] Jean-Marie Rodrigues, Stefan Schulz, Alan Rector, Kent Spackman, Bedirhan Üstün, Christopher G Chute, Vincenzo Della Mea, Jane Millar, and Kristina Brand Persson. Sharing ontology between icd 11 and snomed ct will enable seamless re-use and semantic interoperability. In *MEDINFO 2013*, pages 343–346. IOS Press, 2013.

[170] Cornelius Rosse and José LV Mejino Jr. The foundational model of anatomy ontology. In *Anatomy ontologies for bioinformatics: principles and practice*, pages 59–117. Springer, 2008.

[171] Philippe Roussille and Olivier Teste. TOMATO: results of the 2022 OAEI evaluation campaign. In Pavel Shvaiko, Jérôme Euzenat, Ernesto Jiménez-Ruiz, Oktie Hassanzadeh, and Cássia Trojahn, editors, *Proceedings of the 17th International Workshop on Ontology Matching (OM 2022) co-located with the 21th International Semantic Web Conference (ISWC 2022)*, Hangzhou, China, held as a virtual conference, October 23, 2022, volume 3324 of *CEUR Workshop Proceedings*, pages 210–215. CEUR-WS.org, 2022.

[172] Antonio A Sánchez-Ruiz, Santiago Ontanón, Pedro A González-Calero, and Enric Plaza. Measuring similarity of individuals in description logics over the refinement space of conjunctive queries. *Journal of Intelligent Information Systems*, 47:447–467, 2016.

[173] Antonio A Sánchez-Ruiz, Santiago Ontanón, Pedro Antonio González-Calero, and Enric Plaza. Measuring similarity in description logics using refinement operators. In *International Conference on Case-Based Reasoning*, pages 289–303. Springer, 2011.

[174] Balachandran Sangeetha and Ranganathan Vidhyapriya. A novel accurate and time efficient map reduce approach for biomedical ontology alignment. *Journal of Electrical Engineering & Technology*, pages 1–13, 2023.

[175] Emanuel Santos, Daniel Faria, Catia Pesquita, and Francisco M Couto. Ontology alignment repair through modularization and confidence-based heuristics. *PloS one*, 10(12), 2015.

[176] Najla Sassi, Wassim Jaziri, and Saad Alharbi. Supporting ontology adaptation and versioning based on a graph of relevance. *Journal of Experimental & Theoretical Artificial Intelligence*, 28(6):1035–1059, 2016.

[177] François Scharffe, Ondřej Zamazal, and Dieter Fensel. Ontology alignment design patterns. *Knowledge and Information Systems*, 40:1–28, 2014.

[178] Gilles Serasset. Dbnary: Wiktionary as a lemon-based multilingual lexical resource in rdf. *Semantic Web*, 6(4):355–361, 2015.

[179] Abhisek Sharma and Sarika Jain. Lsmatch and lsmatch-multilingual results for oaei 2023. In P. Shvaiko, J. Euzenat, E. Jiménez-Ruiz, O. Hassanzadeh, and C. Trojahn, editors, *Proceedings of the 18th International Workshop on Ontology Matching (OM 2023) co-located with the 22th International Semantic Web Conference (ISWC 2023)*, CEUR Workshop Proceedings, Athens, Greece, 2023. CEUR-WS.org.

[180] Abhisek Sharma, Sarika Jain, and Archana Patel. Large scale ontology matching system (lsmatch). *Recent Advances in Computer Science and Communications*, 16:1–11, 2023.

[181] Rishi Rakesh Shrivastava and Gerard Deepak. Aioiml: Automatic integration of ontologies for iot domain using hybridized machine learning techniques. In *2023 2nd International Conference on Paradigm Shifts in Communications Embedded Systems, Machine Learning and Signal Processing (PCEMS)*, pages 1–5. IEEE, 2023.

[182] Nicholas Sioutos, Sherri de Coronado, Margaret W Haber, Frank W Hartel, Wen-Ling Shaiu, and Lawrence W Wright. Nci thesaurus: a semantic model integrating cancer-related clinical and molecular information. *Journal of Biomedical Informatics*, 40(1):30–43, 2007.

[183] Barry Smith, Michael Ashburner, Cornelius Rosse, Jonathan Bard, William Bug, Werner Ceusters, Louis J Goldberg, Karen Eilbeck, Amelia Ireland, Christopher J Mungall, et al. The obo foundry: coordinated evolution of ontologies to support biomedical data integration. *Nature Biotechnology*, 25(11):1251–1255, 2007.

[184] G. Sousa, R. Lima, and C. Trojahn. Combining word and sentence embeddings with alignment extension for property matching. In P. Shvaiko, J. Euzenat, E. Jiménez-Ruiz, O. Hassanzadeh, and C. Trojahn, editors, *Proceedings of the 18th International Workshop on Ontology Matching (OM 2023) co-located with the 22th International Semantic Web Conference (ISWC 2023)*, CEUR Workshop Proceedings, Athens, Greece, 2023. CEUR-WS.org.

[185] Guilherme Sousa, Rinaldo Lima, and Cassia Trojahn. Amélioration de l'alignement de propriétés d'ontologies grâce aux plongements et à l'extension d'alignement. In *34èmes Journées francophones d'Ingénierie des Connaissances (IC 2023)@ Plate-Forme Intelligence Artificielle (PFIA 2023)*, number paper 20, pages 1–10, 2023.

[186] Guilherme Sousa, Rinaldo Lima, and Cassia Trojahn. Results of propmatch in oaei 2023. 2023.

[187] Fabian M. Suchanek, Serge Abiteboul, and Pierre Senellart. Ontology alignment at the instance and schema level. *ArXiv*, abs/1105.5516, 2011.

[188] Fabian M Suchanek, Serge Abiteboul, and Pierre Senellart. Paris: Probabilistic alignment of relations, instances, and schema. *arXiv preprint arXiv:1111.7164*, 2011.

[189] Yufei Sun, Liangli Ma, and Shuang Wang. A comparative evaluation of string similarity metrics for ontology alignment. *Journal of Information & Computational Science*, 12(3):957–964, 2015.

[190] Zequn Sun, Chengming Wang, Wei Hu, Muhao Chen, Jian Dai, Wei Zhang, and Yuzhong Qu. Knowledge graph alignment network with gated multi-hop neighborhood aggregation. In *Proceedings of the 34th AAAI Conference on Artificial Intelligence*, February 7-12, 2020, New York, USA.

[191] Boontawee Suntisrivaraporn. A similarity measure for the description logic el with unfoldable terminologies. In *2013 5th International Conference on Intelligent Networking and Collaborative Systems*, pages 408–413. IEEE, 2013.

[192] Péter Szeredi, Gergely Lukácsy, and Tamás Benkő. *The Semantic Web explained: the technology and mathematics behind Web 3.0.* Cambridge University Press, 2014.

[193] Élodie Thiéblin, Ollivier Haemmerlé, Nathalie Hernandez, and Cassia Trojahn. Task-oriented complex ontology alignment: Two alignment evaluation sets. In *The Semantic Web: 15th International Conference, ESWC 2018*, Heraklion, Crete, Greece, June 3–7, 2018, *Proceedings 15*, pages 655–670. Springer, 2018.

[194] Elodie Thiéblin, Ollivier Haemmerlé, Nathalie Hernandez, and Cassia Trojahn. Survey on complex ontology matching. *Semantic Web*, 11(4):689–727, 2020.

[195] Molka Tounsi Dhouib, Catherine Faron Zucker, and Andrea GB Tettamanzi. An ontology alignment approach combining word embedding and the radius measure. In *Semantic Systems. The Power of AI and Knowledge Graphs: 15th International Conference, SEMANTiCS 2019*, Karlsruhe, Germany, September 9–12, 2019, *Proceedings 15*, pages 191–197. Springer International Publishing, 2019.

[196] Hugo Touvron, Louis Martin, Kevin Stone, Peter Albert, Amjad Almahairi, Yasmine Babaei, Nikolay Bashlykov, Soumya Batra, Prajjwal Bhargava, Shruti Bhosale, et al. Llama 2: Open foundation and fine-tuned chat models. *arXiv e-prints*, pages arXiv–2307, 2023.

[197] Cassia Trojahn, Renata Vieira, Daniela Schmidt, Adam Pease, and Giancarlo Guizzardi. Foundational ontologies meet ontology matching: A survey. *Semantic Web*, 13(4):685–704, 2022.

[198] Michael Uschold. *OWL Limitations*, pages 163–184. Springer International Publishing, Cham, 2018.

[199] Line van den Berg, Manuel Atencia, and Jérôme Euzenat. Agent ontology alignment repair through dynamic epistemic logic. In *AAMAS 2020-19th ACM international conference on Autonomous Agents and Multi-Agent Systems*, pages 1422–1430. ACM, 2020.

[200] Line van den Berg, Manuel Atencia, and Jérôme Euzenat. A logical model for the ontology alignment repair game. *Autonomous Agents and Multi-Agent Systems*, 35(2):32, 2021.

[201] Javier Vela and Jorge Gracia. Cross-lingual ontology matching with CIDER-LM: results for OAEI 2022. In Pavel Shvaiko, Jérôme Euzenat, Ernesto Jiménez-Ruiz, Oktie Hassanzadeh, and Cássia Trojahn, editors, *Proceedings of the 17th International Workshop on Ontology Matching (OM 2022) co-located with the 21th International Semantic Web Conference (ISWC 2022)*, Hangzhou, China, held as a virtual conference, October 23, 2022, volume 3324 of *CEUR Workshop Proceedings*, pages 158–165. CEUR-WS.org, 2022.

[202] Petar Velickovic, Guillem Cucurull, Arantxa Casanova, Adriana Romero, Pietro Lio, Yoshua Bengio, et al. Graph attention networks. *Stat*, 1050(20):10–48550, 2017.

[203] Lucy Lu Wang, Chandra Bhagavatula, Mark Neumann, Kyle Lo, Chris Wilhelm, and Waleed Ammar. Ontology alignment in the biomedical domain using entity definitions and context. In Dina Demner-Fushman, Kevin Bretonnel Cohen, Sophia Ananiadou, and Junichi Tsujii, editors, *Proceedings of the BioNLP 2018 workshop*, pages 47–55. Association for Computational Linguistics, July 2018.

[204] Peng Wang and Baowen Xu. An effective similarity propagation method for matching ontologies without sufficient or regular linguistic information. In Asunción Gómez-Pérez, Yong Yu, and Ying Ding, editors, *The Semantic Web*, pages 105–119, Berlin, Heidelberg, 2009. Springer Berlin Heidelberg.

[205] Peng Wang, Baowen Xu, and Yuming Zhou. Extracting semantic subgraphs to capture the real meanings of ontology elements. *Tsinghua Science and Technology*, 15(6):724–733, 2010.

[206] Yaoshu Wang, Jianbin Qin, and Wei Wang. Efficient approximate entity matching using jaro-winkler distance. In *International Conference on Web Information Systems Engineering*, pages 231–239. Springer, 2017.

[207] Zhichun Wang, Qingsong Lv, Xiaohan Lan, and Yu Zhang. Cross-lingual knowledge graph alignment via graph convolutional networks. In *Proceedings of the 2018 Conference on Empirical Methods in Natural Language Processing*, pages 349–357, 2018.

[208] Zhu Wang and Isabel F Cruz. Agreementmakerdeep results for oaei 2021. In *OM@ ISWC*, pages 124–130, 2021.

[209] Xingsi Xue and Qihan Huang. Generative adversarial learning for optimizing ontology alignment. *Expert Systems*, 40(4):e12936, 2023.

[210] Xingsi Xue and Yuping Wang. Ontology alignment based on instance using nsga-ii. *Journal of Information Science*, 41(1):58–70, 2015.

[211] Victor Eiti Yamamoto and Julio Cesar dos Reis. Updating ontology alignments in life sciences based on new concepts and their context. In *SeWeBMeDa@ ISWC*, pages 16–30, 2019.

[212] Yuchen Yan, Lihui Liu, Yikun Ban, Baoyu Jing, and Hanghang Tong. Dynamic knowledge graph alignment. In *Proceedings of the AAAI conference on Artificial Intelligence*, volume 35, This conference was held online, thus there is no venue. Below I provide the DOI of this publication: https://doi.org/10.1609/aaai.v35i5.16585. pages 4564–4572, 2021.

[213] Lan Yang, Kathryn Cormican, and Ming Yu. Ontology-based systems engineering: A state-of-the-art review. *Computers in Industry*, 111:148–171, 2019.

[214] Li Yujian and Liu Bo. A normalized levenshtein distance metric. *IEEE Transactions on Pattern Analysis and Machine Intelligence* 10.1109/TPAMI.2007.1078, 29(6):1091–1095, 2007.

[215] Abir Zekri, Zouhaier Brahmia, Fabio Grandi, and Rafik Bouaziz. τowl: A framework for managing temporal semantic web documents. In *Proceedings of the 8th International Conference on Advances in Semantic Processing (SEMAPRO 2014)*, Rome, Italy, pages 33–41, 2014.

[216] Abir Zekri, Zouhaier Brahmia, Fabio Grandi, and Rafik Bouaziz. Temporal schema versioning in τowl: a systematic approach for the management of time-varying knowledge. *Journal of Decision Systems*, 26(2):113–137, 2017.

[217] Tian Zhang, Dezhi Xu, and Jianer Chen. Application-oriented purely semantic precision and recall for ontology mapping evaluation. *Knowledge-Based Systems*, 21(8):794–799, 2008.

[218] Haiyan Zhao, Hanjie Chen, Fan Yang, Ninghao Liu, Huiqi Deng, Hengyi Cai, Shuaiqiang Wang, Dawei Yin, and Mengnan Du. Explainability for large language models: A survey. *arXiv preprint arXiv:2309.01029*, 2023.

[219] Lu Zhou and Pascal Hitzler. Aroa results for oaei 2020. In *OM@ ISWC*, pages 161–167, 2020.

[220] Shiyi Zou, Jiajun Liu, Zherui Yang, Yunyan Hu, and Peng Wang. Lily results for OAEI 2021. In Pavel Shvaiko, Jérôme Euzenat, Ernesto Jiménez-Ruiz, Oktie Hassanzadeh, and Cássia Trojahn, editors, *Proceedings of the 16th International Workshop on Ontology Matching co-located with the 20th International Semantic Web Conference (ISWC 2021)*, Virtual conference, October 25, 2021, volume 3063 of *CEUR Workshop Proceedings*, pages 167–174. CEUR-WS.org, 2021.

Index

alignment, 27
    concept level, 28, 68, 116
    instance level, 28, 86, 125
    relation level, 28, 76, 122
alignment assessment method
    continuity based, 147
    depth based, 144
alignment inconsistency, 144
    circular inheritence, 30
    disjoint inheritence, 30
attribute, 11
attribute language, 12
attributes' semantics, 12

change significance
    concept level, 112
    instance level, 115
    relation level, 114
concept, 11
concept disjointness, 14
concept equality, 14
concept hierarchy, 16
concept knowledge potential, 131
concept's context, 13
concept's instance, 13

difference function
    concept level, 110
    instace level, 111
    relation level, 110

external ontology aligment, 87

fuzzy alignment method
    concept level, 69

instance level, 88
    relation level, 76

inconsistent alignment, 31
instance, 14

LogMap, 49, 134

OAEI, 41, 68, 142, 154
ontology, 10
ontology alignment methods
    instance based, 39
    semantic, 39
    structural, 38
    terminological, 37
ontology alignment universe, 87
ontology evolution, 107
ontology interoperability, 131
ontology log, 110
ontology repository, 109
ontology timeline, 108

quality metrics
    f-measure, 61
    precision, 60
    recall, 60
    relaxed precision and recall, 61

refinement, 40
relations' semantics, 15

thesauri, 18
Thing, 16

For Product Safety Concerns and Information please contact our EU
representative GPSR@taylorandfrancis.com
Taylor & Francis Verlag GmbH, Kaufingerstraße 24, 80331 München, Germany

www.ingramcontent.com/pod-product-compliance
Ingram Content Group UK Ltd.
Pitfield, Milton Keynes, MK11 3LW, UK
UKHW051941210425
457613UK00028B/242